Recovering the Liberal Spirit

Recovering the Liberal Spirit

Nietzsche, Individuality, and Spiritual Freedom

STEVEN F. PITTZ

Cover image by Caspar David Friedrich (1774–1840); oil on canvas (circa 1818) in public domain (Wikimedia Commons) entitled "Woman before the Rising Sun."

Published by State University of New York Press, Albany

© 2020 State University of New York

All rights reserved

Printed in the United States of America

No part of this book may be used or reproduced in any manner whatsoever without written permission. No part of this book may be stored in a retrieval system or transmitted in any form or by any means including electronic, electrostatic, magnetic tape, mechanical, photocopying, recording, or otherwise without the prior permission in writing of the publisher.

For information, contact State University of New York Press, Albany, NY
www.sunypress.edu

Library of Congress Cataloging-in-Publication Data

Name: Pittz, Steven F., author.
Title: Recovering the liberal spirit: Nietzsche, individuality, and spiritual freedom / Steven F. Pittz, author.
Description: Albany : State University of New York Press, [2020] | Includes bibliographical references and index.
Identifiers: ISBN 9781438479774 (hardcover : alk. paper) | ISBN 9781438479781 (pbk. : alk. paper) | ISBN 9781438479798 (ebook)
Further information is available at the Library of Congress.

10 9 8 7 6 5 4 3 2 1

In memory of Joanne Marie Pittz, who, while raising five children, remained a free spirit until the end

Contents

Acknowledgments ix

Introduction 1

1. The Free Spirit 19

2. A Safe Distance from Politics 41

3. Free Spirits in Action: Practicing Political Detachment 59

4. Free Spirits in Liberal Political Society 91

5. The Possibility of Autonomy: The Progressive Critique 115

6. The Desirability of Autonomy: The Communitarian Critique 145

Conclusion 167

Notes 177

Bibliography 207

Index 215

Acknowledgments

It is no easy task to remember all of the people who helped make this book a reality, but I will do my best to give credit where it is due and to extend my sincere gratitude. First and foremost, I thank my advisors at the University of Texas, Kathleen Higgins and A. P. Martinich. I do not believe I would have completed a PhD, let alone this project, without their guidance. Also from my time in Texas, I thank Jeffrey Tulis, Juliet Hooker, David Edwards, Thomas Pangle, and Devin Stauffer for valuable comments and advice.

Many others have read drafts or portions, and I thank them all for their comments and consideration: Joshua Dunn, Judd Owen, Bill Glod, Bob Irwin, Eric Long, Joe Postell, Allison Postell, Mark Jensen, Justin Dyer, and Francis Pittz. I also thank two anonymous reviewers from SUNY Press and the Political Science Colloquium at the Kinder Institute on Constitutional Democracy, at the University of Missouri, for helpful criticism.

I am grateful for research assistance from several institutions. The Institute for Humane Studies has been a great supporter of my work from the early stages. I also received support from Emory University's Program in Democracy and Citizenship and the Center for the Study of Government and the Individual at the University of Colorado–Colorado Springs.

Last, but certainly not least, I thank my wife, Bethany Miller, who has been an unwavering support throughout the process (including editorial assistance). I also mention my two young boys, Soren and Arthur, who deserve no credit nor gratitude and who actively attempt to prevent any work being done, but still somehow manage to make all the effort worthwhile.

Introduction

> How small, of all that human hearts endure, that part which laws and kings can cause or cure.
>
> —Oliver Goldsmith

> Freedom extends beyond spatial bounds. Liberty presumes an autonomy of self that includes freedom of thought, belief, expression, and certain intimate conduct. The instant case involves liberty of the person both in its spatial and more transcendent dimensions.
>
> —Supreme Court Justice Anthony Kennedy

The liberal political order is under attack. Such a statement would have appeared hyperbolic only a few years ago, but is today not much of a stretch. Populist movements in Europe and America challenge the liberal order both domestically and internationally. These democratic political challenges are mirrored by challenges from scholars and public intellectuals alike. Recent years have seen the publication of titles such as *Why Liberalism Failed*, *The Retreat of Western Liberalism*, *Against Democracy*, and more.[1] The reasons behind such challenges vary: there is backlash to the uneven distribution of economic globalization, there is a strengthening of identity politics as an alternative to liberalism, and there are calls for a return to the smaller communities that characterized the premodern, preliberal world. Yet, there is a deep and enduring question about liberal political order that underpins these prominent recent challenges. The question is whether the liberal order can provide the spiritual nourishment that human beings require. Few, including critics of liberalism, doubt the material benefits that the modern liberal world has made possible. Despite these benefits, however, liberalism ultimately leads to the spiritual impoverishment of citizens, or so the story goes. As Alexander Solzhenitsyn warned us forty years ago, Western liberalism began "the dangerous trend of worshiping man and his material needs. Everything beyond physical well-being and the accumulation of material goods, all other human requirements and characteristics of a subtler and higher nature, were left outside the area of attention of state and social systems, as if human life did not have any higher meaning." Physical security and material wealth are not enough, for the "human soul longs for things higher, warmer, purer."[2]

Solzhenitsyn's warning was echoed by critics of liberalism in the years following his famous address, and those echoes have grown louder in recent years. Patrick Deneen's *Why Liberalism Failed* follows the Solzhenitsynian logic, arguing that the spiritual emptiness we see all around us is the achievement of the liberal promise, a promise that placed the individual's material well-being over all else.[3] The political and economic benefits of the liberal order are no longer enough to produce a society full of steadfast supporters of liberalism. To hear Solzhenitsyn again, "We have placed too much hope in politics and social reforms, only to find out that we are being deprived of our most precious possession: our spiritual life."[4] From communitarians to progressives to recent critics of different stripes, liberalism is under attack for its apparent inability to provide spiritual nourishment and meaning to life. If the broad liberal order that has structured the West for nearly half a millennium is to endure, it must be able to answer the question, Is spiritual fulfillment possible for liberal citizens? Put differently, does liberalism enable, or at least not prevent, the spiritual fulfillment of its citizens?

I attempt to answer these questions, in the affirmative, throughout this book. Liberalism is in need of a *spiritual* defense, and one possible version of such a defense is my goal. Freedom is at the heart of the liberal project, and we need to understand how freedom and spiritual fulfillment might go together. To this end, we will explore what I call spiritual freedom. I suggest that spiritual freedom is a category of liberal freedom, a category that adds to our understanding of what it means to be free in a liberal sense. At the outset, I acknowledge that spiritual freedom eludes precise definition. I do not think there is a determinate answer to what spiritual freedom is, anymore than there is a determinate answer to what justice or moderation are. Nevertheless, political philosophy and the tradition of liberalism can gain from a fuller and richer understanding of spiritual freedom. Moreover, it seems that certain categories of liberty in the Western world get more press; the discourse on liberty is dominated by questions surrounding the categories of political/civil and economic liberty. In the West, concerns about liberty in both political philosophy and practical politics—seen through the prism of our political parties—seem to manifest primarily in debates over institutional form. Classical liberal theorists fight with Rawlsian-type liberals about what the moral aims of liberal democracy should be, and about what institutions best reflect those aims. Classical liberals think of citizens as self-owners, or self-authors, while Rawlsians think of liberal citizens as "free and equal persons." Classical liberals emphasize ownership and individual autonomy; Rawlsian liberals emphasize cooperation and equality. The two camps advocate institutional forms that reflect their divergent aims. They each try to set up institutions to answer questions such as the following: How do we protect civil liberties? How much economic liberty should individuals have? How will property rights be set up? How will taxes be structured? What are the essential public goods, and how ought we to provide them? Do we have an obligation to provide economic assistance for those who are the least well off in society, and if so, what means should be used to provide such assistance?

These sorts of questions dominate the intraliberal debate, and also take center stage in practical politics more often than not. Western liberal politics are predicated largely on questions of economic and political liberty. The task of balancing economic and political liberties is of great importance, but I believe that something is lost if liberty is discussed only, or at least overwhelmingly, in terms of economic and political freedoms. Our sense of freedom—we may say our sense of *feeling* free—extends past economic and political dimensions; it extends to our spiritual life. The category of spiritual freedom is necessary to take fuller account of, if not encompass, our understanding of individual, liberal freedom. Moreover, I think liberals would benefit from a more precise conception of what freedom of spirit is, and how we might defend liberal freedom at least partially on this basis.

Yet a precise definition of spiritual freedom is hard to come by. In order to minimize the difficulty inherent in the task of defining spiritual freedom, we will probe spiritual freedom and its relation to political freedom through the analysis of a "free spirit," a person who embodies the spiritual freedom under our microscope. Once we have a figure of a free spirit, we can then examine how this figure relates to politics and political freedom. We will not be left with an apodictic understanding of spiritual freedom, but my hope is that we will leave with a clearer view of spiritual freedom and its implications for politics, particularly for the liberal political orders prevalent in the West. By exploring the free spirit, we will see a concern with independence of mind and intellectual freedom, but also a concern for spiritual fulfillment. Spiritual freedom, then, contains intellectual freedom, but extends past it through a concern with spirituality as well. Intellectual freedom, it seems, is good for its own sake, it is intrinsically good. If we are not intellectually free, then our thoughts are somehow not our own or our thoughts are not self-generated—we are prisoner to the thoughts of someone or something else. That we wish to be intellectually free is hardly controversial and the vast majority of people would affirm intellectual freedom as a human good. When I use the term spiritual freedom, I intend to include this sense of intellectual freedom within it.

In addition to intellectual freedom, spiritual freedom includes a concern for spiritual fulfillment. One seeks to be spiritually free in order to achieve something greater, some sort of positive spiritual state. To be spiritually free is not as desirable as being spiritually *full*. Spiritual seekers pursue some sort of contented, or full, spiritual state. I will call this a state of "spiritual fullness." We thus arrive at a preliminary definition of spiritual freedom: intellectual freedom plus a concern for spiritual fullness. Likewise, a "free spirit" will be someone who is both intellectually free and who pursues spiritual fullness on his own terms.[5] The free spirit will embody our concept of spiritual freedom, and we will explore the free spirit's relation to politics and liberalism.

A second major goal of this book is to introduce and contemplate the notion of spiritual fullness, or fulfillment. Spiritual fullness may be of great import for political theory. Here, at the outset, I wish to highlight the importance of spiritual fullness to the case for liberalism. As we will see, many critiques of liberalism are predicated on the idea that liberalism produces spiritually empty citizens. The notion of the isolated/empty liberal individual is a primary point of attack of critics of liberalism, largely because it nullifies or trumps whatever other benefits accrue from a liberal political order. The importance of the conclusion reached in this work—that individuals can achieve spiritual fullness *outside of* the common sources of community, religion, tradition, or politics—is that it refutes claims made by various critics that the liberal individual is ineluctably isolated and spiritually empty. In so doing, the conclusion bolsters the case for liberalism.

The free spirit, then, is a human type that poses questions for political philosophy in general, and liberal political philosophy in particular. The free spirit is at once both detached from, and beneficial to, a liberal society. And the free spirit achieves spiritual fullness within the liberal framework. The major themes to be explored are as follows: How does a free spirit relate to a liberal political order? What does this relationship tell us about political order itself? What positive goods can free spirits offer society? What can the free spirit teach us about individual autonomy, and about the possibility of individual consent in liberal democracies? How does a free spirit achieve spiritual fullness in liberal societies? These questions will be addressed throughout the book. First, however, the free spirit in question will need to be introduced and explained, a task to which we now turn.

"Free spirit" is a bit of a hackneyed term in modern culture. It will become clear as we proceed that the free spirit expounded here is quite different than the popular "free spirit" one finds in novels, Hollywood movies, pop culture and the vernacular. Indeed, the latter "free spirit" tends to be portrayed as one who has chosen an alternative lifestyle, an escapist, one who refuses to follow the basic rules of social convention. Moreover, these popularized "free spirits" tend to be portrayed as persons that do not want to face "reality," they are disenfranchised by the "system," they cannot or will not work a "regular" job, and often they display a proclivity towards mysticism. This is not to suggest that the popular version of the "free spirit" is wholly negative, for free spirits are often portrayed as an important and seductive alternative to the overworked and overstressed bourgeois or middle-class working person. What I seek to highlight, however, is the fact that the popularized "free spirit" is generally taken to shun the "real world," to choose to live instead in a world of dreams, illusions, and mystical intuitions.

The free spirit discussed here does not share the worldview of the typical popularized "free spirit." On the contrary, the free spirit at issue here is precisely concerned with ridding himself of dreams and illusions. His spirit is only considered free when he is facing reality head on, without the comforts of religious or mystical beliefs in any form. Our free spirit is not an escapist; rather, he is concerned with avoiding the common pitfalls of escapism. The salient characteristics and the orientation of the free spirit will emerge in detail in the following chapters. Here, however, is a provisional characterization of the free spirit: he is a skeptic[6] who seeks above all to be free of illusions about the world. He is able to face reality without falling to despair. This is possible because of his cheerful disposition, and also because of his ability to view a world without rational meaning as a cause for wonder rather than crushing doubt; as an invitation to create meaning rather than as a terrifying abyss.[7] The free spirit affirms life and creates value in it—that is, he achieves what I will call *spiritual fullness*—through an aesthetic perspective, as opposed to traditional moral perspectives such as communal or religious doctrines, or belief in a teleological human progress of some sort. Consequently, a free spirit is likely to be detached, to a large degree, from the traditions, morals, and general ethos of the community in which he lives. In other words, free spirits make great use of the "negative" liberty—that is, *freedom from*—afforded by liberal regimes. They wish to be free from custom and convention, free from community and associations that interrupt their solitude and create harmful attachments, and free from unconditional or dogmatic claims to truth and authority. These are the basic criteria of a free spirit. They can be met to a greater or lesser extent; there are, as I will argue later, degrees of spiritual freedom. To be a free spirit, however, there must be a considerable presence of these characteristics.

This characterization of the free spirit carries the question, Why do free spirits matter for politics at all? Are they not simply apolitical at best, and political pariahs at worst? While there is inevitable tension between free spirits and politics, I argue that free spirits practice a "politics of detachment," a practice in which individuals carve a space for themselves outside of politics while working towards inner freedom. Prima facie, the notion of a politics of detachment appears paradoxical: Is not detaching from politics tantamount to being apolitical? This paradox can be resolved when one sees that free spirits can work towards the improvement of political society by focusing inward. Free spirits are primarily concerned with their own spiritual freedom, but they retain an important political role. Politically detached free spirits provide two major benefits to liberal democracy: first, they facilitate a loosening of ideology and a weakening of fanaticism; second, they *demonstrate*[8] the independence of mind necessary for resisting the dominance of popular opinion. Free spirits act as a check on the prevailing social forces in liberal societies, leading to greater skepticism, and scrutiny, of the authority of public opinion. Political parties, mass media, and mass marketing are all strong liberal democratic forces that, in some sense, seek to capture the spirit. By selling or promoting certain ideologies, beliefs, and lifestyles, these forces ineluctably encroach upon the individual's spiritual freedom. These forces together constitute a major threat of majority tyranny, a threat that the existence of free spirits may help to combat. One should not need to look further than the history of mass movements in the twentieth century to realize the importance of keeping these forces in check. The presence of free spirits in society works towards this end.

Nietzsche's free spirit is the inspiration for the one investigated throughout this work. However, I have modified the concept of free spirit, and enumerated the basic criteria of spiritual freedom, to fit a broader description as well. It is important to note that I do not claim to be carrying on the work of Nietzsche, and I do not attempt to enlist Nietzsche as a supporter of liberalism, which he certainly was not. In chapter 2, I will introduce the free spirit and further explain my use of Nietzsche's work. Throughout the text, I will distinguish between Nietzsche's specific picture of the free spirit and a broader conception of free spirit based on the criteria above, which is general and abstract enough to allow for a wide spectrum of eligible individuals. However, when the term free spirit is used without qualification (as is often the case), the context in which it is used is compatible with both Nietzsche's specific understanding and the broader, more general one.

Spiritual Fullness

I will use the notion of spiritual fullness as a criterion of success, as a standard by which we can judge political philosophies. First, I suggest that one of the principal aims, whether explicitly or implicitly expressed, of many political theorists is that politics must be organized in such a way as to enable—if not to direct—citizens to achieve spiritual fulfillment. Put differently, I suggest that many political theorists are concerned not exclusively with questions of justice, equality, distribution, political legitimacy, and the like; many are also concerned with the spiritual state of individual citizens and the political community as a whole. This suggestion is justified by the language some prominent contemporary political theorists are wont to employ. They speak of the "malaise of modernity," the loss of "narrative unity" or personal stories, and the loss of "identity."[9] These terms do not denote the traditional metrics for judging political regimes—for example, justice, security, fairness, prosperity, and legitimacy. Rather, these terms denote an interest in the spiritual state of the citizens within political regimes, in this case the modern liberal regimes that dominate the West. On this basis I believe we are justified in using the notion of spiritual fullness as a standard.

The terms used to approach the idea of spiritual fullness vary. "Spirit" itself is a term with many definitions and connotations. Generally, these various definitions include mention of the distinction between some noncorporeal substance—be it the soul, consciousness, personality, and so on—and the material body. "Spirit" is also often thought of as the animating principle in humans or animals. This "animating principle" may, however, be considered to be a mystical soul, a God-given breath of life, or simply the human intellect or consciousness, which may or may not be an immaterial substance. The term "spiritual" is likewise open to several various definitions. For religious believers of different varieties, spirituality may refer to the connection the believers have with their God (or gods) or with their religious beliefs themselves. More recently, spirituality has focused more on subjective experience. On this view, any sort of meaningful or blissful experience—whether connected to religious belief or not—may be considered spiritual.

The uses of "spirit" and "spiritual" in this work are meant to be inclusive. The various meanings of the two terms should be compatible with the idea of spiritual fullness presented here. Often our understanding of spiritual fullness is separate from that of bodily or physical pleasure. The meaningful or blissful experiences, whether viewed as secular or religious, that constitute spiritual fullness are distinguished from the various forms of physical pleasure. To say that one's spirit is full is something different than to say that one's body is satiated. Experiences that constitute spiritual fullness touch on ideas, beliefs, or feelings that help us to explain who we are, how we see ourselves, and how we relate to the world. Fullness of spirit is something that can endure in a way that the fleeting and ephemeral satisfactions resulting from a pleasure-seeking lifestyle cannot.

Nevertheless, spiritual fullness should not be understood *only* as experience separated from physical pleasure. Many religious, blissful, or meaningful experiences do indeed travel through the physical senses. We can imagine, for example, an experience of awe or wonder brought on by sensing or conceiving the unity, or the mere factualness, of existence or reality. Likewise, we may experience the awe or wonder of the unity of reality, even as we experience the variety or intricacy of reality. One may "sense" the presence of God through the smell in the aroma of a field of flowers. Whatever the particular experience, we should bear in mind that many experiences that should count as spiritual are also experiences that are considered physical. Indeed, spirituality and physicality are not mutually exclusive. Spiritual experiences can come in many forms, and spiritual experiences lead to the spiritual fullness we have set up as a criterion for success.

The variety of spiritual experience is necessary to note because where individuals achieve spiritual fullness varies as well. Some theorists speak of the fulfillment that comes from active political life and the pursuit of public honor, others of self-realization through community membership and a strong sense of identity, and others speak more generally of the pursuit of happiness. Political philosophy has something to say about all of these ends, and I think all of these ideas about ends can be understood to have a common goal of enabling spiritual fullness. With that in mind, let us begin to define "spiritual fullness." Most broadly conceived, spiritual fullness is a state an individual has reached when he regards his life to be both desirable and full; a state in which life is not lacking in any significant way, and is therefore subjectively affirmed.[10] One can imagine numerous paths to achievement of such a spiritual state, but the goal remains the same for all.

Political philosopher Charles Taylor describes spiritual fullness accordingly: "We all see our lives, and/or the space wherein we live our lives, as having a certain moral/spiritual shape. Somewhere, in some activity, or condition, lies a fullness, a richness."[11] These activities or conditions "help us to situate a place of fullness, to which we orient ourselves morally or spiritually. They can orient us because they offer some sense of what they are of: the presence of God, or the voice of nature, or the force which flows through everything, or the alignment in us of desire and the drive to form."[12] All of us do or should seek out a sense of spiritual fullness, yet how a place of fullness will be described depends largely on the moral and spiritual outlook of the person doing the describing. The religious woman feels the presence of God, the mystic the energy of the universe, the naturalist the power of nature; but in each such state, they feel spiritually full.

Some examples, from distinct thinkers, may further illuminate the idea of spiritual fullness. For a religious perspective we can listen to St. Ignatius of Loyola, to whom Taylor refers when discussing spiritual fullness. In his *Spiritual Exercises*, St. Ignatius distinguishes between spiritual "consolation" and spiritual "desolation." Consolation, he writes, is when "the soul is aroused by an interior movement which causes it to be inflamed with love of its creator and Lord, and consequently can love no created thing on the face of the earth for its own sake, but only in the Creator of all things."[13] Desolation, on the other hand, is "darkness of the soul, turmoil of the mind, inclination to low and earthly things, restlessness resulting from many disturbances and temptations which lead to loss of faith, loss of hope, and loss of love. It is also desolation when a soul finds itself completely apathetic, tepid, sad, and separated as it were, from its Creator and Lord."[14] Thus, fullness of spirit is marked by gratitude and love for life—and, for Ignatius, the Creator of life—while emptiness of spirit is likened to separation from the Creator of life. We may understand this notion of spiritual fullness as requiring a strong attachment and love for our life; and if we are theists, for the Creator of this life.[15]

Jean-Jacques Rousseau has some very similar ideas about the nature of spiritual fullness, albeit coming from a nontheistic perspective. I quote at length from the fifth walk of *The Reveries of the Solitary Walker*, where Rousseau describes "the sentiment of existence," a sentiment that facilitates spiritual fullness as he understands it:

> In our most intense enjoyments, there is hardly an instant when the heart can truly say to us: *I would like this instant to last forever*. . . . But if there is a state in which the soul finds a solid enough base to rest itself on entirely and to gather its whole being into . . . without any other sentiment of deprivation or of enjoyment, pleasure or pain, desire or fear, except that alone of our existence, and having this sentiment alone fill it completely; as long as this state lasts, he who finds himself in it can call himself happy, not with an imperfect, poor, and relative happiness such as one finds in the pleasures of life, but with a sufficient, perfect, and full happiness which leaves in the soul no emptiness it might feel a need to fill. . . . What do we enjoy in such a situation? Nothing external to ourselves, nothing if not ourselves and our own existence. . . . The sentiment of existence, stripped of any other emotion, is in itself a precious sentiment of contentment and of peace which alone would suffice to make this existence dear and sweet to anyone able to spurn all the sensual and earthly impressions which incessantly come to distract us from it and to trouble its sweetness here-below.[16]

Despite the fact that Rousseau invokes "existence"—whereas St. Ignatius invokes the "Lord and Creator"—we can see the similarities between what these two thinkers consider spiritual fullness to be. Consequently, we can infer that spiritual fullness is not exclusively a religious, theistic concept or exclusively an atheistic or agnostic concept of spirituality. Believer and unbeliever alike may share in the pursuit and experience of spiritual fullness.

Of the shared ideas between St. Ignatius and Rousseau, there is one I wish to emphasize: what distinguishes consolation and desolation—or spiritual fullness and spiritual emptiness—is a feeling of gratitude and love for life as well as an attachment to something other than sensual or physical, material things. Emptiness of spirit is likened to separation from the Creator for Ignatius, and disconnectedness from one's own "existence" in Rousseau. One may argue that Rousseau does not indicate "attachment to existence" in the passage above. He does, after all, implore, "What do we enjoy in such a situation? Nothing external to ourselves. . . ." Nevertheless, it is clear in this passage, and elsewhere in Rousseau's works, that the notion of "existence" is a source of meaning that can facilitate peace and contentment, and that one should seek it out. Existence is the place, or thing, that we are able to connect with when we have stripped ourselves of the earthly things that distract us from it. We may peel off the layers of socialization, as it were, to return to our natural state with existence, the state in which we lived before our spirits were corrupted by socialization.

"Creator" or "existence" might be replaced with some other idea that Taylor mentions, be it "the voice of nature, or the force which flows through everything, or the alignment in us of desire and the drive to form." The source of attachment varies. Yet, the descriptions given by Ignatius and Rousseau are meant to enrich our understanding of spiritual fullness, rather than define it. Taylor further describes spiritual fullness as requiring an idea that provides an attachment to something other than oneself, to some source of greater meaning. The implications of where one seeks attachment—that is, how and to where one is oriented spiritually—will be a major theme, and will be discussed later. For now, however, we can say that spiritual fullness is a spiritual state an individual has achieved when he regards his life to be both desirable and full, a state in which life and existence are affirmed, and that achieving this state requires an attachment to some source of meaning.

Now that we have begun to hone in on what spiritual fullness means, we may also gain clarity by identifying what it is not. Human flourishing conceived in the classical Greek sense, as the individual's achievement of the highest possible human virtue, may be thought by many to be the achievement of spiritual fullness. Yet as we proceed we will see the universal standards of virtue or excellence that Aristotle and other classical thinkers advocate may preclude certain possibilities for the spiritual fulfillment described above. In today's liberal democratic societies, we may find that the ground is particularly infertile for the cultivation of classical virtue, which requires state involvement in the process of inculcating proper virtues. As Charles Larmore points out, Greek and medieval thinkers

> entertained very sanguine prospects about the possibility of reasonable agreement about the good life. For them, it was axiomatic that here, too, reason tends naturally toward single solutions. The result was that, in their different ways, Greek and medieval thinkers usually assigned to the state the task of protecting and fostering the good life.[17]

A defining characteristic of liberal societies, by contrast, is that the state ought to be neutral towards controversial views of the good life. In the classical view, a well-ordered society directs citizens towards virtue and flourishing, which requires widespread agreement about what these are. Such agreement on what counts as virtue and the political will to legislate accordingly is elusive in liberal democracies. It would therefore be very risky, if not futile, to define spiritual fullness as Aristotelian flourishing in a political and historical age that is not suited to its pursuit.

There is a second reason for spiritual fullness to resist definition in terms of Aristotelian flourishing. It is possible that even a great or exemplary man of Aristotelian virtue will not have meaningful attachments nor be in a position to affirm life. For instance, we can imagine a person who dutifully follows the Aristotelian prescriptions for a life of virtue without an attachment to a greater source of meaning, a meaning that is required for our notion of spiritual fullness. Nietzsche repeatedly suggests that free spirits must be free even from their own virtues. A free spirit must know "how to escape from his own virtues occasionally,"[18] in order to gain knowledge and to maintain the strength of his autonomy. Indeed, honing and practicing Aristotelian virtue is not enough, for someone who possesses and practices the virtues deemed necessary for human flourishing may be merely going through the motions of living well.[19] According to the argument here, unless a person has an attachment to some source of meaning that leads to life affirmation, he or she will not be spiritually full. Conversely, we can also easily imagine a spiritually full person who is not a paragon of Aristotelian virtue. For example, Rousseau's "noble savage," who lives naturally without concern for the cultivation of virtue, could still be considered spiritually full in the sense we are using, provided he or she possessed an attachment to life. This is not to say, however, that human flourishing and spiritual fullness are mutually exclusive, as there is no reason that they cannot harmoniously coexist. Nonetheless, human flourishing is not a necessary or a sufficient condition for spiritual fulfillment.

The Free Spirit and Liberalism

The question of what spiritual freedom has to do with political philosophy remains. More specifically, how does spiritual freedom affect our understanding of liberalism? The answer, it seems to me, is that it enriches our understanding of individual freedom. Moreover, in the language of liberalism, spiritual freedom enriches our understanding of individual autonomy. Liberalism is a complex idea in itself, with a long history and various permutations. But all versions of liberalism treat the individual as the primary political unit; that is, any version of liberalism takes individual autonomy as its bedrock. The very idea of liberal government requires autonomous individuals, individuals capable of contracting with each other to found a government and, subsequently, to govern themselves. Yet, the concept of an autonomous individual is often attacked, and these attacks come from two angles. From one angle, individual autonomy is alleged to be impossible; from the other, it is alleged to be undesirable. Attacks on the idea of individual autonomy—both on its possibility and desirability—are, by extension, attacks on the political philosophy of liberalism. I believe the discussion of the free spirit throughout this work will provide a basis for a counterargument to some of the charges against individual autonomy. Specifically, the free spirit demonstrates that individual spiritual autonomy is possible and can be desirable. The idea of the free spirit can also lend support to the basic claim of liberalism, the idea that the individual can and ought to be treated as the foundational unit of political theory.

The first challenge to individual autonomy surrounds the question of its possibility. Many political theorists have doubted the notion that the individual is a discrete unit of analysis. In other words, many theorists have asserted that the individual is but a part of the social whole, a social whole that is prior to—and therefore irreducible to—individuals. Alternatively, some theorists claim that the social whole is the natural and necessary end of the individual. Indeed, if one canvasses the history of Western political thought, a view that society—or the state—is of greater import than the individual will emerge in various forms. To greatly simplify some well-known examples: society is prior to the individual (Aristotle); the individual reaches his highest potential and fulfillment in the state (Plato); the individual realizes the full expression of the ethical life only as a member of the state (Hegel); and the individual experiences true freedom only when he dissolves his particular will into the general will of the state (Rousseau). Notwithstanding important differences, these various theories assert that, for the purposes of political theory, separating the individual from society is impossible. It is unnecessary to recount the arguments here, but it is important to acknowledge the influence they have had on critiques of liberal politics, both of the recent past and of today.

Contemporary critics of liberalism of different stripes argue against the autonomy of the individual. Throughout the book, I will examine and critique thinkers such as Taylor, Alasdair MacIntyre, and Michael Sandel, as well as John Dewey, Charles Merriam, Herbert Croly, and John Burgess. These communitarian and progressive thinkers all argue against the liberal individual in similar ways. Despite their various differences, all challenges to the liberal idea of individual autonomy converge around the claim that the state is a "social organism." The notion of the state as a social organism starts with the premise that individuals cannot be separated from society. John Dewey explains the "social organism" in *The Ethics of Democracy*:

> . . . that theory that men are not isolated non-social atoms, but are men only when in intrinsic relations to men. . . . Society in its unified and structural character is the fact of the case. . . . Society, as a real whole, is the normal order, and the mass as an aggregate of isolated units is the fiction. If this be the case, and if democracy be a form of society, it not only does have, but must have, a common will; for it is this unity of will which makes it an organism. A state represents men so far as they have become organically related to one another, or are possessed of unity of purpose and interest.[20]

In words that echo Hegel and Rousseau, Dewey asserts the idea that men "are men only when in intrinsic relations to men." Hence, the very possibility of individual autonomy is attacked by the idea of the state as a social organism. Naturally, humans are born and raised in society and rely on other humans for an assortment of basic needs, but the idea that individuals are an irremovable part of a social organism with a common will is a much bolder claim, a claim that will be challenged here. As we proceed, my hope is that the idea of the free spirit will challenge the idea that individuals have no role outside of the social organism, or are not truly "men," as Dewey and others suggest.

The importance of refuting the idea that individual autonomy is impossible, that individuals are only parts of the social organism, becomes clear when we recall that liberal government requires individual consent for its legitimacy. Only autonomous individuals can enter into something consensual—for example, a social contract. Thus, by rejecting individual autonomy, one also rejects the social contract. Liberal government cannot exist without some form of contract; hence, if the idea of the free spirit demonstrates individual autonomy, it provides a basis for liberal government legitimated by consent as well. This discussion of the free spirit, then, is meant to provide an alternative method by which to legitimate liberalism through a "proof" of individual autonomy.

The second challenge to individual autonomy surrounds the question of whether it is, or can be, desirable. Many of the critics of liberalism discussed will attempt to uncover—explicitly and implicitly—the spiritual emptiness of liberal society. Indeed, many scholars insist that it is liberal political order that disconnects us from the things that might bring us spiritual fullness, things like religion, politics, community, and traditional values. Taylor, MacIntyre, and Sandel argue in different ways that liberalism disconnects individuals from sources of meaning, sources that offer a place for our attachments and provide a sense of identity. The communitarian challenge focuses on the absence of attachments. Recall our definition of spiritual fullness; it requires some sort of attachment. Thus, prima facie, it appears that this challenge may have some merit. If liberalism precludes meaningful attachments, it thereby precludes spiritual fullness. Meaningful attachments, critics of liberalism emphasize, come from engagement with political and communal life. The nature of these attachments will be described in detail later on.

The aforementioned thinkers find the liberal individual in a state of spiritual emptiness. They identify a need to transcend what they see as an "atomized" self through attachment to something greater than the individual, and the choices they give are politics, the broader community, and tradition (which includes religion). These are the very things liberalism devalues, at least according to their critique. What follows from this is a rejection of liberalism as a political philosophy.[21] One need not criticize the liberal political regime from a macroscopic perspective if its microscopic and foundational unit, the liberal self, is found to be spiritually damaged.

Whatever the wide-reaching political benefits of a liberal regime might be—increased prosperity, rule of law based on the equality of persons, decreased global conflict especially amongst liberal capitalist democracies, and so on—liberalism as a whole cannot be adequately defended if the individuals that follow its teachings are spiritually empty. The arguments of thinkers like Taylor, MacIntyre, and Sandel call for a return to republicanism or a more communitarian form of democracy, and they are predicated on the belief that these forms of government can cultivate spiritually fulfilled citizens, while a liberal regime cannot. The individual autonomy intrinsic to liberalism is deemed to be something like a spiritual disease. It is alleged that even if it is possible to separate from the "social organism," it is dangerous to do so. Thus, the second challenge to individual autonomy is based on the conclusion that even if it is possible, it is not to be desired.

The idea of the free spirit will challenge the claim that liberal citizens are ineluctably spiritually desolate. Indeed, taking seriously the premise that liberal political order allows for, perhaps even encourages, individualism and detachment from politics and community, there are still possibilities for spiritual fulfillment. I will show a type of individual we find in liberal societies, the free spirit, and show that he is—as these thinkers lament—largely detached from political life and the broader community. Despite this detachment, however, we will see that free spirits achieve spiritual fullness. We will also see that liberalism does not hinder this spiritual pursuit. Liberalism, instead, provides the individual with the freedom to seek spiritual fullness on one's own terms. This means, ipso facto, that liberalism allows for affective attachment[22] to something, as affective attachment is required by our definition of spiritual fullness. Liberalism does not, however, assume that politics, community, and tradition are the only, or even the central, locations where such attachment may be found.

The free spirit does not seek attachment in these locations, but creates an affective attachment to existence and life through taking an aesthetic perspective. Moreover, liberalism does not, as a communitarian democracy does, place obligations on individuals that may in fact preclude or hinder a free spirit's pursuit of spiritual fullness, obligations that may preclude the freedom of thought necessary to achieve an aesthetic perspective. I will defend, then, both a weaker and a stronger thesis: the weaker is that progressivism and communitarianism are not capacious enough to include the free spirit; the stronger is that such theories place obligations on individual free spirits that threaten their pursuit of spiritual fullness. The demonstration of these theses will urge us to consider that the state should not attempt to facilitate spiritual fullness, but rather should avoid coercive demands that restrict the possibility of free spirits to behave as such. Indeed, we should think more about what the state should not do than what it should do.

The free spirit is an autonomous individual who is at the same time capable of achieving spiritual fullness. This argument mitigates the criticisms levied at the individual autonomy and the social contract that are central to the liberal political order. At the same time, it presents a possibility for affective attachment and spiritual fulfillment in liberal societies that resides outside of both the spheres of politics and of the broader notion of community: a life of aesthetic appreciation. Once this possibility is presented, we will see that a liberal political order also provides possibilities for the individual to pursue spiritual fullness apart from politics and community. In short, the free spirit will show that individual autonomy is possible and that it can be desirable as well.

Plan for the Book

The examination of spiritual freedom throughout the book leaves us with three principal conclusions. First, spiritual freedom is a desirable category of liberal freedom that should be understood and protected. Free spirits seek detachment from politics in order to pursue more spiritual goals, and they should be allowed to do so without fear of persecution. Second, despite the apparently apolitical nature of free spirits, their political detachment is good for society in several ways, notably for loosening the knot of ideology and weakening fanaticism, and for *demonstrating* independence of mind. Fanaticism of any stripe is a danger to the moderation and sobriety through which a liberal society functions at its best. Third, and finally, spiritual freedom bolsters the case of liberalism in two ways: it shows that liberalism is superior to other forms of political order in its ability to accommodate outsiders, that is, to accommodate free spirits; and spiritual freedom provides us with a different way of thinking about, and a "proof" of, the individual autonomy and individual consent that is required by liberal democracy.

The book proceeds as follows: Chapter 1 introduces the free spirit and lays out the basic criteria for a spiritually free person. Chapter 2 considers the free spirit's proper relationship to politics. Chapter 3 looks to the example of "real life" or empirical free spirits to investigate how they balance the pursuit of spiritual freedom and the demands of public life. Chapter 4 questions whether the free spirit has lessons for liberal political society, and how liberal society benefits free spirits. Chapter 5 discusses the possibility of individual autonomy, its importance to the justification of liberal government, and the progressive critique of autonomy. Chapter 6 contemplates the desirability of autonomy, exploring the relationship between autonomy and spiritual fullness and addressing the criticisms by communitarians regarding the spiritual state of liberal societies. Taken together, the arguments in these chapters will illuminate the question of what it means to be spiritually free and how this knowledge may affect the way we look at politics and political philosophy.

Chapter 1

The Free Spirit

> The whole problem with the world is that fools and fanatics are always so certain of themselves, and wiser people so full of doubts.
>
> —Bertrand Russell

In the following two chapters, I will explore the idea of the free spirit, borrowing heavily from Nietzsche's description of this human type. I will be interested in the free spirit not as a component of Nietzsche's character nor as a "hat" he sometimes wears, as a side of himself, but rather as a human type. The free spirit is presented as an ideal type; as Christine Daigle argues, the free spirit is "a viable ethical idea."[1] Not all Nietzsche scholars see the free spirit as such an ideal, and I will address these views later on. Up front, however, I argue that the free spirit is a viable ethical type and suggest that among individuals we may observe varying degrees of spiritual freedom. We may expect to find the traits and proclivities of the free spirit in various individuals to various extents. Likewise, we may expect to find the spiritual freedom of an individual to vary, to be more or less evident, at given times.

Free spirits must meet certain criteria, and there may be a fairly diverse spectrum of people that meet these criteria. Nietzsche offers one portrayal of the free spirit, and from this portrait we will gather the basic characteristics. But we will also extend past Nietzsche's description at times, and we will be more inclusive in our definition of a free spirit than what we see in Nietzsche. I argue that, once we have determined the salient characteristics of spiritual freedom, the number of eligible individuals becomes substantial. Because there are degrees of spiritual freedom—degrees to which an individual may embody the salient characteristics—we can find free spirits in a greater quantity in society. Nietzsche himself insisted that the free spirit is a "relative concept,"[2] that is, that rather than embodying an absolute sense of spiritual freedom, free spirits are more or less free than others, and the degree of freedom depends on many factors. Nietzsche also portrays the free spirit as rare and elite, however, and I will not precisely follow him in this regard. Instead, I will attempt to describe a free spirit by looking at certain traits, virtues, and orientations that exist in all of them. Therefore, exploring these traits, virtues, and orientations—that is, exploring the free spirit as a human type—will be the focus of this chapter. Once the mold of the free spirit becomes clear it will be possible to see which persons might fit into it.

A few other remarks about both my use of Nietzsche's free spirit and the differences between his free spirit and the one conceptualized here are in order. Concerning my use of Nietzsche: many readers will hesitate at a discussion involving both Nietzsche and liberal political order. Nietzsche was a vociferous critic of liberalism, and his criticisms included the notion that liberalism weakens the spirit and produces citizens with a herd-like mentality. I do not attempt to challenge this reading of Nietzsche, nor do I attempt to make Nietzsche safe for liberal democracy. Further, it is readily apparent that the free spirit ideal is not obviously compatible with some of Nietzsche's later writings (the free spirit belongs to what scholars have coined Nietzsche's "middle period").[3] This, however, hardly negates the value of the ideal. I am interested in a model of spiritual freedom, and my debt to Nietzsche is for his provision of one in his rich description of the free spirit. As other scholars, such as Amy Mullin, have contended, the ideal of the free spirit is of interest to anyone who share's Nietzsche's "enthusiasm for the ability to explore multiple ways of interpreting human behavior and norms."[4] Recent years have also seen an increase in scholarship on the free spirit, with a 2015 volume devoted to "Nietzsche's free spirit philosophy."[5] In other words, many scholars have begun to approach the free spirit as an ideal type that is worthy of study for its own sake. But while recent scholarship has produced a deeper understanding of spiritual freedom, it has not directly raised the question of how it relates to political life, or how we, as contemporary liberal citizens, might benefit from such understanding. That is my aim here, and I do not purport to be uncovering Nietzsche's political project, but merely examining the free spirit and applying that ideal to the liberal political world. I will address this further in the discussion of politics in chapter 3.

In addition, it is necessary to distinguish between Nietzsche's free spirit and the broader conception of free spirit that I develop. While the two conceptions are largely compatible, there are two major differences: First, for Nietzsche it seems that free spirits are rare and exceptional, part of an elite group separated from the mass of society. For Nietzsche, such spiritual freedom is out of reach for most of humanity. Second, Nietzsche's free spirit does not allow for spiritual seeking in the way our more capacious conception does. Our free spirit leaves open the possibility of spiritual seeking—in a limited, liberal way—while Nietzsche's free spirit seems to nearly foreclose some forms of spiritual seeking. Spiritual seekers,[6] as it were, are often seeking some sort of metaphysical comfort. Nietzsche's free spirit, to the contrary, must take leave of all metaphysical comforts—of "metaphysical need," as he puts it—and the strength of their spirits depends on the degree to which they can do this. This point will be drawn out in detail later on. Our broader conception of spiritual freedom leaves some room for spiritual seeking and metaphysical attachments. Certain requirements limiting such seeking will emerge out of our discussion, but it is important for us to be cognizant of these differences before exploring the free spirit.

The best way to introduce ourselves to the free spirit is through Nietzsche's description. The free spirit is prefigured in section 34 of *Human, All Too Human*. It will be helpful to provide some context for his emergence. Section 34 follows three others that ask whether humans can face the truth about what is essential to our acceptance of life. These sections are about (1) what is illogical, (2) what is unjust, and (3) the errors we have regarding life.[7] Nietzsche wonders whether humankind, coming face to face with these truths, may in fact turn its back on life; would "death not be preferable?"[8] Nietzsche's first claim is that much of what is good in life is or proceeds from what is illogical. Secondly, as illogical beings we are also bound to be unjust, as we have no "fixed standard to be able justly to assess the relation between ourselves and anything else whatever."[9] Finally, Nietzsche contends that if man allows himself to see truly humankind as it is, "if in all he does he has before him the ultimate goallessness of man, his actions acquire in his own eyes the character of useless squandering," and he will be led to despair.[10] Our "error" is refusing to acknowledge the "goallessness of man," preferring instead to believe in metaphysical illusions or human "progress."

After showing us what he believes is a clear-sighted view of life and existence, Nietzsche proceeds to imagine a person who could face all of these truths—that is, resist the temptation to lie to himself about the nature of man or the value and meaning of human actions—and still contentedly accept life as it is. This person is a free spirit, and Nietzsche emphasizes that, above all, a free spirit's positive reaction to the reality of existence is due to the person's temperament. For Nietzsche, temperament means something closer to disposition, a distinction that I will clarify later. For now, let us quote Nietzsche at length, for this initial image of the free spirit will guide my further discussion of this human type. When confronted with the true knowledge of reality, reality free of illogic and error, Nietzsche asks:

> Is it true, is all that remains a mode of thought whose outcome on a personal level is despair and on a theoretical level a philosophy of destruction? I believe that the nature of the after-effect of knowledge is determined by a man's *temperament*: in addition to the after-effect described I could just as easily imagine a different one, quite possible in individual instances, by virtue of which a life could arise much simpler and emotionally cleaner than our present life is: so that, though the old motives of violent desire produced by inherited habit would still possess their strength, they would gradually grow weaker under the influence of purifying knowledge. In the end one would live among men and with oneself as in *nature*, without praising, blaming, contending, gazing contentedly, as though at a spectacle, upon many things for which formerly one felt only fear. One would be free of emphasis, and no longer prodded by the idea that one is only nature or more than nature. For this to happen one would, to be sure, have to possess the requisite temperament, as has already been said: a firm, mild and at bottom cheerful soul. . . . A man from whom the ordinary fetters of life have fallen to such an extent that he continues to live only so as to know better must, rather, without envy or vexation be able to forgo much, indeed almost everything upon which other men place value; that free, fearless hovering over men, customs, laws and the traditional evaluations of things must *suffice* him as the condition he considers most desirable.[11]

There is much to analyze in this section, and some unpacking is required. It is helpful to break the section into parts by asking three questions: (1)

How is this free spirit able to face the "terrible truths" that what is good in life comes from illogic, injustice, and error? (2) In the absence of belief in any of these "untruths," how is the free spirit to evade despair and find a way to value and affirm life? How does the free spirit achieve spiritual fullness? (3) What does this section intimate about the free spirit's relationship to the traditions of his historical and political community? Of these three questions I will be focusing on 1 and 2 in this chapter. Question 3 will be more appropriately answered in the next chapter.

In attempting to answer the first question, let us begin by delving further into Nietzsche's "terrible truths" about human existence. In the section "Why I Am a Destiny," in *Ecce Homo*, Nietzsche claims that the truth is terrible. We must bear in mind Nietzsche's epistemological standpoint when we approach the term "truth" here.[12] Nietzsche did not believe in metaphysical, unitary, universal truth; he does not believe in truth with a capital "T." When he speaks of "terrible truth," he is therefore employing a more casual definition of truth, yet also with an implication that if one wants to see the reality of existence and human life as clearly as possible, one is going to come to some terrible and difficult conclusions. What might these conclusions be, exactly? Brian Leiter provides a helpful map for this question, dividing Nietzschean "terrible truths" into three basic categories. According to Leiter, there are three kinds of "terrible" truths: existential, moral, and epistemic.[13] These truths align quite well with Nietzsche's claim, while introducing the free spirit, that much in life comes from "illogic, injustice, and error."

Let us address each in turn, starting with the terrible existential truths. For Nietzsche, it is the fear of accepting the existential truths that leads us to prefer "error." Especially in his youth, Nietzsche was heavily influenced by the work of Arthur Schopenhauer, and the existential truths enumerated here borrow much from him. First, Leiter states that it is a terrible fact of life that we will all die. The notion of the immortal soul is an illusion, the existential truth being that we will literally vanish from the world, "our sentience and sapience will be extinguished for eternity."[14] A second existential truth is that we are all vulnerable to suffering throughout our lives, and are sure to be close to others—family members, friends, coworkers—who suffer as well, perhaps greatly. Worse yet, much of this suffering does not appear to us to have any clear cause, reason, or purpose.[15] Finally, we are all stuck in a state of constant desire, or in Schopenhauerian terms, we are imprisoned by our will. We cannot will what we want and always receive it, according to Schopenhauer, but we must *will*. We have no choice about what desires we have; they are imposed upon us, and we can't help but will them. What this means, as Leiter points out, is that "we are cursed, as it were, to reenact this pointless routine of striving and disappointment again and again for as long as we remain sentient, constituting the final perverse pointlessness of our existence in Schopenhauer's view."[16]

Now we must ask, how does the free spirit face these truths? The defining, and redeeming, characteristic of the free spirit is his capacity for affirming life in the face of these truths. The "terrible" existential truth is overcome by the free spirit's temperament. Temperament was long a subject of import for Nietzsche, dating back to his notes in 1861, when he was seventeen years old. His recognition of temperament as a crucial factor in human behavior and an individual's interpretation of events seems to have been stimulated when he was introduced to the writings of Ralph Waldo Emerson. Nietzsche poses the matter rhetorically: "What determines our happiness in life? Do we have to thank events whose whirlpool carries us away? Or is it not our temperament, as it were, the coloration of events? Do we not encounter everything in the mirror of our personality? And do not events provide, as it were, only the key of our history while the strength or weakness with which it affects us depends merely on our temperament? Ask gifted doctors, Emerson says, how much temperament decides."[17] We will return to the subject of temperament later on, but we may note now that temperament was crucial for Nietzsche's analysis of the self and of human behavior generally, and his interest in it is observable from his earliest writings to the end.

For those with the proper temperament, mortality is a cause for passion and enthusiasm rather than depression and despair. The brevity of life renders it more precious, thrilling, and intense than it would be if one's life were eternal. This is a clear case where "the nature of the after-effect of knowledge is determined by a man's *temperament*"—that is, how a man reacts to the knowledge of his own mortality depends on what kind of man he is, and a free spirit does not find mortality to be a cause for despair. Nietzsche ultimately came to reject strongly Schopenhauer's condemnation of existence. He came to the view that Schopenhauer was successful in presenting an accurate description of the world, but he also went a step further by judging the world. To describe accurately is one thing, to pass judgment is another, and one need not condemn existence when faced with these existential truths.

Helpful here is Nietzsche's idea of "Dionysian" pessimism, the insistence that pessimism need not lead to despair.[18] Joshua Foa Dienstag explains Nietzsche's view accordingly: "All pessimisms conclude that the universe has no order and human history no progress; the Dionysian variety is the only one that can find something to like about this situation."[19] The free spirit can still achieve spiritual fullness without belief in cosmic, metaphysical unity or human progress.[20] Furthermore, the Dionysian pessimist does not find suffering to be cause for rejecting the idea that life has value on the whole: "The problem is that of the meaning of suffering: whether a Christian meaning or a tragic meaning."[21] Identifying the problem in this way means, stated most simply, that suffering need not result in a negation of this world in the hope of a better world after death (Christianity). Instead, a free spirit may view suffering as simply an unalterable part of life; one can affirm life as a whole in spite of suffering.[22]

Now that we have seen how the free spirit faces existential truths, let us turn to the other two categories of "terrible truths," the epistemic and moral. Leiter's headings here again align quite closely with Nietzsche's claim that what is good in life comes from what is "illogical" and "unjust," respectively. Regarding epistemology, it is easy to see why, according to Nietzsche, we are wont to resist the idea that the world is not comprehensible to us. Indeed, we would like to think that what we see, hear, and feel—the world of the senses—is made up of stuff that we can understand in a basic sense. As Leiter puts it, we'd like to think that "at least we *know* a few certain things about the world, like what our senses tell us about the immediate environment." But Nietzsche reminds us throughout his writings that this is not the case, he "understood the point in terms of the illusion of 'being' or stable things, when the reality was one of constant flux and change, but the basic epistemic point is the same: ordinary beliefs about the world around us are illusory."[23]

Nietzsche questions our commonsensical understanding of our immediate environments, and he also judges our foundational spiritual beliefs—those residing in our religious doctrines and metaphysical philosophies—to be illusory as well. To make a claim of true knowledge in any of these areas is to succumb to "illogic," according to Nietzsche. He further claims that much of what is good in life, and what preserves life, comes from what is illogical. Indeed, Nietzsche claims that the constant flux and change of existence *necessitated* a belief in the illogical notions of "being" and "substance" for logic to exist in the first place. "In order that the concept of substance could originate—which is indispensable for logic although in the strictest sense nothing real corresponds to it—it was likewise necessary that for a long time one did not see nor perceive the changes in things."[24] The belief in logic stems from belief in what is illogical—unchanging substance or being—and Nietzsche's claim that much of what is good in life coming from what is "illogical" reflects this understanding. In a similar manner, our foundational spiritual beliefs also arise from what is false or fantasized, and the vast majority of humans will recoil at the thought that they have no true knowledge of the physical world or of metaphysics. Moreover, we will see that this lack of true knowledge extends to morality as well.

The "terrible" moral truth flows from the epistemic truth that we have no iron-clad, dependable knowledge of the world. As Leiter suggests, "There is the terrible epistemic truth (which implicates a moral one), namely, that all of our moral beliefs are based on lies and falsehoods, as Nietzsche never tires of emphasizing."[25] Moral systems tend to be based on belief in some sort of enduring and eternal knowledge. Such knowledge provides a solid foundation upon which to create moral laws. It may be knowledge of human nature and therewith natural laws; it may be a Kantian version of ethical imperatives that result from the constitution of human reason; or it may be knowledge of a supernatural kind, manifest in revelatory decrees from a deity. Nietzsche endeavors to pull the rug from under all of these possibilities, intimating instead that such types of moral truths, moral truths that are objective and universal, are illusory.[26] Therefore, the "terrible" moral truth is that there is no moral truth, at least no universal moral truth.

Nietzsche's philosophical nominalism is well documented, as is his position on the idea of universal moral laws. He famously calls himself the "immoralist," and often alludes to the folly of searching for universal moral laws. For Nietzsche, the real ethical task is creating one's self or character, and the proper way to do this depends on *who* is doing it.[27] Moral truth, if we were to undergo the dubious process of stretching Nietzsche's thought to incorporate these two terms side-by-side, would be that a man's morality depends on what type of man he is and what he seeks to become. Ultimately, the "terrible" moral truth is that traditional moral laws—howsoever they manifest—are not truths at all. Like the "terrible" existential and epistemic truths, one can either face the "terrible" moral truth with a clear mind or reject it in favor of the comfort of traditional moral illusions. Most humans will choose the latter, Nietzsche is convinced, but he believes strong souls will choose the former. The free spirit possesses this strength of soul, and refuses to clench the various life preservers presented by traditional, moral, metaphysical, or epistemological doctrines that obscure or distort the fact that the truth can be terrible. The free spirit will remain at sea, so to speak, and we will dig a little deeper to determine why this is so.

Skepticism

We still want to know *how* and *why* the free spirit deals with those terrible epistemic and moral truths. What is it about free spirits that makes them different from others, those who would prefer the comfort of a belief in certain knowledge? In addition to his cheerful temperament, the free spirit seeks no escape from these truths through denial, because the free spirit is a skeptic. Skepticism, we will see, is an essential part of the free spirit's character, a part that cannot be traded in, as it were, without one ceasing to be a free spirit. Nietzsche insists on this skepticism from the initial image of the free spirit cited earlier all the way to his later works. In one of Nietzsche's last works, we see him reaffirm the importance of skepticism. Although not explicitly a description of the free spirit, the following passage from *The Anti-Christ* recalls the free spirit from earlier works:

> One should not let oneself be misled: great intellects are skeptics. Zarathustra is a skeptic. The vigour of a mind, its *freedom* through strength and superior strength, is *proved* by skepticism. Men of conviction simply do not come into consideration where the fundamentals of value and disvalue are concerned. Convictions are prisons.[28]

Such convictions can be of the religious or scientific variety. Examples of Nietzschean attacks on convictions could be presented *ad abundantiam*.[29] That they are prevalent in both religious believers and scientists Nietzsche asserts in the aphorism "Believers and their need to believe": "How much one needs a *faith* in order to flourish . . . that is a measure of the degree of one's strength (or, to put the point more clearly, of one's weakness). Christianity, it seems to me, is still needed by most people in old Europe even today; therefore it still finds believers." The need for faith is not confined to religion. He goes on to say, "Metaphysics is still needed by some; but so is that impetuous *demand for certainty* that today discharges itself among large numbers of people in a scientific-positivistic form."[30] The free spirit, conversely, "would take leave of all faith and every wish for certainty, being practiced in maintaining himself on insubstantial ropes and possibilities and dancing even near abysses. Such a spirit would be the *free spirit* par excellence."[31]

As a brief yet related aside, it warrants mentioning that, despite Nietzsche's negative critiques of Christianity, he places the historical Jesus in the category of free spirit in the *Anti-Christ*:

> One could, with some freedom of expression, call Jesus a "free spirit"—he cares nothing for what is fixed: the word *killeth*, everything fixed *killeth*. The concept, the *experience* "life" in the only form he knows it is opposed to any kind of word, formula, law, faith, dogma. . . . On this point one must make absolutely no mistake, however much Christian, that is to say *ecclesiastical* prejudice, may tempt one to do so: such a symbolist *par excellence* stands outside of all religion, all conceptions of divine worship, all history, all natural science, all experience of the world, all acquirements, all politics, all psychology, all books, all art.[32]

Nietzsche interprets the historical Jesus as essentially antidogmatic, resistant and determined to avoid the fixed convictions that free spirits must be free of. Christian doctrine represents a dangerous and common pitfall for free spirits, but for Nietzsche the case of Jesus himself is more complicated. Jesus is treated as a free spirit to some degree, and at the least this conclusion should leave us with a cautious attitude regarding the easy presumption that anyone associated with the Christian faith is thereby excluded from the possibility of spiritual freedom. The case, rather, is that unflinching adherence to ecclesiastical doctrine or dogma imprisons the spirit, while following the teachings of Jesus—particularly by following the example of his life—may in fact help one to achieve spiritual freedom.

In sum, these statements, culled from works that span Nietzsche's writing, provide a glimpse of how the free spirit avoids the pitfalls of belief in "untruths." In large part, the free spirit avoids such pitfalls because of her cheerful temperament. In addition, however, the free spirit resists such pitfalls through her active skepticism. The free-spirited skeptic refuses to place belief in religious, metaphysical, or scientific traditions, viewing them—despite their usefulness in alleviating "terrible truths"—as illusions. "What characterizes the free spirit is not that his opinions are the more correct but that he has liberated himself from tradition, whether the outcome has been successful or a failure. As a rule, though, he will nonetheless have truth on his side, or at least the spirit of inquiry after truth: he demands reasons, the rest demand faith."[33] As this passage suggests, by choosing skepticism, the free spirit liberates herself from traditional claims to knowledge.

For us to truly grasp what is at stake in adopting a skeptical outlook, we need to delve further into the practice of skepticism itself. The term "practice" here is of great importance. The ancient, Pyrrhonist variety of skepticism is a way of life, not merely an epistemological position. The emphasis on skeptical practice is one of the most important differences between ancient and modern schools of skepticism. Jessica Berry views Nietzsche as an inheritor of a variety of ancient Pyrrhonian skepticism. Viewed this way, many of the problems, contradictions, and difficulties surrounding skepticism—that it is self-refuting; that one cannot truly "live" a skeptical life—disappear. We must distinguish between ancient and modern skepticism, and then show that Nietzsche belongs in the former camp. Let us listen to Berry, whom I quote at length:

> What needs to be abandoned . . . is our indentification of all skepticism with the two-dimensional view. . . . The skeptic of post-Cartesian and contemporary epistemology has been rightly condemned as "an abstract theoretical construct who lacks all psychological authenticity" and who is "saddled with an uninteresting thesis about the unattainability of certain knowledge." This is the skeptic against whom "the alleged dangers of self-refutation are used to render him vulnerable to the charge that he arbitrarily disputes the rational credentials of one class of beliefs while inconsistently maintaining that other beliefs susceptible to similar regressive difficulties are nevertheless actually rationally justified." Once we appreciate fully that this skeptic is largely a creature of the modern philosophical imagination and come to understand how little he has in common with his flesh-and-blood predecessors in antiquity, who espoused skepticism as a genuinely practicable way of life, the affiliation of Nietzsche with skepticism should no longer be unpalatable.[34]

Modern, "post-Cartesian" skepticism is, for Nietzsche, "philosophy reduced to 'theory of knowledge,' in fact no more than a timid epochism and doctrine of abstinence—a philosophy that never gets beyond the threshold and takes pains to deny itself the right to enter."[35] Nietzsche is unequivocal about the worth, or lack thereof, of modern, epistemological skepticism, but he does not condemn skepticism generally. He finds another skepticism, "the skepticism of audacious manliness," which "despises and nevertheless seizes; it undermines and takes possession; it does not believe but does not lose itself in the process; it gives the spirit dangerous freedom, but it is severe on the heart."[36] As we can infer from Nietzsche's description, this sort of skepticism is an active—we might even say positive—way of life, not a denial of knowledge. Berry shows how this difference pertains to our understanding of ancient skepticism: "The fact that skepticism in antiquity advertised itself as a genuinely practicable way of life (*agoge*) makes it both more difficult to refute than modern skepticism and more meaningful to examine."[37] With the aim of defending a non-self-refuting, meaningful, and practicable version of skepticism, let us dig deeper into the fundaments of ancient skepticism.

Pyrrhonism, or the school of skepticism developed by Pyrrho of Elis in the fourth century BCE, was best preserved and promulgated through the works of Sextus Empiricus, who was a Greek physician and philosopher who lived and worked in the late second century CE. Sextus questioned all types of knowledge and raised doubts about induction and the problem of infinite regress well before modern skeptics like Hume and Descartes brought such philosophical puzzles into the intellectual mainstream. Pyrrhonism emerged not as a progressive philosophical method, but rather as a reaction to the certitude claimed by other branches of philosophy. In *Outlines of Skepticism*, in which Sextus lays out the basic framework of Pyrrhonism, he identifies three branches of philosophy—dogmatic, Academic, and skeptical:

> Those who are called Dogmatists in the proper sense of the word think that they have discovered the truth—for example, the schools of Aristotle and Epicurus and the Stoics, and some others. The schools of Clitomachus and Carneades, and other Academics, have asserted that things cannot be apprehended. And the Skeptics are still investigating. Hence the most fundamental kinds of philosophy are reasonably thought to be three: the Dogmatic, the Academic, and the Skeptical.[38]

Regarding the skeptics, Sextus intimates that they are not "pro-skepticism," as it were, but rather "anti-dogmatism." As Berry notes:

> While all three groups are seekers after knowledge, Dogmatists as Sextus presents them give up seeking and say they are satisfied once they arrive at an answer. It is this attitude toward inquiry that is the standard target of skeptical attack in the sense that it is a common, even essential, feature of the groups Sextus names. Skeptics identify themselves by contrast to Dogmatists—those who make a professional habit of forming theories and beliefs (*dogmata*) and who subsequently stop investigating. In this respect, Skepticism is an ad hominem enterprise.[39]

The goal of the skeptic is not to promote skepticism, not even to *refute* established theoretical claims through attempts to *prove them* wrong. Instead, the goal is to incessantly call into question any claims of certitude (dogmata) on the part of the dogmatists.

A clear conception of what things count as dogmata is crucial to recognizing the Pyrrhonist approach to knowledge (it would be misleading to call this a Pyrrhonian epistemology, as suggesting that skeptics have a "theory of knowledge" further suggests that they make certain claims about what knowledge is[40]) and its practical manifestations. Tad Brennan remarks that "Sextus says on many occasions that the skeptic examines not all beliefs, but only '*dogmata*.' And by '*dogmata*' Sextus means the principles and tenets characteristic of the professional schools of philosophy, as for instance the Epicurean's belief in invisible atoms, or the Platonist's belief in eternal, unchanging forms."[41] Skeptics need not be dubious about bits of knowledge that most, if not all, of us take for granted, such as whether a car truly could hurt someone who doesn't look before crossing the street. They are not interested in unsettling all the beliefs that allow for everyday activity to occur; the doubt they propose is of a limited and focused kind. Berry reminds us that "the Skeptic is entitled to maintain a number of beliefs about perfectly ordinary and everyday matters, which he arrives at in the ways ordinary, everyday people do."[42] Indeed, "the Sextan skeptic is on no sort of mission to question things generally, he simply finds the views proffered by the Dogmatists brash and arrogant and puts them to question."[43] Brennan goes so far as to suggest that many, if not most "ordinary people are Sextan skeptics."[44]

The question that remains, however, is whether Nietzsche viewed his own skepticism in this way, or whether he was a skeptic at all. Indeed, there is no shortage of strong declarations in his works, declarations that would seem to rest on claims of objective, even metaphysical, knowledge. Surely, statements Nietzsche makes about the will to power or the eternal recurrence, for example, seem to be "dogmata" themselves. There may be no conclusive or satisfactory answer to this apparent contradiction,[45] but I am sympathetic to Berry as she tries to ameliorate the problem: "What I would like to say here is that the passages in which Nietzsche does embrace caution, *ephexis*, and suspicion and in which he steadfastly refuses to sully himself in the arena of metaphysical mudslinging far and away outnumber those in which he sounds adamant and dogmatic."[46] In terms of volume, then, Nietzsche appears to be more of a skeptic than a dogmatist.

Of course, we need to do more than count beans to establish Nietzsche as a Pyrrhonist. I will follow Berry in her attempt to evince Nietzsche's Pyrrhonist stance, but with an important caveat. Our more limited goal here is to better understand the skeptical nature of the free spirit. It is not essential that we find conclusive evidence that Nietzsche is a skeptic, or more precisely a Pyrrhonist.[47] We have noted already that Nietzsche himself is not equivalent to the free spirit. But we also know, via Nietzsche's numerous proclamations, that the free spirit is a skeptic. Therefore, what we want to glean from our investigation is a clearer conception of the skeptical free spirit, that is, how Nietzsche was thinking about skepticism as he declares his free spirit a skeptic. Berry endeavors to interpret Nietzsche as a Pyrrhonist, but, whether she succeeds or not, we are left with a much clearer view of the free spirit's skeptical nature.

Berry produces abundant textual evidence that the skepticism we see in Nietzsche's works mirrors that of the Pyrrhonist tradition. She looks, for instance, at early *Nachlass* passages for Nietzsche's comments on the purpose and value of philosophy:

> Consider, for example, "The Philosopher as Cultural Physician," in which Nietzsche notes at several points that part of the "value of philosophy" is that it "cleanses muddled and superstitious ideas. Opposes scientific dogmatism." . . . Among its most valuable contributions, he thinks, are both "*the destruction of rigid dogmatism*: (a) in religion, (b) in mores, (c) in science," and "the *skeptical* impulse. Every force (religion, myth, knowledge

drive) has barbarizing, immoral, and stultifying effects when it is taken to extremes as an inflexible master (Socrates)."[48]

Philosophy's central purpose is to oppose dogmatism and cleanse one of "muddled and superstitious ideas." Essentially, philosophy is not the search for truth—specifically universal truth or Truth with a capital "T"—but instead a remedy for poor or sick thinking. Moreover, Nietzsche's style of philological interpretation—his academic training was in philology, not philosophy—aims at the same suspension of judgment that the Pyrrhonists were after. Again, it is helpful to quote Berry at length:

> Philology, understood in a broad sense as Nietzsche does here, is an interpretive art. Though he often uses the language of *textual* interpretation, much of his talk is metaphorical in these contexts, and his use of "interpretation" is by no means restricted to the exegesis of academic or philosophical texts. We are doing important interpretive work whenever we perceive and try to understand the everyday, phenomenal world.... And to do it well, Nietzsche says, is to employ "caution, patience, [and] subtlety." Now perhaps these attitudes alone would not indicate that a genuine suspension is what Nietzsche has in mind. But he makes the further claim in this passage that philology *means* "*ephexis* in interpretation." As Nietzsche is well aware, the Greek term *ephexis* means "a stopping or checking," and it comes from the verb *epechein*, which itself means "to hold back" or "to check." In Hellenistic skepticism, "holding back" or refraining from judgment is precisely what characterizes the activity of a Skeptic; the term *epechein* is the *source* of the Pyrrhonian skeptics' concept *epochē* ("suspension of judgment").[49]

There is much to untangle in this passage. The concepts of *epochē* and the also relevant *ataraxia*, and their relation to Pyrrhonist skepticism, will be addressed in the following section. Presently, however, we should note that Berry has shown a direct connection between Nietzsche's method of interpretation and the method of the Pyrrhonists. Nietzsche consciously employs skeptical methods, and the aim of these methods likewise mirrors the aims of the Pyrrhonists.

A third and final piece of evidence supporting Nietzsche's Pyrrhonian outlook is his notion of "perspectivism." Perspectivism, or the notion that all knowledge is of a perspectival nature, is unsurprisingly an epistemological approach that is heavily debated, but again our purpose here will be limited to demonstrating a connection between Nietzsche and Pyrrhonism. Nietzsche forcefully claims the importance of perspective in *Beyond Good and Evil*: "perspective, the basic condition of all life."[50] Dogmatists want objective, irrefutable truth, but this desire is based on a "metaphysical need"; it is "a dogmatist's error"[51] that stems from the desire for intellectual security and stability. The intellectually honest person doesn't hide from the perspectival nature of knowledge. The wisdom of perspectivism finds a home in Sextus's writings as well. He proffers several examples in the physical world—to prove a much harder case, of course, than that of discovering varying perspectives in the metaphysical or moral world—to illuminate perspectivism: "Eggs appear soft in the bird but hard in the air. . . . Coral appears soft in the sea, but hard in the air. And sound appears different when produced in a pipe, in a flute, or simply in the air."[52] We perceive material facts differently depending on where they come from. "Since, then, all apparent things are observed in some place and from some interval and in some position, and each of these produces a great deal of variation in appearances, as we have suggested, we shall be forced to arrive at a suspension of judgment."[53] Knowledge is situated in a certain way and in a certain context; we cannot assume that what appears to be a "truth" today will also be a "truth" tomorrow, in a different time and context.

The evidence suggests that this is Nietzsche's view as well: "If we examine the best textual evidence we have for Nietzsche's perspectivism, we will find little more than a commitment to the view that all knowing is 'situated' in a sense to be explained presently. The claim that all knowing is perspectival is intended to undermine philosophical claims to 'objectivity' that Nietzsche regards as symptomatic of the ascetic ideal."[54] The epistemological assumptions made by Nietzsche are similar to those of the Pyrrhonists, and the goal—that of attacking the claims of dogmatists—is likewise the same. Moreover, this kinship should give pause to those who attempt to find bold metaphysical claims in Nietzsche (e.g., will to power, eternal recurrence) and attempt to build a Nietzschean system out of them. As Nietzsche remarks in *Twilight of the Idols*, "I distrust all systematizers and avoid them. The will to a system is a lack of integrity."[55] Berry reaches a similar conclusion: "A recognition of the likeness between perspectivism and Skepticism, and an understanding of the roots of that skepticism in a tradition with which Nietzsche is well familiar, should together force us to appreciate his unwillingness to defend the audacious positions attributed to him by the metaphysical readings."[56] Regardless of how one comes down on the debate over the nature of such metaphysical readings, it should be clear by now that skepticism was an important epistemological stance for Nietzsche, and certainly that it is the epistemological stance of the free spirit.[57] A skeptical outlook is one of the main methods through which the free spirit faces the truths of existence.

Skepticism and Cheerfulness

As we have seen, the free spirit's skepticism is practicable—a way of life rather than a mere epistemological theory; it is antidogmatic, and it is ever open to investigation. What is more, however, is what such skepticism allows for in terms of spiritual fulfillment. How can skepticism result in a positive spiritual state? Recall Nietzsche's claim when describing the free spirit that a "free, fearless hovering over men, customs, laws and the traditional evaluations of things must *suffice* him as the condition he considers most desirable."[58] The passage suggests that skepticism need not be viewed as a negative reaction to what the moral and epistemic traditions offer; it is not world denial. It can be, instead, a positive reaction to the unknown, a "free, fearless hovering." The free spirit seeks out a skeptical attitude as a means to the liberation that is "the condition he considers most desirable"; skepticism is an indication that the free spirit's goal of spiritual liberation from tradition has been achieved.

This goal, and the positive spiritual state that results from its achievement, also have roots in the ancient skeptical tradition. The concepts of *epochē*, translated as "suspension of judgment," and *ataraxia*, "tranquility" or "freedom from disturbance," illuminate the intellectual process of a skeptic. A skeptic differs from most other persons by the relentless nature of her investigating and inquiring. Being unsatisfied with typical or common answers to big questions, the skeptic investigates further. What happens eventually, according to Pyrrhonism, is that she will come to find multiple arguments that seem relatively persuasive and possibly true. Arguments are "equipollent," they have equal or close to equal strength, and no one claim can be accepted as true. The next natural intellectual move, then, is to suspend judgment (*epochē*). The skeptic reaches equipollence of argument while reflecting, which leads to suspension of judgment, and what follows is *ataraxia*, or a certain sort of spiritual satisfaction. Satisfaction is reached not because a conclusion has been reached, but because one can go no further. John Laursen explains it accordingly: "In their own terms, the Pyrrhonists adopted an attitude of suspension of belief or judgment (in Greek, *epochē*). This, in turn, led to freedom from disturbance or tranquility (*ataraxia*). Rather than seek the reality that was somehow behind or beneath the surface of things according to competing philosophies, they were content to live with appearances (*phainomena*)."[59] The intellectual process of the skeptic terminates in a positive spiritual state, contrary to the conventional view of the knowledge-denying skeptic as lost at sea. In fact, the skeptic becomes cheerful through her unceasing intellectual investigation. Berry concludes that "upon closer inspection we will find that the roots of both the Epicurean and late Pyrrhonian senses of [*ataraxia*] make more than enough room for thinking of it not negatively, as the avoidance of suffering, but in a wholly positive way, as a state of psychophysical balance and indication of strength, life, and health—and in fact, *as a state of cheerfulness.*"[60]

The ties between ancient skepticism and spiritual freedom begin to clearly emerge. Nietzsche states that the free spirit finds the condition of spiritual freedom, "free, fearless hovering," to be the most desirable condition. The notions of *epochē* and *ataraxia* describe the path one takes to reach such a state of spiritual freedom. Moreover, the pursuit of this spiritual freedom will naturally affect what types of activities one engages in and what types of behavior one exhibits. The free spirit prefers this condition over other conditions that many would never consider leaving or would at least prefer to such spiritual freedom: the sense of peace and consolation that stems from participating in traditions like religious ceremonies; the sense of identity that comes from being part of a certain nation, race, or people; or the sense of fellowship that may result from seeing oneself as a member of a political community. Living without such attachments may be difficult for many, and for this reason Nietzsche takes pains to warn would-be free spirits that the condition of spiritual freedom "must *suffice* him" as the most desirable condition.

But what is it about breaking with tradition and community that will "suffice" one—that is, will be sufficient to one—as the most desirable condition? Spiritual liberation is well and good, but how can mere freedom be all that one desires? Why should I think of freedom and skepticism as positive conditions, when they seem instead to negate so many things? Even *ataraxia*, if thought of in terms of tranquility, seems to be a sort of sedated state, after all. I will attempt to answer these questions later on, but first we must take note of the importance that the idea of a cheerful temperament, or disposition, has to any answer we may come up with. Like the Pyrrhonists who claim that *ataraxia* is a state of cheerfulness, so too does Nietzsche assert the role of cheerfulness in the life of the skeptic.

We should remember that Nietzsche asserts the importance of one's temperament in confronting the truths of existence. A spirit who is naturally free by temperament, possessing "a firm, mild and at bottom cheerful soul," is capable of inwardly facing up to the existential, moral, and epistemic truths we have described. But how does one come to possess such a temperament? In the language of contemporary psychology, temperament is not something one has any control over. Temperament is a predisposition one is born with, or a "configuration of inclinations" we are given, as opposed to a "configuration of habits" that we may arrange and that constitute our character.[61] Thus, temperament is fixed, while character is changeable. Moreover, psychologists like David Keirsey argue that internal temperament, when influenced by the external environment, *determines* character.[62] It would therefore be impossible, in this psychological picture, for one to achieve the cheerful soul requisite for free-spiritedness if one were not born with it.

When Nietzsche employs the term "temperament," however, he does not adhere to the sharp distinction between temperament and character psychologists make today. Rather, Nietzsche asserts that one may indeed be born with a certain temperament—in this case "cheerful"—but does not believe that such a temperament is impossible for one not born with it. In section 486 of *Human, All Too Human*, entitled "One thing is needful," Nietzsche states that "there is one thing one has to have: either a cheerful disposition by nature, or a *disposition made cheerful* by art and knowledge."[63] Hence, while Nietzsche acknowledges a difference between temperament one is born with and character that can be cultivated, one does not preclude the other. Instead, we may work towards having a cheerful soul. To understand how Nietzsche thinks this can be done, we should look at his understanding of drives, which we may treat as equivalent to the term "inclinations" that is used by Keirsey. For Nietzsche, there are numerous methods (six, to be precise) one can use to resist, and thereby to shape and mold, the "vehemence of a drive."[64] Individuals are able to shape their drives, and they are therefore able to shape their characters—at least to a limited extent. Character formation is a result of *arranging* one's drives in order to form a coherent character or personality. One may not choose one's drives, but one may choose which to cultivate and which to combat, which to weaken and which to strengthen, and in doing so form a chosen character. Nietzsche describes it accordingly: "One can dispose of one's drives like a gardener and, though few know it, cultivate the shoots of anger, pity, curiosity, vanity as productively and profitably as a beautiful fruit tree on a trellis."[65] As a gardener cultivates his plants to create a coherent and beautiful garden, a free spirit may arrange one's drives to form a "firm, mild and at bottom, cheerful soul."

It is important to note that the notion of drive cultivation as being somehow "self-directed" (i.e., not *determined*) is controversial. After all, Nietzsche himself wonders whether the drive to cultivate and master the drives is not simply another drive itself. There is considerable scholarship surrounding this question, which will be addressed later along with a discussion of spiritual autonomy. For now, however, it is sufficient to assert that the free spirit's cheerful disposition is something that can be both naturally occurring and artificially changed. One can be born with such a temperament, or one can become so. In either case, cheerfulness is a necessary condition for the free spirit as she faces the truths of existence. Yet the idea that free spirits possess the requisite temperament for a world free of illusion still does not fully explain how the condition of spiritual freedom is sufficient for them. An arrival at *ataraxia* constitutes an important spiritual goal and contributes to spiritual fulfillment, but the emphasis on tranquility doesn't quite render it a sufficient condition for spiritual fullness. At some level, skepticism remains a negation of the "traditional evaluations of things," but it does not do enough to provide one with a positive direction. If the free spirit is merely a skeptic, albeit one of the Pyrrhonist variety, we may be hesitant to claim she has achieved spiritual fullness through *epochē* and *ataraxia*. The orientation of the free spirit would still be characterized in terms of what it is oriented *away from*, and we are seeking an orientation *towards* something. Later on in the book we will take a look at a potential positive orientation for the free spirit. Our conclusions now, however, are that the free spirit is a skeptic with a cheerful temperament who seeks above all to confront life and existence directly, fearlessly hovering over the illusions of tradition, metaphysics, and customary morality.

Now that we have discovered and enumerated the criteria for being a free spirit, we can see that free spirits might be found in many different walks of life.[66] We could find free spirits among the ranks of myriad artists, such as writers, composers, painters, and others. We might find free spirits amongst persons that would not be considered members of the literati, persons who may work in agriculture, industry, services, and the like. There may also be degrees of spiritual freedom, that is, these traits may emerge at various points in a person's life but not all of them, or at times with great intensity and other times with less. Treating the free spirit as a practical ethical ideal presumes that the ideal will be participated in at some times but not at others. Spiritual freedom may be a demanding ideal, but it is not impractical. We can practice it, even improve our ability to achieve it, even if we cannot maintain it in perpetuity. We never live up to our ideals constantly or even consistently, but this is precisely what makes them ideals. This is how I suggest we view spiritual freedom. Wherever we find free spirits, it is clear that they will experience a certain kind of relation to the human community at large. We must now ask some questions about how a free spirit relates to society. I will argue that what is important for us to focus on is not where a person is positioned—socially, economically, politically, and so on—in society, but *how a person positions himself in relation to society.* How free spirits choose to relate to society will be explored in the next chapter.

Chapter 2

A Safe Distance from Politics

> A man can be himself only so long as he is alone, and if he does not love solitude, he will not love freedom, for it is only when he is alone that he is really free.
>
> —Arthur Schopenhauer

Perhaps many people can identify, or sympathize, with the free spirit and can recognize free-spirited traits to a greater or lesser extent in both themselves and others. As a political theorist, I am interested in how knowledge of spiritual freedom affects the way we think about politics, about relations amongst humans and engagement in political behavior. To approach this subject, we need to better grasp how a free spirit relates to society. Society can be defined as civil society, the political regime, a religious or ethnic community, or just a group of friends or acquaintances. Society can mean all of these things, so we must break it apart if we are to inspect it further. I am interested in understanding the free spirit's relation to three different types of society: that of friends, that of politics, and that of what political theorists call community. I will show in what follows that the free spirit avoids deep engagement with the practice of politics[1] and the community, but in doing so does not necessarily choose reclusive solitude. The pursuit of spiritual freedom and fullness requires distance—perhaps even active disentanglement—from politics and community, but it need not prevent one from enjoying the society of friends. Regarding politics and community, we will find that the distancing and disentangling that free spirits undergo does, however, constitute a sort of social role for them. Consciously or not, free spirits have an effect on the spheres of politics and community. The following discussion should illuminate this effect and the ways in which free spirits relate to different types of society more broadly, and it will culminate in some real-world examples of how they do this in practice.

A free spirit aimed at spiritual liberation does, necessarily, walk on a more deserted road than most. Such spiritual independence is not common. Nor should one who seeks it expect to be surrounded by peers. Nietzsche makes multiple claims to this effect: "Independence is for the very few; it is a privilege of the strong";[2] these very few strive "instinctively for a citadel and a secrecy where [they are] saved from the crowd, the many, the great majority";[3] and, finally, "insofar as we are born, sworn, jealous friends of solitude, of our own most profound, most midnightly, most middaily solitude: that is the type of man we are, we free spirits!"[4] Such strong statements lead one to think of the free spirit as a solitary spiritual hermit. Nietzsche himself spent the bulk of his productive writing years largely in his own company—in Switzerland during the summers and Italy and France during winter months—staying in modest bunkhouses and mostly keeping to himself.[5]

Some scholars have remarked that such statements are indicative of Nietzsche's radical individualism, which is a natural offshoot of his epistemological skepticism. Leslie Paul Thiele argues, for example, that "the road to radical individualism, which has its greatest ramifications in the realms of politics and morality, finds its origin in epistemology. The starting point is the limitation of man's mind. Nietzsche's individualism is above all the extension of his skepticism." Thiele continues, "The individual, like the species, cannot see around his own corner. Each is locked into a world of his own."[6] If one believes that all knowledge is peculiar, to some degree, to the person who holds it, social interaction may be strained. Shared understanding and mental connection with others at a deep level would certainly be more difficult to come by.

For Thiele this radical individualism leads to a general rejection of society: "The individual is a law unto himself, unpredictable and unmanageable. Society, then, cannot be composed of individuals. It requires members. . . . The price of social membership is the forfeiture of self-rule, this by means of establishing social norms."[7] This argument suggests that the radically individualistic free spirit will shun the constraints imposed by social membership, and that maintaining a strong solitary life may be a practical necessity for her. Social interactions for the basic necessities of life, and for human connection and friendship, are available to the free spirit, but the forfeiture of self-rule and unquestioned obedience to social norms required for social membership are costs free spirits are unwilling to pay. Social membership often requires these costs, according to Thiele, and the true individualist will therefore shun social membership. Whether or not we agree with Thiele's assessment of Nietzsche as an individualist, the figure of the free spirit seems to fit with such a position.[8]

I think, however, that it is important to dig a little deeper to see whether the free spirit is truly required to be so solitary. First, we should question if Nietzsche thought the free spirit must wholly take leave of society. My reading suggests that, on the contrary, the free spirit must abstain not from all societal interaction but from the arena of practical politics and the identification with her community. Free spirits can still be members of society, while maintaining their distance from certain aspects of it. The society of others is not necessarily dangerous to spiritual liberation; it is a question of society with whom. This is consistent with Nietzsche's view as well. A case in point is Nietzsche's flirtation, on several different occasions, with the idea of creating a "monastery for free spirits" like himself.[9] A second consideration regarding the free spirit as presented here, which may not necessarily be Nietzsche's view, is that the tendencies of spiritual freedom may be more or less evident at given times. Free spirits may choose when and how much to engage in social interaction, and sometimes this interaction may connect with politics and political community. However, free spirits will always be wary of identifying too closely with the traditions of their community, or of becoming too involved in practical politics; both of these potential problems will be discussed in more detail later.

The best way to understand how a free spirit deals with these problems is to leave abstract theorizing aside and observe some real-life free spirits in action. I will discuss the lives of Johann Wolfgang von Goethe, Herman Hesse, Ralph Waldo Emerson, Henry David Thoreau, and C. S. Lewis to demonstrate the role of a free spirit. Nietzsche's archetypal free spirit, Goethe, creates distance between himself and politics and between himself and community while at the same time cultivating friendships of the spirit with those like himself. Hermann Hesse, who lived after Nietzsche, shares Goethe's method, as it were, of cultivating friendships while avoiding political and communal connections. In like manner, Emerson, Thoreau, and Lewis all endeavored, consciously and deliberately, to minimize contact with society in order to focus on spiritual pursuits. As we hear their stories it becomes clear that a free spirit need not be an awkward, asocial, solitary hermit. Nevertheless, a tension between free spirits and those two spheres of society—politics and community—undoubtedly exists. The arena of politics and the choice of taking one's identity to be a matter of community membership are obstacles to spiritual liberation, according to both Nietzsche and the argument I will make here. So what does Nietzsche have to say about these spheres of life?

During the period in which Nietzsche was writing and publishing *Human, All Too Human*, he wrote in his notebooks the "Die zehn Gebote des Freigeistes" (Ten Commandments for Free Spirits).[10] We should probably assume that these commandments were written with quite a bit of Nietzsche's tongue in his cheek, as the idea of commandments for a free spirit isn't free of irony. Nevertheless, these commandments guide one to a better understanding of the orientation of the free spirit and what sorts of life-activities threaten his spiritual freedom. Some are quite predictable—for example, "Thou shalt not submit yourself to any religious ceremony"; "Thou shalt avoid the famous and influential." Others are less obvious—for example, "Thou shalt not regret an offence, but rather perform one more good deed." Our focus will be on those commandments that give us a sense of how a free spirit should position herself in relation to society, politics, and community.

The following commandments show what Nietzsche considered threatening to spiritual freedom. The first arena is politics, where the message is unambiguous: "Thou shalt not practice politics." This blanket statement about practicing politics seems to cover both the stronger sense of politics as political rule and also the weaker sense of engaging in the political process through methods available to a common citizen. We will spend much more time unpacking the sorts of political activities a free spirit should avoid later.

The second arena, society with others, or friends, is touched upon in a commandment about the education of children: "Thou shalt let your children be educated by your friends." This presupposes that the free spirit *has* friends, and should lead us to be more skeptical of the claim that the free spirit must be a solitary hermit.[11] It also suggests that free spirits *choose* their own society, they desire to interact with those they deem worthy; worthy in the sense that they allow for, or even help facilitate, their spiritual goals. It is not complete isolation that the free spirit is after, but an individual pursuit of knowledge and self-discovery that might find assistance in others. Other scholars have noted this as well. Daigle claims that "the free spirit's search for truth will only be successful if he engages with others who can be his friends.... The free spirit's association with the right individuals, namely those that are deemed equals, will lead to his flourishing and self-knowledge."[12] In a similar manner, Christa Davis Acampora discusses the way in which free spirits avoid burdensome attachments to some in order to create more meaningful and useful attachments to others: "It is not a matter of being radically unbound. Ideally, it includes being *enabled* in a certain way, that is, to be *free to* form significant relations with others."[13] Resisting "addiction" to negative attachments and partiality towards others may even allow for a better love of others, according to Acampora.[14] I will not delve any deeper into the question of a "proper" friend for a free spirit, but Nietzsche clearly does find value in friendships and does not advocate complete isolation.

Finally, there are two commandments that are at least loosely tied to the idea of community and the identification of oneself as a member of a particular community. The first commandment is "Thou shalt neither love nor hate peoples or nations." This commandment indicates the importance to love oneself and other selves but never *Völker*, that is, peoples or nations. The message here, it seems, is that one should not identify oneself with—or attach oneself too closely to—one's community or nation to the extent that one may love or hate it. In other words, one should resist fanatical and dogmatic attachment to one's *Völker*. Spiritual autonomy requires the treatment of others as *individuals*, as opposed to members of a particular community. The free spirit, who seeks above all individual autonomy in the form of spiritual freedom, thereby requires individualized identity. The fifth commandment returns to this theme: "Thou shalt take your wife from a people or nation other than your own." We can infer from the fifth commandment that to prove one's commitment to liberation from tradition a free spirit shall look past his particular community for a spouse, ostensibly in order to reduce the influence of tradition on one's marriage and life. This should ensure that one is conscious of the way of life one is leading, rather than merely assuming the way of life most often lived by those in one's community and tradition. Moreover, one's individuality might be better maintained if one's spouse is from another people, as the contrast of diverse backgrounds illuminates individual differences. Again, from these two commandments we can infer that Nietzsche wants the free spirit to abstain from strong identification with one's nation or community.

It would be a mistake to consider the "Ten Commandments for Free Spirits" as an authoritative moral code for two basic reasons. First, Nietzsche never published the commandments himself; we find them in his notebooks, and perhaps they are best understood as thought exercises. Secondly, Nietzsche was fond of bits of wit and irony in his writings, and of attempts to shake up his readers, and it seems reasonable to think crafting rules for a spirit that wishes to "hover" over traditional moral rules was one of these bits. Nietzsche's thorough skepticism virtually precludes the idea of strict moral rules, and he is well aware of this as he playfully creates his own. Thus, while we ought not to take these commandments too seriously, they do provide a rough guide to what Nietzsche thinks free spirits are like both individually and as members of society. Again, our examination of the free spirit as a member of "society" separates into three spheres: societies of friends, politics, and community. The free spirit finds obstacles, or perhaps more accurately threats, to spiritual liberation in both politics and community. I will address the free spirit's relationship to each of these spheres now, beginning with politics. It is sensible to look to the sphere of politics first because it is less ambiguous than the idea of "community," and because Nietzsche directed many of his attacks at the politics of his day.

Eschewing Practical Politics

The message Nietzsche has for free spirits regarding the political sphere is straightforward: stay away from it. "Thou shalt not practice politics" if you are a free spirit, but why exactly is this? The growth of all great individuals—all free spirits—is stunted or destroyed by the burdens of politics:

> Questions and cares of the public weal, renewed every day, devour a daily tribute from the capital in every citizen's head and heart: the sum total of all these sacrifices and costs in individual energy and work is so tremendous that the political emergence of a people almost necessarily draws after it a spiritual impoverishment and enfeeblement and a diminution of the capacity for undertakings demanding great concentration and application.[15]

The free spirit must exist above and outside the "ephemeral chatter of politics and national egoism"[16] or risk his own destruction, that is, the imprisoning of his spirit. Nietzsche rhetorically implores, how many "more spiritual plants and growths . . . have to be sacrificed to this coarse and gaudy flower of the nation?"[17]

Nietzsche makes it clear in these passages that he thinks political activity takes a toll on one's spirit, and he further makes it clear that some should be allowed to evade such a toll. I think a plausible way to think about this is to take as given that a spirit has a finite amount of energy, energy it needs to cultivate itself. Considered this way, one can argue that political activity—both in the sense of one devoting one's life to politics (e.g., running for office, taking a job in political administration) and in the lesser political engagement one may choose (e.g., public discourse, electioneering, involvement with political groups, diligently following the news as opposed to being "rationally ignorant"[18])—saps one's limited spiritual energy. Such spiritual energy is needed to cultivate a free spirit; therefore the possibility of a spirit marked by "free, fearless hovering over men, customs, laws and the traditional evaluations of things" rests to some extent on the evasion of politics.

Nietzsche is hardly alone in his condemnation of politics. All of the free spirits we discuss in the next chapter share similar sensibilities, and we shouldn't be surprised to find voices in agreement with such condemnation on a wide scale in society. This is as true today as in Nietzsche's time. Several scholars of different disciplines have recently begun to question the effects of politics on individuals as well.[19] Jason Brennan claims that "we no longer have to speculate, as Mill did, about what politics does to us. Psychologists, sociologists, economists, and political scientists have spent more than sixty years studying how people think about, react to, and make decisions in politics."[20] Brennan finds, as do Christopher Achen and Larry Bartels, that political participation is not, by and large, motivated by a desire to engage in rational debate. The impulses that drive political participation are irrational, partisan, and group-based rather and individualized. John Stuart Mill hoped that the spread of political involvement would improve society; he "hypothesized that getting citizens involved in politics would enlighten them."[21] But what we have found instead is that participation stultifies people, it makes them worse off than they would otherwise be. In characteristically acerbic form, Brennan concludes, "Politics tends to make us hate each other, even when it shouldn't. We tend to divide the world into good and bad guys. We tend to view political debate not as reasonable disputes about how to best achieve our shared aims but rather as a battle between the forces of light and darkness. It's especially bizarre that mainstream political discussion is so heated and apocalyptic, given how *little* is at stake."[22] Whether or not we fully agree with Brennan's quite negative account of political participation, we can understand the motivation behind it. The daily dose of political information is enough to harm the patient, and Brennan further alerts us to the irrational way in which we process this information. It is far from clear that deliberation makes us better or more understanding, as a society or as individuals. The dangers of politics as Nietzsche saw them remain dangers today; perhaps, for us, it is even more difficult to resist the pull and prevalence of politics because it is harder to consistently avoid contact with political media.

The salient point is that tension between spiritual freedom and politics is evergreen, and wariness of and skepticism toward political participation seems a mark of health. Free spirits, if they are to achieve spiritual liberation and maintain it, require some distance from politics. Indeed, Nietzsche advocates the privacy of these individuals. He remarks, "If the purpose of all politics really is to make life endurable for as many as possible, then these as-many-as-possible are entitled to determine what they understand by an endurable life." But, he rejects the notion that these can demand "that *everything* should become politics in this sense, that *everyone* should live and work according to such a standard." The free spirits must be allowed to detach themselves from politics:

> For a few must first of all be allowed, now more than ever, to refrain from politics and to step a little aside: they too are prompted to this by pleasure in self-determination; and there may also be a degree of pride attached to staying silent when too many, or even just many, are speaking. Then these few must be forgiven if they fail to take the happiness of the many.[23]

The standards of the many do not apply to some few, and these few, the free spirits, should not be coerced into adopting those standards.

Nietzsche does not detail precisely how these few are to "step a little aside"; that is, we cannot tell from this statement what sort of political system he means to advocate, if any. What is clear, however, is that a life-consuming or coercive politics, which seeks to force a particular way of life on its citizens,[24] cannot be reconciled with Nietzsche's apparent call for freedom of the few from politics. For regimes that place the cause of the nation above the cause of the individual—and which enforce strong membership and obedience on its citizens—are the "coarse and gaudy flowers" to which so many "spiritual plants and growths" are sacrificed.

For the few—these free spirits—the cause of the nation will forever be dangerous, which gives us another clue as to what sort of politics is harmful to them. The nationalist political regimes emerging throughout Europe beginning at the end of the eighteenth century, which declared the state to be of primary importance—both at the expense of the individual and of all other states—were not constituted with Nietzsche's call for separation and privacy for the "few" in mind. Nietzsche also confronts political perfectionism in *Human, All Too Human*. That is, he challenges the claim that one of the state's functions is to improve and perfect the citizens within it. In the aphorism entitled "Genius incompatible with the ideal state," Nietzsche argues that a perfect state[25] is one that puts the good of society, of the social (political) body, above that of the individual. For Nietzsche, even if mankind were able to produce an ideal state, "mankind would have become too feeble still to be able to produce the genius." The free-spirit "will refrain from promoting the foundation of the 'perfect state,' inasmuch as only enfeebled individuals can have any place in it."[26]

Nietzsche's position on the relation of free spirits to politics appears straightforward on this reading. Indeed, there can be little doubt that he considered deep engagement with politics to be anathema, to put it mildly, to free spirits. Active partisan membership jeopardizes spiritual freedom, as adherence to political platforms and political ideologies is required for the promotion of political causes. We can imagine that some political positions may be compatible with a free spirit's spiritual pursuits, such as administrative positions that require no political allegiance or active political participation.[27] We can also say with reasonable judgment that a free spirit can vote without giving up too much. Nonetheless, deeper engagement should be shunned, which leaves out many common political roles and occupations: those of political officials, journalists, campaign workers, lobbyists, and so on. Likewise, even if one's occupation is apolitical, intense or obsessive engagement with current events and political media should also be avoided. The key argument I want to make here is that active participation in politics, understood as making political life at least a large and important aspect, if not the driving force, of one's life, is not something a free spirit can do without ceasing to be one.

With this conclusion in mind, it may be hard to imagine a political role for free spirits. Yet despite appearances to the contrary, and whether or not free spirits intend to do so, free spirits do play an important political role. To identify such a role, however, requires a more abstract notion of politics than what we have defined as political activity heretofore, a notion we can find throughout Nietzsche's works. Nietzsche often talks of a battle over ideas and values when referring to politics. Put differently, Nietzsche distinguishes between practical politics and political philosophy. The free spirit avoids the former, but may engage in the latter. By entering the battle over ideas and values—for example, by doing political philosophy—free spirits can to some extent influence political culture.

The Free Spirit in Nietzsche's Political Philosophy

As previously argued, I do not attempt to investigate and determine Nietzsche's political views. We are focused squarely on the free spirit. Nonetheless, some preliminary remarks about Nietzsche's politics are in order before analyzing the political culture that a free spirit may influence. Nietzsche's views on politics are often dissected but seldom agreed upon. Nevertheless, many have attempted to paint Nietzsche as a political thinker, perhaps even primarily a political thinker.[28] Herman W. Siemens claims that three moments stand out in the "standard" political reading of Nietzsche:

> Nietzsche is first and foremost an autarkic individualist (Stern, MacIntyre), philosophically insensitive to the sphere of social relations and deaf to the ethical claims of community. In the wake of a total critique of reason as will to power, Nietzsche (secondly) *abandons the claims of reason* altogether, turning instead to aesthetic and archaic values such as the "Tragic," the "Dionysian" and the "Noble" (Habermas). Since, on his own terms, modernity is too decadent or depleted to sustain such values, he (thirdly) entrusts our salvation to a *mighty act of will* on the part of superhuman redeemers (e.g., the Übermensch, Dionysos) who are yet to come.[29]

I do not intend for the discusson about the free spirit made here to fall entirely into any of these camps. I do not want the question of Nietzsche's politics to distract from the purpose at hand, which is to better understand spiritual freedom and to reflect on how this understanding applies to the citizen of the modern, liberal democratic order. We do, however, need to acknowledge some of the common perceptions of Nietzsche's political philosophy in order to disentangle them from the political philosophy of the free spirit. Moreover, we need to distinguish the free spirit from other human types that Nietzsche presents, notably the type he calls the "new philosopher."

In most cases, scholars who focus on Nietzsche's political philosophy note the elitist, neo-aristocratic proposals Nietzsche appears to proffer in his later works.[30] From this perspective, tying Nietzsche to liberal political order, as I am doing here, is at best an ignorant "stretch" and at worst a willful misrepresentation. I defend myself against such potential criticism by narrowing the focus to Nietzsche's figure of the free spirit. Whatever Nietzsche's true political views are—a point of contention unlikely to be resolved anytime soon—I believe I am justified in suggesting that the free spirit is of import for liberal political order. As Amy Mullin concludes:

> I hope also, now that we can recognize that Nietzsche's free spirit is neither associated with particular values, nor an exception to his general denial of freedom of the will, that we can begin to examine what may be appealing about the ideal of the free spirit. *Furthermore, we can see that Nietzsche's free spirit may be of interest even to those who do not share his repudiation of liberal democratic values, but who do share his enthusiasm for the ability to explore multiple ways of interpreting human behavior and norms.*[31]

Thus, regardless of Nietzsche's alleged elitism and aristocratic leanings, one of his most important human types—the free spirit, whom Siemens calls one of Nietzsche's favored conceptions of "genius"[32]—has much to offer to liberal political thought.

The free spirit desires not to be burdened with cultural or political goals. This does not mean, as mentioned earlier, that free spirits do not play—consciously or unconsciously—a political role. To see this role clearly, we must focus on politics as political philosophy: on a grand scale, as a battle over ideas and values. Paul Glenn examines this view of politics and how it applies to the debate over Nietzsche as a political philosopher: "At times Nietzsche does not seem like a political thinker at all because he does not discuss the best regime or details of what a good society would be. But this is the point: Nietzsche is attempting to redefine politics, to move beyond the narrow realm of the state and see the important struggles occurring quietly and, at times, invisibly."[33] These important struggles are over competing epistemologies, according to Glenn, and these so-called epistemologies[34] render competing moral and cultural values. The most significant political events, then, are "not what we often think they are, namely, wars, treaties, and the creation of legislation. Instead, the greatest events are the creation of values. Therefore, most of what we think of as politics is rather petty and minor; truly great politics are the battles over values and ideas."[35] Indeed, the free spirit is not required to take leave of all political and cultural *thinking*, and we may wonder if it would be possible in any case to leave all such thinking aside. Nonetheless, there is a distinction to be made between political thought and political action. This is made clear by Nietzsche in several places, as shown by Anthony K. Jensen in "Anti-politicality and Agon in Nietzsche's Philology." Jensen suggests that "although Nietzsche's self-appellation as the 'last anti-political German' is contained in a section of *Ecce Homo* (EH weise 3) whose publication he rather emphatically rejected, the phrase is still a fair characterization of Nietzsche's attitude toward what may be termed 'institutional involvement' in political affairs."[36] Such involvement should be avoided, but in the same work Nietzsche affirms the task of influencing cultural ideas and values, looking to the Greek poet Theognis as an example. Jensen demonstrates that in Theognis, Nietzsche found "a way to influence culture on a grand scale without resorting to governmental politicking."[37]

In other words, engaging in truly great politics is akin to engaging in political philosophy, specifically political philosophy that deals with the battle over values and ideas. To find where free spirits "fit," we may contrast them with another Nietzschean type, the "new philosopher."[38] Nietzsche's new philosopher, it turns out, is a sort of free spirit turned cultural creator. Compared with the new philosopher, the free spirit appears likely to be more contemplative than active, more private than political. As Jeremy Fortier claims, "The task of the free spirits is negative and destructive, rather than positive and constructive." They are Nietzsche's model "for how to criticize *existing* ideals, without aiming to refurbish or replace them."[39] According to Nietzsche, however, out of the free spirit this political—or to be more precise cultural—type might be born: the new philosopher, whose public role is the creation and teaching of new cultural values. When Nietzsche first introduces the free spirit he states, "if more is nonetheless desired of him [than his solitary freedom], he will, with a benevolent shake of the head, point to his brother, the free man of action," but of this latter man "there is a curious tale still to be told." The more active nature of the new philosopher is foreshadowed again at the end of *Human, All Too Human*, if and when a free spirit "and his heart grow weary of wandering."[40] In *Beyond Good and Evil* Nietzsche most clearly suggests the shortcomings of the free spirit, as detached spiritual hermit, if the goal in mind is cultural or political change. If he remains "quietly and proudly hidden in his citadel, one thing is certain: he was not made, he was not predestined, for knowledge. If he were . . . he would go *down*, and above all, he would go 'inside.'"[41] The free spirit is unwilling to leave his citadel and "go down" to the political community. The new philosopher, on the other hand, takes on the challenge of politics; he will go as a cultural creator, attempting to impose his revaluation of values. Zarathustra, and at times Nietzsche himself, especially as he presents himself in *The Anti-Christ*, exemplify the new philosopher.[42]

How do we know that the free spirit is distinct from the new philosopher? These other types, claims Richard Schacht, "would be not only interpreters but also leaders."[43] The free spirit, on the other hand, is contemplative rather than active, solitary rather than political. Some Nietzsche scholars dispute this characterization, notably Laurence Lampert and Paul Kirkland, who argue that the free spirit is not a model human type, but rather a mask that Nietzsche uses to further a political agenda. A thorough examination and challenge to these scholars' arguments is too large a task to engage here, but a few considerations warrant discussion.

According to Lampert, Nietzsche must don the mask of a free-spirited skeptic in his later works, particularly *Beyond Good and Evil*, in order to evade the annoyance of modern philosophers who consider skepticism to be the final stop on a philosopher's journey. Nietzsche's new philosopher is a legislator and commander who understands the will to power as the basis of real philosophy, so in *Beyond Good and Evil* Nietzsche appears "for now as a free spirit merely preparing the way for philosophers of the future who are beyond scepticism" in order to parry "the annoyance of the newly liberated free spirits for whom scepticism itself is the highest philosophical achievement."[44] For Lampert, scholars who defend Nietzsche's free spirit mistake the mask for the "real article," primarily on account of the fact that scholars think of themselves as free spirits and prefer their own type. In his later work, *Nietzsche's Task*, Lampert maintains this basic position, explaining that "the free mind" (which is now Lampert's translation for *der freie Geist*) is "enslaved to the ideals of the democratic enlightenment" and is therefore in need of overcoming.[45] But Lampert blurs the lines between free spirits and what Nietzsche calls free-thinkers when Lampert discusses the "free mind." Lampert misinterprets Nietzsche for his own rhetorical purposes here, for it is obvious that this distinction between free spirit and liberal democratic free-thinker is very important to Nietzsche, made evident in *Beyond Good and Evil* and also discussed by Mullin and Berkowitz.[46]

In a similar vein, Kirkland argues that inventing the free spirit was a rhetorical strategy used by Nietzsche to make readers aware of the shortcomings of the understanding of freedom as liberation from traditional values (as is argued here) and move them toward "higher goals and new modes of evaluation." Kirkland claims that "in this way, Nietzsche will prepare those committed to freedom understood as liberation from prejudices for freedom understood as the capacity for command, self-command, and responsibility."[47] For Kirkland, it is a mistake to think of a free spirit as actually existing; instead, it is a mask used to represent the "radicalization of the modern spirit" and the modern emphasis on enlightened rationalism.[48] Nietzsche's many critiques of modernity, Kirkland claims, show us that the free spirit was something to be overcome, replaced by the new philosopher.

The accounts of Lampert and Kirkland, however, ignore two major themes that recur throughout Nietzsche's works: first, the consistent emphasis Nietzsche places on the importance of solitude both in his writings on the free spirit and in his own life, and, second, the fact that Nietzsche takes pains in his writings to separate the free spirit from the more political types. Firstly, Nietzsche's insistence on solitude is well documented, and can be traced from his very first autobiography—authored at age fourteen—all the way through his later writings.[49] Moreover, many secondhand accounts have confirmed Nietzsche's penchant for solitude.[50] Secondly, we ought to follow Nietzsche's treatment of these as distinct human types, rather than to treat the new philosopher (or Übermensch) as the final overcoming of the free spirit. In every work, Nietzsche treats them as kindred but separate—for example, after his remark "That is the type of man we are, we free spirits!" he asks, "And perhaps *you* have something of this, too, you that are coming? You *new* philosophers?"[51] In addition, the free spirit is required to deviate from the cultural creation of the new philosopher once that creation has become strong, fixed, and stable (which signals its imminent decay). The free spirits must till the soil, so to speak, for new philosophers to plant their cultural seeds (to create new values), and this crop rotation continues in perpetuity.[52] Finally, it is unclear whether Nietzsche would have considered himself a free spirit or a new philosopher. He assumes both roles; the former as he remains a solitary author throughout his life and in his admiration of

Goethe, the latter in his creation of Zarathustra and in his cultural call to arms in *The Anti-Christ*.

Thus, while Lampert and Kirkland are certainly correct in suggesting that Nietzsche is interested in goals other than free-spirited liberation, it does not follow that the free spirit is merely a rhetorical mask. It appears, instead, that from the free spirit these political—or to be more precise cultural—types may be born. The new philosopher and the Übermensch seem to have a public role to play in the creation and teaching of new cultural and political values, or, in Kirkland's phrasing, "higher goals and new modes of evaluation." They therefore seek to integrate themselves into the political community in some way. Conversely, the free spirits require a strong, fixed, and stable political community to evolve *out* of. Again, Nietzsche paints the free spirit as a spiritual hermit, a solitary man.

We are thus pointed to a political role for free spirits. The free spirit prepares the ground for new philosophers by breaking with old traditions and values. This connection between the two types can be interpreted in two ways, with vastly different ramifications. One is that free spirits—as a sort of societal group—all work towards the goal of liberating society from the traditional values and morals of the past. Once this is done, the new philosophers enter, revaluing values and beginning a cultural renaissance. The other way to interpret the connection between free spirit and new philosopher, to which I subscribe, is that before one is to become a new philosopher—a creator of culture—one must necessarily be a free spirit. At the level of the individual, a spirit liberated from the old cultural values is essential for one to be able to create new ones. Michael Gillespie arrives at a similar conclusion, as he charts the stages of human development leading up to the idea of the superman. Gillespie identifies the free spirit as a skeptic who, like the lion-spirited in Zarathustra's "The Three Metamorphoses," uses his critical faculties "not to obtain truth but to shatter our subjection to all transcendent ideals."[53] The free spirit prepares the way for the Übermensch or new philosopher, but remains his own type, with his own methods. In like manner, J. Harvey Lomax argues that the free spirit represents an intermediary stage in the maturation of a philosopher. One must pass through the stage of spiritual freedom—much like one must pass from camel to lion to child in Nietzsche's *Zarathustra*—to ultimately become a genuine philosopher. As Lomax concludes, "Whatever might be said of the possibility of the superman, certain it is that the free spirit can exist: Nietzsche implies that he himself is a free spirit, and on first and second scrutiny Socrates would appear to qualify, too."[54] For both

Gillespie and Lomax, the free spirit is a separate and important human type that can be understood on its own terms.

For Nietzsche himself, the evidence suggests that he moved beyond the free spirit ideal in his later writings. *Thus Spoke Zarathustra* and *Twilight of the Idols*, for example, appear to be the work of a "new philosopher" or cultural creator rather than that of a free spirit. They do not represent detachment but the headlong entrance into political and cultural contests. These works explicitly endeavor to "create new values," rather than merely separating Nietzsche and his readers from the accepted values of one's time. The reasons for this shift are surely many, and it is beyond the purview of this book to investigate its causes and implications. There is also evidence of a change in his personal life between the "free-spirited" years and his later years, focused particularly around his relationship to Lou Salomé. Indeed, Nietzsche goes so far as to seemingly renounce his commitment to the free-spirited ideal in a letter to Salomé, but we must interpret this in the context of his courtly pursuit of her.[55] Furthermore, Nietzsche's lifelong struggle with loneliness may have played a role as well. He conveys his isolation at times in his personal writings, and desired to increase his interaction with others. Again, a thorough discussion of this shift in Nietzsche's writings and attitude is too far afield of the argument here, but we do need to acknowledge that the shift away from the free spirit ideal occurred. Other scholars, particularly Paul Franco, have engaged with this discussion in earnest.[56]

Despite the scholarly dissensus on Nietzsche's "true" understanding of the free spirit, what is important for our purposes here is that we follow Nietzsche's treatment of these as two distinct human types, rather than to treat the free spirit as merely a stepping stone to the new philosopher. Freedom of spirit, and its relationship to liberal politics, is my primary goal. Strong political engagement is to be avoided. As we saw earlier, the goals of nationalism and socialism are harmful to the free spirit, but these are not the only unworthy political goals. The free spirit is reluctant to pursue any final or all-encompassing goal. As Nietzsche says, "There are people who repose so steadily within themselves and whose capacities are balanced with one another so harmoniously that any activity directed towards a goal is repugnant to them."[57] And he emphasizes this again later: "He who has attained to only some degree of freedom of mind cannot feel other than a wanderer on earth—though not as a traveler to a final destination: for this destination does not exist."[58] The free spirit searches for an inner nobility that trumps any other pursuits, including political ones.

Even so, it is possible for the free spirit to practice what Robert Galbreath calls a politics of detachment, to carve a space for him or herself outside of politics while working towards inner freedom. To practice a politics of detachment is not to be apolitical; rather it is to avoid deep engagement with politics while working for the improvement of society by focusing inward. Individual liberation in the sense Nietzsche understands it does not come from constructing a political platform aimed at liberation as the goal. Instead, it requires *inner* transformation aimed at individual self-realization. Prima facie this does not seem like a political role; instead it appears wholly private. But as we will see in their lives and actions, the free spirits can have an effect on politics, an effect that constitutes a political role, albeit in an unconventional sense. In the following chapter, we will explore how some "real life" free spirits practice a politics of detachment, remaining spiritually free while having a beneficial effect on society.

Chapter 3

Free Spirits in Action

Practicing Political Detachment

> But your isolation must not be mechanical, but spiritual, that is, must be elevation. At times the whole world seems to be in conspiracy to importune you with emphatic trifles.
>
> —Ralph Waldo Emerson
>
> What is the value of any political freedom, but as a means to moral freedom?
>
> —Henry David Thoreau

In his writings, Nietzsche mentions Goethe as a free spirit more than any other figure. Goethe is Nietzsche's free spirit par excellence,[1] and the term "free spirit" also turns up in Goethe's corpus, particularly his conversations with Eckermann.[2] Goethe shows up often in *Human, All Too Human*, where Nietzsche introduces the free spirit and explains his virtues and solitude.[3] His opinion of Goethe as a model free spirit (and genius) did not waver over time, made evident by his praise in the late work *Twilight of the Idols*. Here he celebrates the traits of the free spirit that Goethe embodied:

> Goethe was, in an epoch disposed to the unreal, a convinced realist: he affirmed everything which was related to him in this respect. . . . Goethe conceived of a strong, highly cultured

> human being, skilled in all physical accomplishments, who, keeping himself in check and having reverence for himself, dares to allow himself the whole compass and wealth of naturalness, who is strong enough for his freedom; a man of tolerance, not out of weakness, but out of strength, because he knows how to employ to his advantage what would destroy an average nature.... A spirit thus *emancipated* stands in the midst of the universe with a joyful and trusting fatalism.[4]

The characteristics attributed to Goethe here are very similar to the characteristics Nietzsche presents in *Human, All Too Human* 34, when he first introduces the free spirit. In Goethe we have a real, living free spirit, and for this reason Goethe warrants further investigation. Goethe was Nietzsche's chosen free spirit, and by understanding how Goethe viewed his own relationship to politics we will better understand a free spirit's relation to politics in general.

Unlike the other free spirits to be examined in the following pages, Goethe was actively engaged in politics in his lifetime, holding a position as an important administrator in the small German state of Weimar. Goethe moved to Weimar in 1775 for at least partially political reasons. While the principal draw was a culturally and artistically active setting for his various projects, he also moved at the urging of a young duke, Carl August, who greatly admired Goethe and wanted him in his inner political circle.[5] "Goethe arrived in Saxe-Weimar as a favorite of the new eighteen-year-old duke, Carl August (1757–1828), but within a few months found himself appointed Legation Councillor with a seat in the four-member Privy Council, the highest governing organ in the duchy."[6] Goethe was like a chief of staff to the young duke, perhaps with a view towards shaping the younger man into an enlightened ruler. Goethe spent nearly a decade heavily burdened with administrative responsibilities. As Daniel Wilson notes, "The next 9 years—until his virtual withdrawal from the daily work of the Council in the spring of 1785—found Goethe so immersed in the minutiae of absolutist government that he published very little literature and was written off by the world of letters as a complete loss."[7]

Despite the fact that Goethe possessed a considerable political—in particular, administrative—record, the evidence suggests that he considered this experience as a distraction from his poetic and scientific pursuits, even a burden. The constant requirement of attending to official and unofficial meetings also took their toll. This is clearly observed, by Goethe himself, in his conversations with German poet Johann Peter Eckermann. For example, he confesses to Eckermann, "My real happiness was my poetical sensibility and creative power. But how much was this disturbed by my outward position, limited and hindered. If I had kept myself back more from public and business working and activity and been able to live more in solitude, I would have been happier and would have done far more as a poet."[8] Goethe was, however, unable to extricate himself from many public duties. Here is a representative example of his attitude, which we see recurring in the *Conversations*: "This morning the Archduke was with me, for to-morrow midday the Archduchess has had herself announced. I have to value such visits as a high favour, they embellish my life, but they make, however, demands on my inner being."[9] Eckermann himself witnesses the toll that Goethe's high public position placed on him, and he reports one especially dutiful period accordingly: "Above all [Goethe] was threatened with visitors from all neighborhoods. The meeting of famous Naturalists in Berlin had set in motion many men of importance, who, on their way passing through Weimar, had let themselves be partly announced and their arrival was to be expected. Disturbances for weeks in length which took away the inner feeling and turned things from their accustomed course, and all the other unpleasantness which are connected with such worthy visitors, all this must be felt in anticipation by Goethe in a ghost-like manner, as soon as he set foot on the threshold and walked through the spaces of his rooms."[10] Goethe was aware of the benefits of his high position, as well as its duties,[11] but he keenly felt the loss of time for the creative, artistic, scientific, spiritual goals he preferred to pursue.

Frustrated and worn out by a decade of Weimar politics, Goethe took an extended leave to Italy in 1786 to dissolve his political ties and recreate himself by resuming his poetic and scientific pursuits. In fact, on returning to Weimar in 1788, it was on the condition that he would have no further administrative duties, to which Carl August agreed. As Lesley Sharpe explains, "Carl August respected the fact that Goethe wished after his Italian sojourn to remain free of the administrative burdens that had oppressed him in the early 1780s."[12] We may conclude that Goethe was a reluctant politician, born into privilege (to a family of Frankfurt patricians) and later granted a noble title, who was more or less thrown, or dropped, into positions of leadership. Thomas Saine sums this fact up nicely: "Goethe occupied a position that often placed him closer to historical events than he might have liked and forced him to come to terms with them, not only personally, but above all for the sake of Duke Carl

August (1757–1828) and the small German state of Saxe-Weimar-Eisenach that Goethe served throughout his adult life."[13]

The same reluctance characterized Goethe's nonadministrative forays into politics. Many read Goethe's early novel *The Sorrows of Young Werther* as a romantic and politically revolutionary work, but it is not clear that Goethe viewed it as such. In the end, Goethe did not favor drastic political change, because it got in the way of his preferred pursuits: poetry, philosophy, science, and self-realization. Wilson disabuses us of the notion that Goethe was a sort of romantic revolutionary:

> The myth prevails, however, that when Goethe left his non-monarchist home town in 1775, at the age of twenty-six, he switched allegiances from a sort of youthful revolutionary élan to deference to princely authority. In truth, the pre-Weimar Goethe had merely toyed with social or political dissidence. He was no more revolutionary than his first novel's hero Werther, who seems to reject the boundaries between classes—or, more accurately, between estates—only to say in the next breath that he realizes they are necessary, and expresses frustration merely because they stand in the way of his very individualistic striving for self-realization.[14]

Indeed, Goethe's detachment from politics is evident from his early works. He was well aware that active engagement came at great cost, in terms of compromising both other intellectual pursuits and the journey of self-discovery he had embarked upon.

The crucial idea for Goethe, all throughout his life, was that it was not the outer political world, but the inner world that was of interest and that ought to be explored and expressed.[15] Politics were of the outer world and were, at best, of passing interest and, at worst, a distraction from Goethe's focus on expressing his inner life. Barker Fairley explains how Goethe's nature led him ultimately to be interested only in nonpolitical aspects of humanity:

> It was only to be expected that a poet who began, as Goethe did, by having such a lengthy struggle with himself, one inner problem leading to another till it seemed the inner problems would never cease, would be drawn into seeing life from this point of view, privately rather than publicly, and that he would

have no choice but to concentrate on those aspects of humanity which detached themselves, or came nearest to detaching themselves, from social and political questions.[16]

This explanation of Goethe's interests is supported by the opinions of his friends and associates. Georg von Reinbeck remarks in 1806 that "I can't remember [Goethe] ever talking about politics," and in January 1814 Wilhelm von Humboldt concluded that "Goethe was by nature indifferent to politics and nationalism."[17] Goethe never tried to repudiate such claims; indeed, he himself often spoke of his indifference to politics. He was a free spirit in the Nietzschean sense, believing that individuals like himself could only be burdened or even destroyed by politics, rendering them unable to produce and contribute what they could in philosophy, science, poetry, and literature. In a letter to F. F. Buchholtz in February 1814, Goethe relates that "he and private individuals like him did right to leave the troubled affairs of state to those whose business it was to deal with them and that he knew no better service he could perform for his part than by going on with the literary and philosophical survey of the recent history of his country that he was endeavoring to provide in his autobiography."[18] In other words, Goethe found it necessary to "step a little aside" from the political arena in order to properly utilize his talents and time.

Goethe's insistence on privacy did not result in total solitude, however. He maintained his distance from politics and community, but not from other human beings simply. He cared little for societal trends or grand politics, but he sought out those people "who could share his ideals and his enthusiasms with him."[19] As we may recall from our earlier discussion on the society of friends in chapter 2, this is precisely the notion of friendship that a free spirit ought to practice. Indeed, Goethe claims that "the poet who fails to establish his solidarity with the rest of mankind and to shape his life accordingly is a child not yet out of tutelage."[20] In the dedicatory poem that opens the first authorized edition of his printed works in 1784, he shows, speaking through the Muse, that he already (he was in his early thirties at the time) saw himself "as a man not so very different from other men, and that it is his duty to put his gifts at their service and to live with them in peace."[21] Thus we see that Goethe sought out connections with other humans, simultaneously maintaining his distance from politics and the political community. His contributions to other humans took the form of expressions of his inner world. His "gift" was that of expressing his inner world as a poet and of demonstrating the cultivation of the spirit.

Goethe famously stated that we are "pantheists as natural scientists, polytheists as poets, and monotheists as moral beings." He, of course, had experience and success in all of these fields; his quip, therefore, should provoke serious consideration. One serious conclusion we might draw is that here Goethe demonstrates his free-spirited nature. H. B. Nisbet comes to such a conclusion, claiming that in this statement Goethe "was not defining precise ideological differences. . . . He was simply pointing out that no one set of doctrines can do full justice to the complexity of the universe and of human existence, although all of them have their distinct value if they are approached in a sympathetic and non-dogmatic spirit."[22] Goethe was ever resistant to dogma and ideology. He was skeptical of philosophy—understood by Goethe as the study of ideas rather than nature (German philosophy was very much under the influence of Kant at the time) and advocated a return to close observation of nature. Speaking of his contemporary Schiller, "I cannot help believing that Schiller's philosophical leaning has damaged his poetry, for through it he came to hold the idea higher than all nature, indeed by it to abolish nature. What he can imagine, must happen, whether it is in accordance with nature or the contrary."[23] Philosophy, if it succumbs to dogmatic belief in ideals, runs the risk of ideological possession and a spirit that is captured by it. Goethe's resistance to ideology and dogmatism mirrors that of Nietzsche's skeptical free spirit.

Goethe's own spiritual growth is a model to follow, he was a free spirit intent on practicing a politics of detachment. Moreover, he was cognizant of the favorable political climate in which he found himself in his later years, writing to Friedrich von Müller, in 1824, that he would not choose to have lived at any other time, and that German people were happy as long as each one was allowed to go his own way.[24] In other words, Goethe was able to pursue his own spiritual fulfillment both because he detached himself from politics and because of the political regime he lived under. Goethe's spiritual freedom was enabled in part by a regime liberal enough to allow for it.

Hesse

Another instructive example of how a free spirit may practice a politics of detachment comes in the form of German-Swiss writer Hermann

Hesse. The story of Hesse also portrays a free spirit practicing a politics of detachment, though in a political period with greater challenges than those that Goethe faced. Hesse wrote several books in the early mid-twentieth century revolving around the questions of inner transformation and spiritual fulfillment. Unlike Goethe, however, Hesse wrote in a tumultuous time for politics, and his works fell victim to a repressive regime; his books were eventually banned in Nazi Germany. Hesse was a free spirit who found himself in a political situation that threatened his spiritual freedom. Fortunately, however, Hesse's dual citizenship—he became a Swiss citizen in 1924 after he was denounced in Germany as a pacifist traitor—allowed him to peacefully leave Germany and live out his days in Switzerland.

Hesse was profoundly influenced by Nietzsche and treated many Nietzschean themes in his novels.[25] Hesse is therefore an appropriate choice as a model for Nietzsche's free spirit, as he both possessed the characteristics of the free spirit outlined here and was an avid student of Nietzsche himself. Moreover, Hesse is the model Robert Galbreath uses to describe a politics of detachment. According to Galbreath, "Hesse was detached from politics by temperament and conviction. As an emigrant, he was detached from the German scene; as an intellectual, a certain amount of detachment was an inherent part of his calling. Yet this does not mean that Hesse, or any free spirit, is somehow prohibited from taking a stand on anything whatsoever. Hesse, for example, still took an active interest in current affairs or in speaking out in defense of his ideals in ways which he deemed appropriate."[26] These "ways which he deemed appropriate" are not, however, the means typically associated with political action. Let us hear Galbreath speak of Hesse again:

> He had a strong aversion to the politics of parties, protests, and propaganda, but he did not see himself as irresponsible or as an escapist. His politics of detachment implied neither indifference nor lack of feeling. "Detachment" is used here rather to suggest a distancing effect which is intensely personal, a withdrawal from the frantic pursuit of chimerical external solutions so that a calming of the self may ensue through which brotherhood and peace may be experienced directly as living knowledge.[27]

We see from Galbreath's description that Hesse was extremely skeptical of arriving at peace and brotherhood via the right political project. Left/right, liberal/conservative, even Nazi/Jew membership does not help the progress of peace, according to Hesse. Indeed, joining in political causes may reduce the *quality* of society, even if it increases its *quantity*. This is the message Hesse has for fellow intellectuals, whom he believes mistakenly assume that they have a responsibility to play an active role in politics. Politics is a realm of quantity—of aggregating political will—whilst the intellectual realm should be one of quality. The work of intellectuals may be powerless to realize peace in the short term, but he has faith that in the long term such work is the best chance for the progress of peace. Instead of engaging in political action, Hesse believed that intellectuals should transcend politics, focusing instead on the spiritual bonds of a common humanity. This is what Hesse attempted to do during his experiences of both world wars, experiences that were chronicled by his pen, but not to drum up political support for either side. Hesse's position was certainly influenced to some extent by his experience taking care of war prisoners for the Imperial Army during World War I. After initially volunteering to aid the war effort Hesse gradually came to oppose it. He also became disillusioned when his appeals to his countrymen fell on deaf ears. This experience led him to write a few polemical articles against the war under the pseudonym "Sinclair."[28] On November 3, 1914, in the midst of war hysteria, Hesse published a short piece entitled "O Friends, Not These Tones" (taken from Schiller's "Ode to Joy") asking Germans to consider the human bond that transcends belligerency and patriotism.[29] Ralph Freedman sums up Hesse's method of expressing his sentiments accordingly: "[They were] non-activist, indeed, non-political, for whatever pacifist sentiments were voiced were channeled into comments about literature and art."[30] I do not mean to suggest that this position taken by Hesse stands in for all free spirits. Free spirits are not required to be pacifists, and many may in fact view conflict as a means to spiritual strength. What political end Hesse deems worthy—in this case the progress of peace—is not what compels me to place him in the category of free spirit. It is, rather, the means by which he seeks to achieve this end that makes Hesse an instructive example of a free spirit's possible political role. In short, political engagement was avoided and replaced by cultural commentary.

There are many examples of Hesse's practice of political detachment throughout his life, and Galbreath presents several. Perhaps the most striking example is Hesse's public silence about the Nazi party. Galbreath explains:

At no time did he openly condemn them, although his detestation of their policies is beyond question. The result was that his writings were neither condemned nor recommended when the Nazis assumed power. Twenty of his books in fact were published in Nazi Germany for a total of some 481,000 copies. This was a source of considerable pain to those—including the Manns—who knew full well that Hesse was not a Nazi supporter. He preferred, however, to express his opposition more indirectly: by upholding the ideals of the German classics in articles for a Swedish periodical, by reviewing the books of Jewish, Catholic, and other proscribed authors as long as German magazines would accept his contributions; by refusing to edit some of his writings in accordance with Nazi preferences; by opening his home to refugees, among them Thomas Mann and Martin Buber. He was often condemned in the German press for these activities, for his Jewish wife, and for his record during the previous war.[31]

Rather than engaging with institutional, party politics and with public defiance of Nazi power, Hesse believed continuing his work to further the goals of peace, common humanity, and intellectual culture was the higher road to travel. Another example of political detachment is found in Hesse's refusal to join other intellectuals in protesting against Arab aggression in Israel, despite Hesse's Jewish connections, in 1948. The political cause, whether noble or ignoble in Hesse's eyes, did not determine his involvement or lack thereof. Political detachment was practiced in all of these instances, and, as Galbreath concludes, "his stand is a highly principled one."[32] Whatever political impact Hesse could have had on these political events, if he had taken a firm public stance, would have paled in comparison to the good he could do focusing on his inner life and his more spiritual endeavors.

The literary characters that fill Hesse's novels also reveal his concern for spiritual freedom. We find nearly all of his protagonists mired in inner struggle, highly introspective and concerned more fervently with their own actions and beliefs than the external political and social world. Many of his works examine the tension between spirit and flesh. *Narcissus and Goldmund* exposes the insuperable tension between intellect and action, and between art and science. *Steppenwolf* portrays its protagonist, Harry

Haller, as a man torn between his higher, spiritual nature and his lower, animalistic nature, all the while struggling with the demands of modern bourgeois society. Yet the work that best demonstrates our theme of spiritual freedom might be Hesse's last, *The Glass Bead Game*. The protagonist, Joseph Knecht, struggles throughout his life with the obligations he feels, on the one hand, to the whole or collective, and, on the other hand, to his authentic self. Knecht is an ambivalent yet passionate character, pulled strongly between these two sets of obligations.

Hesse employs a third-person narrator to chart the course of Knecht's illustrious life, and we get a sense of the struggle early on in the novel. The narrator tells us, "For us, a man is a hero and deserves special interest only if his nature and his education have rendered him able to let his individuality be almost perfectly absorbed in its hierarchic function without at the same time forfeiting the vigorous, fresh, admirable impetus which make for the savor and worth of the individual."[33] The goal, it seems, is to harmonize the demands of order and spiritual freedom within the individual. In a more practical sense, this struggle is played out through Knecht's attachment and importance to the Order of Castalia (a sort of perfected academy, serving only matters of the pure intellect and spirit), and his own private spiritual longings. The highest calling within Castalia is the Glass Bead Game, a fictional intellectual competition that both harnesses and encompasses all human art and science—indeed, all human knowledge. We hear from our narrator again: "The Glass Bead Game is thus a mode of playing with the total contents and values of our culture; it plays with them as, say, in the great age of the arts a painter might have played with the colors on his palette. All the insights, noble thoughts, and works of art that the human race has produced in its creative eras, all that subsequent periods of scholarly study have reduced to concepts and converted into intellectual property—on all this immense body of intellectual values the Glass Bead Game player plays like an organist on an organ."[34]

The greatest intellects play the Glass Bead Game, and Knecht becomes the greatest of all, earning the title Magister Ludi, Master of the Glass Bead Game. Thus, Knecht is an essential and esteemed member—the most esteemed, in fact—of the Castalian Order, climbing its ranks while providing valuable service to it. This is an important point to remember as one reads the novel, for Knecht continually experiences doubts and remains unfulfilled by his belonging to the order and his distinguished post within it. These misgivings ultimately lead to Knecht's self-driven departure from the order, surrounded by much drama and scandal. The reasons surrounding this fateful choice are important for my purposes here, but first we need to recognize that Knecht was not a traitor or a quitter, but a dedicated and conscientious member of the order. As Theodore Ziolkowski explains in his forward to the novel, "Joseph Knecht is no impetuous radical thrusting non-negotiable demands upon the institution and demanding amnesty from the consequences of his deeds. He attains through disciplined achievement the highest status in the Order and commits himself to action only after thoughtfully assessing its implications for Castalia and the consequences for himself."[35] Moreover, as Peter Roberts points out, "The name Knecht is highly significant here, for it means "servant." Even in the most prestigious role within the Castalian hierarchy—the position of Magister Ludi—it is clear that Knecht becomes a servant for others."[36]

Despite his fantastic success at serving and climbing the order, Knecht was never spiritually fulfilled by it. Clues foreshadowing his eventual departure from the order surface throughout the novel, and show that Knecht saw further than the order from a young age.[37] His self-reliance and individualism could even be found in his approach to the game, which was that of an autodidact: "Advice and information on all questions of detail would have been available to him at any time, and in addition he could have pursued his studies among other scholars in the same field, young men with the same devotion to the Game, instead of struggling alone in a state that often amounted to voluntary banishment. Be that as it may, he went his own way."[38] Knecht maintained a vigilance against possible encroachments on his spirit—on his independence of mind and action. He pursued knowledge for his own purposes, not merely for the purposes of the game or for ascendance in the order. Moreover, he refused to let the process of serving the order prevent him from seeking the truth and achieving spiritual awakening. Knecht's character is more fully revealed later in the novel, where the narrator explains, "The two tendencies or antipodes of his life, its Yin and Yang, were the conservative tendency toward loyalty, toward unstinting service of the hierarchy on the one hand, and on the other hand the tendency toward 'awakening,' toward advancing, toward apprehending reality."[39]

Ultimately, Knecht finds his existence in the order too constraining to continue. The order represents something very similar to the proverbial ivory tower, and Knecht no longer sees any way to maintain his position as Magister Ludi and remain true to his authentic self. Thus, he decides to leave his position, much to the shock and dismay of the elites of the order.[40] Far from being granted an honorable discharge, Knecht is essentially disowned by Castalia, a result which he had anticipated as a distinct possibility. Nevertheless, Knecht evinces no regret for his decision, as our narrator reveals: "He had already explored all the possibilities the office provided for the utilization of his energies and had reached the point at which great men must leave the path of tradition and obedient subordination and, trusting to supreme, indefinable powers, strike out on new, trackless courses where experience is no guide."[41] Much like the other free spirits discussed, Knecht abandoned his conventional role, and what was expected of him, to pursue spiritual freedom. Further, he demonstrated a willingness to take risks, particularly a risk that might lead to self-knowledge and self-improvement. Roberts concludes that Knecht's "actions can be seen as a sacrifice not only of the trappings of Castalian power but of all that was familiar to him. In so doing, he lives out one of the most important educational virtues: the ability to take risks—to make oneself uncomfortable, to go beyond one's prior experiences and existing understanding of the world."[42] Indeed Knecht, Hesse's final protagonist, shows the path of the free spirit, and the practice of detachment, in striking clarity.

To conclude, Hesse represents the free spirit in both his literary characters and his own life. For Hesse, progress, whether political or otherwise, comes from the inner transformation of individuals in society, not from the political transformation of society itself. Free spirits will always first focus inward, plumbing the depths of their inner life. The increase in the number of self-realized individuals, who have attained a higher consciousness, is what leads to the increased quality of society.[43] As quality increases, so too will the possibility that "brotherhood and peace" will be "experienced as living knowledge." Hesse's goal of altering the quality of society is manifestly long in view. Indeed, one who seeks such a goal cannot reasonably expect to enjoy the fruits of one's labor in one's lifetime. It may take many generations for such change to be effected on a large scale. It would not be surprising, therefore, to see concerned citizens argue that the means that Hesse advocates are unsatisfactory. Galbreath addresses this accordingly:

> There is the further problem that by rejecting traditional politics, force, compromise, and collective protest, Hesse drastically reduces the range of effective action in society to that which can be accomplished by the self-realized individual. From Hesse's viewpoint, of course, he is not reducing effective action, but

clarifying its real scope: through inner transformation and by personal example the quality of society will alter. To those individuals who cannot accept Hesse's premise, his conclusion may seem impractical—a pious hope and, in immediate effect at least, a defense of the status quo. Perhaps a clash of premises can never be resolved, but Hesse shies away from the confrontation. His method is an appeal to the inner spirit, not debate.[44]

This passage prescribes a dose of realism about the politics of detachment. There will undoubtedly be individuals who are skeptical about the possibility of inner transformation, believe that it is blind to the problems of evil they perceive within their midst, or, we might add, who are simply too impatient to acquiesce to Hesse's insistence that real, worthwhile change takes a very long time. Nonetheless, this passage does illuminate the practice of politics desired by and appropriate to Nietzsche's free spirit. As Keith Ansell Pearson concludes, free spirits "are to look askance at impatient political invalids who seek change through the bloody quackery of revolution and instead carry out small, personal experiments, establishing ourselves as our own *reges*."[45] The free spirit's focus on individual self-realization and liberation from historical and contemporary values and authority does not entail any immediate political goals. Nor can it be said that the free spirit is concerned, primarily or even tangentially, with the improvement of society. Yet inner transformation can result in societal change over time, little by little, individual by individual.

Lewis

Prima facie, Clives Staples Lewis does not seem like a candidate appropriate to the category of free spirit. Lewis is famous for his literary support of Christianity, revealing in creative ways the role of faith, God, and the Holy Spirit in human life. He fights skepticism about truth and natural law—albeit the modern variety of skepticism, not precisely the Pyrrhonist version—and seeks to win readers over to the Christian faith. As Justin Dyer and Micah Watson, who have written the authoritative treatise on Lewis's relationship to politics, argue, "Lewis has had an enormous impact of the thinking of hundreds of thousands of people in several countries and across several decades since his death. It is impossible, in particular, to fully understand evangelicals and evangelical thought without understanding

C. S. Lewis."[46] Lewis was firmly entrenched within the Christian tradition—at least later in his life—and therefore rejected the ideas of both skepticism and detachment from tradition.

Surely, C. S. Lewis does not meet the criteria of spiritual freedom to the extent that Goethe does; nonetheless, there are many good reasons to consider Lewis a free spirit. First, we ought to remember that there are degrees of spiritual freedom—individuals may fit the concept to a greater or lesser degree. Second, Lewis provides an example of a religious person who is also spiritually free to a large extent. He is wary of social pressure and the power of public opinion. He is not dogmatic nor does he seek to catechize others on the doctrines of the Christian Church. Lewis disdained politics, both governmental and ecclesiastical, and sought instead to refocus his readers' imaginations on enduring questions, "eternal realities, and lasting earthly concerns."[47] Moreover, his intellectual humility—which results from the fallen nature of man—is a sort of practical counterpart to Pyrhhonian *epochē*, or suspension of judgment. Reason is weak and imperfect, which leads Lewis away from a perfectionist politics, and toward adoption of liberal principles of the Lockean and Millian variety. Thus, Lewis is a worthy addition to our discussion of free spirits in action.

Like Nietzsche, Lewis did not hide his disdain for politics, particularly "institutional" politics. He made countless remarks to this effect, from the beginning of his career until the end. As Dyer and Watson discover, "The evidence for Lewis' disdain for and ignorance of day-to-day politics is not hard to come by. 'Jack was not interested in politics,' writes Lewis' stepson, Douglas Gresham. Warnie Lewis, noting his brother's reputation for having 'contempt for politics and politicians,' explains that the household conversation in their childhood was dominated by a rather one-sided 'torrent of grumble and vituperation' about Irish politics such that Lewis simply equated adult conversation with politics."[48] Much later in life, in fact six days before his death in November 1963, "Lewis responded to a Mrs. Frank Jones, noting that 'our papers at the moment are filled with nothing but politics, a subject in which I cannot take any interest.'"[49] Lewis was quite cynical about the prospects of political participation facilitating virtue or improving human beings. "In practice, democracy 'neither allows the ordinary man to control legislation nor qualifies him to do so.' What is more, Lewis noted, the 'real questions are settled in secret and the newspapers keep us occupied with largely imaginary issues. And this is all the easier because democracy always in the end destroys education.'"[50]

Many more statements could be culled to prove Lewis's wariness of politics, but doing so seems unnecessary here. It is illuminating, however, to observe his wariness of conformity and social pressure as it pertains to individual spiritual growth. Consider, for example, his character Mark Studdock in the novel *That Hideous Strength*. Studdock is a sociologist being recruited by the National Institute for Coordinated Experiments (NICE), which is a fictional representation of a totalitarian state, controlling all aspects of human existence. Studdock is aware throughout his recruitment that the NICE may be dangerous, but his will is often broken by the pressures of conformity. Early on, we see into Studdock's need for social approval as he observes a fellow colleague: "Stone had the look which Mark had often seen before in unpopular boys or new boys at school, in 'outsiders' at Bracton—the look which was for Mark the symbol of all his worst fears, for to be one who must wear that look was, in his scale of values, the greatest evil."[51] Studdock's inclination to conform ultimately leads to his entrance and integration into NICE, despite its apparent evil, and he soon joins in the evildoings:

> This was the first thing Mark had been asked to do which he himself, before he did it, clearly knew to be criminal. But the moment of his consent almost escaped his notice; certainly, there was no struggle, no sense of turning a corner. There may have been a time in the world's history when such moments fully revealed their gravity, with witches prophesying on a blasted heath or visible Rubicons to be crossed. But, for him, it all slipped past in a chatter of laughter, of that intimate laughter between fellow professionals, which of all earthly powers is strongest to make men do very bad things before they are yet, individually, very bad men.[52]

In the character of Studdock, we see that detachment from groups can be quite important, indeed. The power of a collective will is often enough to lead to terrible consequences, as many mass movements throughout history have shown. Studdock finds himself almost unconsciously acquiesce to the machinations of a totalitarian regime, thereby becoming partly responsible for great atrocities. The role of conscience is only truly in play when one confronts moral decisions as a self-realized individual. Strong, independent-minded individuals are a necessity for combatting collective evils, and Lewis is keenly aware of the pitfalls that conformism holds for spiritual freedom, and human virtue.

Also like Nietzsche, Lewis took a bird's-eye view of politics, and he distinguished between direct and indirect engagement. Lewis took his view of politics from the Greeks. As Dyer and Watson observe, "The word 'politics' comes to us from the Greeks, whom, as we have seen, Lewis knew and read intimately. In the Aristotelian sense, politics refers to the business of the polis . . . which combined spheres and identities we moderns tend to keep separate: religion, government, family, school, and business." Politics includes the most fundamental questions about human nature and purpose, and "Lewis spent his life wrestling with those fundamental questions, and drew on his considerable gifts and his faith in attempting to provide answers to them."[53]

This effort represents Lewis's practice of political detachment. He avoids involvement in "institutional politics," but he is quite cognizant of the larger political battles—over ideas, values, and fundamental questions—and uses his pen to join in them. Through novels, fairy-tales, and theological/philosophical works, Lewis tried to remind society of forgotten truths of human nature and Christianity. Opponents of Lewis knew he was a threat to their political designs, even if Lewis stayed out of political debates. Francis Schaeffer observed that the great pioneer of behaviorism, B. F. Skinner, attacked Lewis on two occasions: "Why? Because [Lewis] is a Christian and writes in the tradition of the literatures of freedom and dignity. You will notice that he does not attack the evangelical church, probably because he doesn't think it's a threat to him. . . . But he understands that a man like C. S. Lewis, who writes literature that stirs men, is indeed a threat."[54] In other words, the indirect, long-term effect of a politics of detachment may be more powerful than entering the debates of the day.

Clearly, however, Lewis wasn't entirely detached from society, nor was he as skeptical as Nietzsche or the other free spirits here discussed. He was a Christian author with Christian intentions, one of which was to convert others to Christianity. Moreover, he devoted much time to uncovering traditional modes of understanding, notably in his development of a "Medieval Model" of the universe in his last work, *The Discarded Image*.[55] Here he carefully reconstructs the worldview of the characteristic medieval person, and in doing so his affection for the coherence and richness of the tradition is manifest. Lewis finds the "Medieval Model" superior to the modern, reductionist, scientific worldview in many ways, and in

The Discarded Image and his *Narnia* series we clearly see advocacy of an earlier, Aristotelian and Christian worldview. Indeed, Lewis does not seem skeptical when he is in the mode of defending his cherished beliefs. Still, he stops short of calling his preferred worldview the "truth," even as he believes in it and passionately recommends it. And while, as a believer, he ipso facto is not a skeptic, he remains antidogmatic amid his beliefs.

Indeed, Lewis's Christian belief in the fallen nature of man yields a practice of politics that is similar to that of the Pyrrhonist skeptic. Human beings are imperfect, and reason cannot be trusted to fully triumph over appetite and passion. According to Dyer and Watson, Lewis understood that "human imperfection is the fact of which the doctrine of the fall takes account. With Chesterton, Lewis would agree that *we* are what is wrong with the world, but both would add that what is wrong with us is that our reason does not rule as it ought."[56] The implications for politics are clear: we should never trust our rulers to be more blessedly endowed with reason than we are, we should never assume they are wise and good. Lewis makes this clear in his essay "Equality," where he argues that democracy can never be defended on the grounds that democratic rulers are wise and good:

> The danger of defending democracy on those grounds is that they're not true. And whenever their weakness is exposed, the people who prefer tyranny make capital out of the exposure. I find that they're not true without looking further than myself. I don't deserve a share of governing a hen-roost, much less a nation. Nor do most people—all the people who believe advertisements, and think in catchwords and spread rumors. The real reason for democracy is just the reverse. Mankind is so fallen that no man can be trusted with unchecked power over his fellows.[57]

In other words, Lewis *is skeptical* about the ability to use reason to determine for others what is in their interest. Moreover, he observes the typical citizen's vulnerability to fanaticism. Even Christians cannot claim a monopoly on truth, and they must be humble about what they can know and what they can reasonably expect non-Christians to accept. Naturally, it follows that he also is skeptical about the power of government, and he advocates a limited role for it. Lewis, despite his Christian faith, advocates for a liberal political order, one that allows for all types of faith and all types of spiritual pursuits. Dyer and Watson note the many similarities between Lewis and an early defender of toleration, John Locke. Lewis was a partisan of liberal democracy for the same reasons as Locke: "Since Christians do not have a monopoly on moral truth, and given the fall of man, both thinkers detested theocracy and feared the abuses that would accompany governments that understood their primary role to be producing virtuous or pious citizens. Given this fear—despite believing in a hierarchical universe—Locke and Lewis have a very limited view of government's role and warrant."[58] Far from supporting a Christian theocracy, "Lewis endorsed a version of John Locke's social contract theory to ground political legitimacy, and he adopted a version of John Stuart Mill's harm principle in his approach to questions about the legislation of morality."[59] Lewis's intellectual humility is antidogmatic, much like the free spirit's skepticism, and led him to adopt liberal values.

Not only is liberalism the only political order appropriate to the epistemological constraints of human beings, but Lewis also recognized the importance of ordinary citizens to the maintenance of a free society, a society that resists the allure of perfectionist politics. He understood that ordinary citizens—if, we might add, they are free spirits to some degree—have a positive role to play in society. "Although Lewis' political temperament at times places him within the 'just leave me alone' brand of conservatism, he nevertheless did believe in a positive political role for the ordinary citizen, if only to serve as a check on the overly ambitious schemes of planners and optimists."[60] Throughout Lewis's writings, we see remarks about the need to resist fanaticism caused by advertising and political slogans, to scrutinize and even mock the arrogance of central planners, to refocus our attention on enduring and essential questions.

In the end, C. S. Lewis adds to our understanding of free spirits in action, even if some incompatibility remains. As a devout Christian and apologist for the faith, he does not perfectly align with our criteria. But he remains, to a large degree, a model of spiritual freedom. Recall, again, that spiritual freedom admits of degrees, as it ought if it is to be a choice-worthy ideal. Lewis also urges us to heed the important distinction between skepticism and antidogmatism. A believer need not be dogmatic, even if she is also not what most would call a skeptic. Lewis may begin with different premises and believe in a traditional worldview, but he ends up reaching many of the same conclusions—wariness of dogmatists and fanatical social movements, detachment from institutional politics, skepticism about human rule and support of liberalism—that our other model free spirits reached.

Emerson and Thoreau

A final venture into the lives of free spirits comes through exploration of two American thinkers, Ralph Waldo Emerson and Henry David Thoreau. Each might warrant his own consideration, but because both were contemporaries, both part of the American transcendentalist movement, and both took similar positions regarding politics and society, we have cause to view them together. Emerson, of course, greatly influenced Nietzsche, especially the latter's views on fate and history.[61] Nevertheless, Emerson's influence on Nietzsche is not of interest to us here.[62] We are interested in how Emerson was a free spirit, embodying the characteristics of spiritual freedom we have discussed, and how he practiced a politics of detachment. Also, it warrants mentioning that while Emerson influenced Nietzsche, the reverse is not true. Emerson was not influenced by Nietzsche, and was not aware of the latter's conception of a free spirit. Perhaps Nietzsche had Emerson in mind while writing about the free spirit, but Nietzsche does not explicitly identify Emerson as a free spirit in any of his texts. In any case, we are not concerned with Emerson's relationship to Nietzsche, but only with how Emerson's life and works can inform our understanding of spiritual freedom.

Emerson is the intellectual forefather of transcendental principles, and the younger Thoreau tried to live out those principles to great extent. According to Brian-Paul Frost:

> Emerson and Thoreau merit a place together in American political thought for several reasons. First, while Emerson was the philosophical spokesman for what became known as American transcendentalism, Thoreau most famously attempted to put its principles into practice. Second, both men shared a reverential attitude toward nature; a belief that a divine spirit animated all creation; and that each individual was part of a greater whole or oneness. Third, both men were staunch individualists who saw the individual as the sole source of moral authority and worth, and they encouraged creative

self-expression, spontaneous action, and hearkening to one's inner voice or intuition. And finally, fourth, Thoreau is one of the most noted expositors of civil disobedience to unjust government, and many of his views are shared by Emerson.[63]

We can see evidence of both individualism and concern for spiritual fullness, as well as a politics of detachment. As Frost concludes later on the same page, "[Emerson and Thoreau] kept to the sidelines politically and argued that genuine political regeneration could only come through individual spiritual renewal."[64] We find in both Emerson and Thoreau a fervent individualism and antidogmatism that shares in the free spirit ideal.

Abundant examples of free-spirited behavior can be found in the lives and writings of these transcendentalists, but here it will suffice to provide just a few, beginning with Emerson. We need to understand a little about transcendentalism before we uncover the affinity, and the discrepancy, it has with spiritual freedom. Emerson's focus on spirituality was beyond doubt. As well, his concern for his inner life was primary, and this is reflected in his transcendental ideas. Mary Oliver found that "the greater energies of his life found their sustenance in the richness and steadfastness of his inner life."[65] The inner life is complex, Emerson believed, and more importantly it is our inner life that determines our perceptions. This is a principal tenet of Emerson's idealism, which he calls transcendental in reference to the idealism of Immanuel Kant.[66] Like Kant, Emerson believed in the "moral law within," the idea that our moral compass is written on our hearts, so to speak, and is not given to us from external sources. In his essay, "An Address," he touches on the idea of natural laws: "These laws refuse to be adequately stated. They will not be written out on paper, or spoken by the tongue. They elude our persevering thought; yet we read them hourly in each other's faces, in each other's actions, in our own remorse. The moral traits which are all globed into every virtuous act and thought—in speech we must sever, and describe or suggest by painful enumeration of many particulars."[67] In other words, natural laws are not apprehendable, articulable, or susceptible to dogmatic definition. They are ineffable and they are only available to individuals, not to society as a whole. As Emerson declares in "Self-reliance," "No law can be sacred to me but that of my nature. Good and bad are but names very readily transferable to that or this; the only right is what is after my constitution; the only wrong what is against it."[68] This does not devolve immediately into an easy moral relativism, however. In "Character," Emerson claims that "a healthy soul stands united with the

Just and the True, as the magnet arranges itself with the pole; . . . he is thus the medium of the highest influence to all who are not on the same level. Thus men of character are the conscience of the society to which they belong."[69] Emerson is not a relativist, because he believes that moral truth can be discovered by the introspective individual, plumbing the depths of her own soul.

But Emerson is a skeptic, a certain type of skeptic that should remind us of the Pyrrhonists. In his essay "Montaigne; or, the Skeptic," in *Representative Men*, Emerson portrays the type of skepticism he deems choiceworthy, and it is not the radically skeptical modern variety: "But though we are natural conservers and causationists, and reject a sour, dumpish unbelief, the skeptical class, which Montaigne represents, have reason, and every man, at some time, belongs to it. Every superior mind will pass through this domain of equilibration."[70] Like the Pyrrhonists, the goal of the good skeptic is not to merely doubt everything ("a sour, dumpish unbelief"). Rather, "this then is the right ground of the skeptic,—this of consideration, of self-containing; not at all of unbelief; not at all of universal denying, nor of universal doubting,—doubting even that he doubts; least of all of scoffing and profligate jeering at all that is stable and good."[71] Furthermore, Emerson upholds the importance of suspending judgment, and of resisting the urge to dogmatize: "If there is not ground for a candid thinker to make up his mind, yea or nay,—why not suspend the judgment? I weary of these dogmatizers. I tire of these hacks of routine, who deny the dogmas. I neither affirm nor deny. I stand here to try the case."[72] Emerson is sensitive to the charges against skepticism, and he wants to defend himself against them. He responds accordingly in "Circles":

> And thus, O circular philosopher, I hear some reader exclaim, you have arrived at a fine Pyrrhonism, at an equivalence and indifferency of all actions, and would fain teach us that if we are true, forsooth, our crimes may be lively stones out of which we shall construct the temple of the true God! . . . Let me remind the reader that I am only an experimenter. Do not set the least value on what I do . . . as if I pretended to settle any thing as true or false. I unsettle all things.[73]

In this passage, Emerson simultaneously condemns the potential moral bankruptcy of Pyrrhonism while praising the skeptical, experimental spirit.

If we take this passage in conjunction with Emerson's other remarks on skepticism, however, we see that what he opposes is not Pyrrhonism but radical skepticism and moral relativism.[74] Like the free spirit, Emerson is antidogmatic and takes a skeptical approach to moral systems.

Emerson's great hope is that individuals look within themselves to discover moral laws, and it is the act of discovery that is essential for self-reliance. He is not advocating simple rejection of the thoughts and opinions of others, but the creation of one's self through individual discovery. Alex Zakaras explains Emerson's view accordingly: "Being one's self presumably requires, in some instances, the willing affirmation of inherited convictions; in others, it surely requires their revision or abandonment. Whether we accept or discard them, however, it is most important for Emerson that we make the judgment deliberately and remain attentive to other possibilities."[75] A free individual must make her own judgments, even if those judgments ultimately align with established opinions, conventions, traditions, and so on. The key issue to determining one's intellectual freedom is whether one's positions are self-discovered or whether they are adopted from authorities. "Freedom, then," Zakaras writes, "resides in the act of becoming, through which we detach ourselves not only from old habits but also from old teachers and commitments."[76] Emerson finds the need for independent thought increased in his democratic age. He believes that as the authority held by tradition and institutions has decreased or been removed by democratic revolution, authority "must be taken up by each individual for himself."[77]

These free individuals and modern democratic citizens will be, of course, transcendentalists. Emerson presents his own human type, one very similar to the free spirit. Here are some pertinent passages from "The Transcendentalist": "They are lonely; the spirit of their writing and conversation is lonely; they repel influences; they shun general society. . . . Society, to be sure, does not like this very well; it saith, Whoso goes to walk alone, accuses the whole world; he declares all to be unfit to be his companions; it is very uncivil, nay, insulting; Society will retaliate."[78] Transcendentalists detach from society, and Emerson is not naive about the challenges that such behavior presents. Society will retaliate, but detachment is still choiceworthy for transcendentalists, and they are not driven by resentment or social anxiety: "These persons are not by nature melancholy, sour, and unsocial—they are not stockish or brute—but joyous, susceptible, affectionate."[79] Again, they do not reject society for reasons of insecurity or fear of social engagements; they do not view themselves as *outcasts*, but rather choose to be *outsiders*. They shun society because it cannot give them what they seek. They seek spiritual fullness, and "with this passion for what is great and extraordinary, it cannot be wondered at that they are repelled by vulgarity and frivolity in people. They say to themselves, It is better to be alone than in bad company. And it is really a wish to be met—the wish to find society for their hope and religion—which prompts them to shun what is called society."[80]

It is evident that transcendentalists have little taste or need for society. Emerson found society much more likely to produce conformity than freedom. In his numerous poems and essays, Emerson directly confronts the pernicious effects of politics and society. In "Self-reliance," Emerson identifies what society deems the principal virtue: conformity. "Society everywhere is in conspiracy against the manhood of every one of its members. Society is a joint-stock company, in which the members agree, for the better security of his bread to each shareholder, to surrender the liberty and culture of the eater. The virtue in most request is conformity. Self-reliance is its aversion."[81] This places not just a suggestion but a requirement on the individual; in Emerson's words, "Whoso would be a man, must be a nonconformist."[82] Achieving self-reliance—true independence of mind and action—requires nonconformity, or detachment from society. This includes, of course, detachment from political activity as well, particularly "institutional" politics. Again speaking of transcendentalists, Emerson claims, "What you call your fundamental institutions, your great and holy causes, seem to them great abuses, and, when nearly seen, paltry matters."[83]

Such detachment does not require, however, that a transcendentalist become a hermit. True independence of spirit—self-reliance in Emerson's terms—can be had even in the midst of modern society. Indeed, maintaining spiritual freedom while living in society is the real challenge, shunning society is relatively easy: "It is easy in the world to live after the world's opinion; it is easy in solitude to live after our own; but the great man is he who in the midst of the crowd keeps with perfect sweetness the independence of solitude."[84] Detachment, then, is not isolation, but the practice of spiritual freedom within the structure of society. Moreover, the purpose of detachment is clear: to enable and facilitate spiritual goals. Emerson avers, "But your isolation must not be mechanical, but spiritual, that is, must be elevation. At times the whole world seems to be in conspiracy to importune you with emphatic trifles."[85]

Much like the free spirit, the transcendentalist places great value on aesthetic perspective: "But this class are not sufficiently characterized if we omit to add that they are lovers and worshippers of Beauty.... They have a liberal, even an aesthetic spirit."[86] More will be said about Emerson's views on aesthetics in the following chapter, but here we ought to note its importance. As Zakaras finds, Emerson believes aesthetic experience can help us resist conformity and see the world anew; that is, "aesthetics can serve the important negative function of disengaging us from our habitual ways of seeing.... Wonder is, for Emerson, an expression of curiosity about the world, and a catalyst for intellectual and artistic activity.... Beauty is something that we can discover and respond to ourselves, and in sharing our own perceptions of beauty with others, we give expression to our own singular relation to the world around us."[87] Aesthetic receptivity is connected to independence of mind and the act of detachment precisely because it disrupts the way in which we normally perceive the world: "Emerson constantly celebrates our capacity to have new thoughts, to inhabit new perspectives, to suddenly see beyond the limits of conventional understanding.... Emerson often locates these revelations, which he likens in 'Fate' to being 'born again,' in moments of aesthetic contemplation and intimate conversation."[88] The role of aesthetic perspective in maintaining freedom of spirit is evidently an important one for Emerson's transcendentalist.

It should by now be clear that the transcendentalist is kindred with the free spirit, so much so that the resemblance is uncanny. They share nearly all the salient characteristics of free spirits defined at the outset of our investigation, with the possible caveat that the transcendentalist may be less skeptical about natural or universal laws. Yet even this difference is mitigated by the fact that for the transcendentalist these laws are ineffable and only reveal themselves to individuals. Natural laws that are "discovered"—and then articulated and promulgated—are impossible; they remain for the transcendentalist the false hope of the dogmatist. In any case, pride of place is given to skepticism, political detachment, and aesthetic perspective in both the case of the free spirit and the transcendentalist. In short, Nietzsche and Emerson appear uncannily aligned in their presentation of these two human types.

While Emerson repeated these philosophic themes throughout his voluminous writings, Thoreau skirted philosophical exposition in favor of attempting to live like a transcendentalist, or free spirit. Most famously, Thoreau underwent a "life experiment" when he lived away from society, at Walden Pond (on land that was owned, in fact, by Emerson's family), for over two years. As Frost remarks, "Thoreau went to Walden Pond in order to live the good life as he understood it—a life of independence, leisure, and personal self-enlightenment."[89] Thoreau was a naturalist, transcendentalist, and staunch individualist, and this comes out in his reflections from life at Walden and in later writings. Here, I wish to emphasize only his thoughts on the spirit and the individual's relation to society, and have culled some representative passages. In 1863, the *Atlantic Monthly* published Thoreau's essay "Life without Principle" posthumously. What Thoreau is after in this essay, to put it in the form we have adopted here, is a skeptical life free of dogma and the business of modern social life. He begins the essay by observing (or better put, complaining) that a lecturer he went to see said nothing about his own thoughts, about ideas most important and private, and instead resorted to parroting the prevailing ideas and principles of the day. He continues on to lament how hectic is the everyday world, concluding that "I think there is nothing, not even crime, more opposed to poetry, to philosophy, ay, to life itself, than this incessant business."[90] What Thoreau esteems, he makes abundantly clear, is an individualism marked by self-reliance, independent thought, and a preference for introspection, philosophy, and poetry over what we might call bourgeois business (or, perhaps better put, *busy*-ness).

He isn't coy about the value of close engagement with society and politics: "I often perceive how near I had come to admitting into my mind the details of some trivial affair,—the news of the street; and I am astonished to observe how willing men are to lumber their minds with such rubbish,—to permit idle rumors and incidents of the most insignificant kind to intrude on ground which should be sacred to thought."[91] Earlier in the essay he evinces his feelings towards public opinion: "Whenever a man separates from the multitude, and goes his own way in this mood, there indeed is a fork in the road. . . . His solitary path across-lots will turn out the *higher way* of the two."[92] We may detect contempt in such quotes, but it is also the case that Thoreau was keenly aware of the negative effects that political engagement could have on the spirit: "If I am to be a thoroughfare, I prefer that it be of the mountain-brooks, the Parnassian streams, and not the town-sewers. . . . I believe that the mind can be permanently profaned by the habit of attending to trivial things, so that all our thoughts shall be tinged with triviality."[93] Behind his contempt for society,[94] we discover a very real concern: achieving spiritual freedom—both independent thought and spiritual fullness—does require detachment. Moreover, like Goethe and our other free spirits, Thoreau did not shun all forms of society, only political society and the broader community. As Brooks Atkinson observes, "The last eight years of his life were conspicuously social. He visited and was visited."[95] He may have been reluctant to associate with groups of people, but in his private life he enjoyed the society of friends.

What Thoreau recognized was that one cannot routinely engage with trivial things and expect to simultaneously cultivate the spirit, and, for him, virtually all the activities of politics are trivial things: "What is called politics is comparatively something so superficial and inhuman, that practically I have never fairly recognized that it concerns me at all."[96] Thoreau was not only wary that too much engagement with politics would crowd out opportunities for more properly spiritual pursuits, but also believed there was something lower—more connected to the material body and our senses, and to interest and power—that drove politics. He made this clear in his famous 1849 essay "Civil Disobedience." The state ought often to be resisted because of the manner in which it rules: "The State never intentionally confronts a man's sense, intellectual or moral, but only his body, his senses. It is not armed with superior wit or honesty, but with superior physical strength. I was not born to be forced. I will breathe after my own fashion."[97] It logically follows that the best government is that which governs least—a motto Thoreau "heartily accepts"[98]—and that places the rights and interests of the individual above those of the group: "There will never be a really free and enlightened State until the State comes to recognize the individual as a higher and independent power, from which all its own power and authority are derived, and treats him accordingly."[99] In other words, a state that recognizes and protects spiritual freedom will be "enlightened," at least more enlightened than it currently is. A free spirit like Thoreau can be a subject—he is not advocating disobedience in all times and places—but only if the state recognizes the independent power of the individual. He sums this up pithily early in the essay: "I think that we should be men first, and subjects afterward."[100] Whether or not the state offers such recognition, we might at least require something less demanding, that both state and civil society allow individuals like Thoreau their detachment, their right to create the distance required for their spiritual pursuits.

Transcendentalists are wary of delving too deeply into the issues of the day, and they value their spiritual freedom above any and all public concerns. Nonetheless, there were occasions when public life took hold, desired or not. In fact, Goethe, Emerson, and Thoreau were the most politically involved of the free spirits discussed here. There are times, in all of our lives, when public issues and perhaps duties emerge, and it is instructive to see just where Emerson and Thoreau became engaged in politics, even associational politics. Most prominently we see their involvement in the abolitionist movement. What is remarkable about this involvement is that it both illuminates the ambivalence of free spirits in action and intimates the sort of political goals that might be proper to them. We need to take not only their actions into account, but also the manner in which Emerson and Thoreau think about their public involvement.

Emerson was a reluctant entrant into the politics of abolition, but ultimately became a firm and vocal abolitionist, delivering many public addresses between 1844 and 1862. Our first glimpse of the compulsion Emerson felt comes in his 1844 address "Emancipation in the British West Indies." While attempting to look with praise upon the progress against slavery made by England in her colonies, Emerson instead finds himself reflecting on the scope of the injustice of slavery in New England:

> Whilst I have meditated in my solitary walks on the magnanimity of the English Bench and Senate, reaching out the benefit of the law to the most helpless citizen in her world-wide realm, I have found myself oppressed by other thoughts. . . . I could not see the great vision of the patriots and senators who have adopted the slaves's cause—they turned their backs on me. No: I see other pictures—of mean men; I see very poor, very ill-clothed, very ignorant men, not surrounded by happy friends—to be plain—poor black men of obscure employment as mariners, cooks or stewards, in ships, yet citizens of this our Commonwealth of Massachusetts—freeborn as we—whom the slave-laws of the states of South Carolina, Georgia and Louisiana have arrested in the vessels in which they visited those ports. . . . This man, these men, I see, and no law to save them.[101]

Emerson begins at this time to engage with the problems of slavery, but it is the Fugitive Slave Law of 1850 that brings him unflinchingly into the heart of the abolitionist cause. Now that his own Massachusetts was morally complicit in the institution of slavery, Emerson fought it without reservation. In his address "The Fugitive Slave Law," he writes:

> I said I had never in my life up to this time suffered from the Slave Institution. Slavery in Virginia or Carolina was like Slavery in Africa or the Feejees, for me. There was an old fugitive law, but it had become, or was fast becoming, a dead letter, and, by the genius and laws of Massachusetts, inoperative. The new Bill made it operative, required me to hunt slaves, and it found citizens in Massachusetts willing to act as judges and captors. Moreover, it discloses the secret of the new times, that Slavery was no longer mendicant, but was become aggressive and dangerous.[102]

The shift that Emerson perceived led him to engage more and more in abolitionist politics, notably into a friendship with John Brown and a public address to defend Brown after Harper's Ferry in 1862.

Clearly, then, Emerson did not reject political activity outright. Nonetheless, he was always a reluctant participant, and his public speeches nearly always included paeans to self-reliance, or spiritual freedom. A pertinent example comes in the very first paragraph of the Fugitive Slave Law address. Even while agitating against proslavery forces, he devotes his first remarks to self-reliance and a politics of detachment:

> I do not often speak to public questions—they are odious and hurtful, and it seems like meddling or leaving your work. I have my own spirits in prison—spirits in deeper prisons, whom no man visits if I do not. . . . The one thing not to be forgiven to intellectual persons is, not to know their own task, or to take their ideas from others. From this want of manly rest in their own and rash acceptance of other people's watchwords come the imbecility and fatigue of their conversation. For they cannot affirm these from any original experience, and of course not with the natural movement and total strength of their nature and talent, but only from their memory, only from their cramped position of standing for their teacher. They say what they would have you believe, but what they do not quite know.[103]

He prepares the gathered assembly not by condemning the evils of slavery, but by admonishing his audience to use their own intellectual faculties. He does this, we later see, because he believes the eloquence and charisma of

Daniel Webster—the Massachusetts senator who allowed the slave law to pass and was responsible for garnering public support—was the cause of the evil legislation. Instead of thinking for themselves, the citizens of Massachusetts had allowed themselves to fall under the spell of an admittedly great man. Self-reliance was what Massachusetts needed to avoid such calamities, and Emerson was forced to compromise his free-spirited ideals to fight the evil of slavery. Here is how George Kateb summarizes Emerson's experience:

> With the passage of the Fugitive Slave Law of 1850, Emerson embarks on a lengthy episode of agitation for one reform: the containment or abolition of slavery. This spreading of evil—this evil which is truly evil, not only apparently so—forces him to change his attitude on the subject of associating for reform. . . . That profound change is a deviation from his theory of self-reliance, not its transformation. Or, we can say that Emerson accepts the sacrifices of every sort—including the abandonment of aspirations of free persons to self-reliance—which are needed to give all Americans, not just some, the chance for self-reliance. Perhaps a society has no self-reliance anywhere in it if there are slaves anywhere in it.[104]

As Kateb notes, Emerson's foray into abolitionist politics was in one sense a "deviation" from his theory of self-reliance, or his politically detached nature. It was a difficult action to take, and Emerson was ambivalent about it. Yet, in another sense, the action was taken on behalf of his devotion to self-reliance. All citizens must be allowed to achieve self-reliance—much like citizens must all be allowed their spiritual freedom—for Emerson to properly live out his own.

Thoreau's experience is similar to Emerson's. Brian-Paul Frost does a good job of limning the tension that we see in Thoreau:

> In the final analysis, it is hard not to see a tension in Thoreau's position in respect to slavery. On the one hand, he is both horrified at the practice of slavery and increasingly indignant at those who do little or nothing to stop it; on the other hand, he cannot bring himself to admit that one has a positive moral duty to eliminate this evil. He seems caught between his passion to set the world aright and his desire to pursue activities he feels are higher than politics.[105]

Indeed, the tension seen here is one that is basic to the free spirit. There will always be cases where action seems to be required, and this action could be predicated on protecting the spiritual freedom of others. Slavery is both physical and spiritual, and no free spirit or liberal can comfortably stand by and watch its practice or progress. Ultimately, the chosen action of the free spirit will rely on a good deal of prudence. Some extreme injustices must be confronted, but in general the little one individual can do to sway political opinion is not worth the risk to spiritual health. And the protection of spiritual health—pursuing "activities he feels are higher than politics"—allows an individual like Thoreau to remain a positive example in all times and places.

We have now caught a glimpse, at least, of some free spirits in action. All of the figures discussed—Goethe, Hesse, Lewis, Emerson, and Thoreau—are meant to demonstrate how free spirits relate to the political sphere. We see among these individuals all the characteristics necessary to a free spirit: skepticism, or antidogmatism, and intellectual humility; detachment from politics and a focus on inner, spiritual life; a yearning for affective attachment to something greater than oneself; and a stubbornness in the face of public opinion and a strong resistance to conformity (if not, in all cases, a staunch individualism). Not all characteristics are present in each example, but taken together every characteristic of spiritual freedom can be found among them. More important, however, is the idea that there are degrees of spiritual freedom within these examples and within persons everywhere. These examples help to flesh out the concept of spiritual freedom, to make what is quite abstract at least a little concrete.

Free spirits may not be compelled to influence the political climate at all, but if they are, they will do so in ways that bypass or avoid common political channels, such as political parties and political media. In some cases, like that of Goethe, this method may be enough to escape the wrath of a suspicious political regime. The fate of Hesse and his work in Nazi Germany, however, evinces the potential tension between free spirit and political regime. As Freedman tells us in his biography, "Despite his caution, Hesse was ultimately unable to escape the regime's disapproval." In 1943 the works of Hermann Hesse were prohibited; reading them inside Germany had become a crime.[106] The fate of Hesse and his novels show that the spiritual freedom that Hesse sought so dearly came at the expense of his political freedom. In order to retain both, Hesse would have had to live within a political order that guarantees some cluster of political rights for the individual against the state. A liberal political order may be necessary for free spirits to achieve spiritual fulfillment while retaining their political freedom. This will be a subject we return to later on.

We should acknowledge, however, that our examples may be exceptional cases of free spirits; men who had great direct influence on culture and at least some indirect influence on politics. These free spirits reveal the public—if not political—role that free spirits *can* play if they choose to or if they find themselves in a condition of sufficient fame and public recognition that makes it very difficult for them not to play *some* role. But what about free spirits that are not so exceptional? As discussed earlier, there are degrees of spiritual freedom, and there may be people that meet the criteria of a free spirit, albeit to a lesser extent than Goethe, Hesse, Emerson, Thoreau, and Lewis. For these, playing the role of free spirit may involve more common but still important acts, such as resisting the overtures of political activists, remaining skeptical of fleeting, ephemeral, and often-damaging political talking points, or focusing on long-term ends like liberty, prosperity, and peace while ignoring prevailing intellectual fashions; above all, by placing one's inner/spiritual life above those demands society places on each of us individually.

Chapter 4

Free Spirits in Liberal Political Society

In the part which merely concerns himself, his independence is, of right, absolute. Over himself, over his own body and mind, the individual is sovereign.

—John Stuart Mill

Beauty is nothing other than the promise of happiness.

—Marie-Henri Beyle (Stendhal)

At this point, it should be quite clear that free spirits are wary of politics and political activity. This would seem to be true of politics in any regime: communist, authoritarian, theocratic, democratic, and so on. I've promised that the free spirit's import to liberal political society would be discussed, and that is the focus of this chapter. What we find is both that liberal freedom is essential to spiritual freedom and that free spirits are essential to liberal political society. In the first section of this chapter, we will explore the conception of liberal society put forward by John Stuart Mill. We find that strong natures capable of spiritual freedom are essential ingredients to a well-functioning liberal society. In other words, Mill observes the need for individuals very much like the free spirit, for these individuals test the authenticity of a society's liberality and provide crucial checks on the putative authority of public opinion. Free spirits should not only be tolerated, then, but embraced. The second section of this chapter asks what benefits free spirits get from liberal political society. We find that the negative freedom—in the form of civil liberties—afforded to liberal citizens is essential to the free spirit's pursuit of spiritual fullness. As she evades the perspectives of tradition, community, conventional morality, and the like, the free spirit may choose an aesthetic perspective instead. By viewing life and existence aesthetically, she opens up possibilities for achieving spiritual fullness. The liberal, negative *freedom from* creates the space necessary for a positive *freedom to* in the form of aesthetic perspective. The issues addressed in this chapter will leave us with a clearer understanding of why free spirits are good for liberalism and vice versa.

The Millian Test

Many readers may already recognize the affinity between the role of free spirits in society and the role that strong individuals play in Mill's vision of a liberal society. Mill's *On Liberty* is the text that sets the standard for evaluating liberal societies. It places the tension between individual and society in stark relief, attempting to identify and define "civil, or social liberty: the nature and limits of the power which can be legitimately exercised by society over the individual."[1] Whether or not a society respects the nature and limits of societal power determines its liberality. Individuals must be free to think and judge for themselves, and must come to their own worldviews. A truly liberal society cannot threaten eccentricity and independent belief. Alex Zakaras shows that "it is the manner in which beliefs and values are held, and the way dissenters from orthodoxy are treated, that determines the extent of a culture's openness; this, in any case, is what Mill teaches."[2] A liberal society must have a plurality of worldviews, opinions, belief systems, and so on; it must allow for dissent among these various ways of thinking. It also must treat the individual as the container of thought, not groups within society or society at large.

Mill therefore also seeks to help us to understand the true range of individual freedom. As Gertrude Himmelfarb concludes, *On Liberty* leaves us with "what John Stuart Mill, more than anyone else, bequeathed to us: the idea of the free and sovereign individual."[3] Most scholarship on Mill's theory of liberty focuses on the necessity of free thought and free discussion (speech) for the emergence of truth, and on the famous harm principle, which holds that the actions of individuals should only be limited in order to prevent harm to other individuals. These two pillars of liberal freedom were crucial to the establishment of liberal political and economic institutions. In our discussion here, however, I wish to focus more on Mill's understanding of the ways in which society—not institutions, but the collective body itself—affects or threatens the individuals that comprise it. I will rely heavily on Mill's own words, with the twin goals of evincing his commitment to strong individuals and exposing the congruity of these individuals with the free spirit.

Mill's recognition of the variety of individuals stands in stark contrast to the utilitarianism of his father, James Mill. The utilitarian maxim "The greatest good for the greatest number" could not, the son John Stuart came to realize, accommodate the variety of individuals in society. According to Himmelfarb, "*On Liberty* stands as a decisive rebuttal of his father. For it is here, more than in any other work, that he tried to provide an alternative view of man and society which would take proper account of both the 'intellectual culture'—reason and truth—and the 'internal culture'—the individual's feelings, passions, impulses, natural inclinations, personal idiosyncrasies."[4] Remarkably, the inner life of individuals—the "internal culture"—occupies an important place in Mill's theory of liberty. Indeed, Mill argues that "the appropriate region of human liberty" comprises "the inward domain of consciousness, demanding liberty of conscience in the most comprehensive sense, liberty of thought and feeling, absolute freedom of opinion and sentiment on all subjects, practical or speculative, scientific, moral, or theological."[5] We might say, perhaps, that Mill is a strong proponent of spiritual freedom, that in many respects Mill shares the same concerns as the free spirit.

Mill sets out to evaluate the compatibility of Western liberal societies with his notion of human liberty. Unlike his father, John Stuart recognized the problem of majority tyranny, and this problem was at the forefront of Mill's mind as he wrote *On Liberty*. Echoing Tocqueville, Mill claimed that while liberal institutions had freed men from oppressive monarchic and aristocratic regimes, where formal political and economic power was concentrated in few hands, a new form of tyranny emerged as liberal societies evolved:

> There has been a time [in history] when the element of spontaneity and individuality was in excess, and the social principle had a hard struggle with it. The difficulty then was to induce men of strong bodies or minds to pay obedience to any rules which required them to control their impulses. . . . But society

has now fairly got the better of individuality; and the danger which threatens human nature is not the excess, but the deficiency, of personal impulses and preferences.[6]

In other words, a strong society and perhaps even a strong government was once needed to combat the tyranny of individuals. In Mill's time, however, society has become the tyrant:

> But reflecting persons perceived that when society is itself the tyrant—society collectively over the separate individuals who compose it—its means of tyrannizing are not restricted to the acts which it may do by the hands of its political functionaries. Society can and does execute its own mandates; and if it issues wrong mandates instead of right, or any mandates at all in things with which it ought not to meddle, it practices a social tyranny more formidable than many kinds of political oppression, since, though not usually upheld by such extreme penalties, it leaves fewer means of escape, penetrating much more deeply into the details of life, and enslaving the soul itself. Protection, therefore, against the tyranny of the magistrate is not enough; there needs protection also against the tyranny of the prevailing opinion and feeling, against the tendency of society to impose, by other means than civil penalties, its own ideas and practices as rules of conduct on those who dissent from them; to fetter the development and, if possible, prevent the formation of any individuality not in harmony with its ways, and compel all characters to fashion themselves upon the model of its own. There is a limit to the legitimate interference of collective opinion with individual independence; and to find that limit, and maintain it against encroachment, is as indispensable to a good condition of human affairs as protection against political despotism.[7]

It is not enough, then, to establish liberal institutions that protect individuals from government interference. The maintenance of a truly liberal society requires resistance to the tyranny of society, to the "interference of collective opinion with individual independence."

Mill takes pains to drive this point home throughout the essay, and we see that, in his estimation, resisting majority tyranny is akin to resisting human nature. Zakaras concludes that Mill, throughout his works, was of the opinion that "human beings left to their own devices will tend toward conformity and mutual (group) antagonism."[8] The natural or most likely scenario is one where the individual merely adopts the beliefs, values, and thoughts of those around him, and those prevailing social orthodoxies ultimately become forced on those who dissent. Mill is unequivocal about humankinds' proclivity for controlling the thought of others:

> The disposition of mankind, whether as rulers or as fellow citizens, to impose their own opinions and inclinations as a rule of conduct on others is so energetically supported by some of the best and by some of the worst feelings incident to human nature that it is hardly ever kept under restraint by anything but want of power; and as the power is not declining, but growing, unless a strong barrier of moral conviction can be raised against the mischief, we must expect, in the present circumstances of the world, to see it increase.[9]

The majority naturally seeks to expand its dominance in the realm of ideas, and it is not hesitant to quash voices that resist its dominance. Outsiders who embody or seek novel ways of thinking and speaking are not seen as beneficial innovators, but as threats:

> But the evil is that individual spontaneity is hardly recognized by the common modes of thinking as having any intrinsic worth, or deserving any regard on its own account. The majority, being satisfied with the ways of mankind as they are now (for it is they who make them what they are), cannot comprehend why those ways should not be good enough for everybody; and what is more, spontaneity forms no part of the ideal of the majority of moral and social reformers, but is rather looked on with jealousy, as a troublesome and perhaps rebellious obstruction to the general acceptance of what these reformers, in their own judgment, think would be best for mankind.[10]

Mill anticipates that his critics will respond that liberal governments do not stifle free thought, speech, or assembly, and they do not put to death those who challenge social authority. In short, liberal institutions instantiate the principle of tolerance. Yet, while such criticism contains an important truth, Mill claims that, while government may be tolerant, the majority in society can remain intolerant. This "social intolerance kills no one, roots out no opinions, but induces men to disguise them or to abstain from any active effort for their diffusion."[11] Such intolerance is as bad in its practical effects, in terms of the emergence of truth and of individuality, as outright government prohibition. In fact, Mill's contemporary, Tocqueville, suggests it might even be worse. In a chapter entitled "On the Power That the Majority in America Exercises over Thought," Tocqueville argues that majority tyranny in democracies imprison the soul in a manner even oppressive authoritarian regimes cannot muster:

> Under the absolute government of one alone, despotism struck the body crudely, so as to reach the soul; and the soul, escaping from those blows, rose gloriously above it; but in democratic republics, tyranny does not proceed in this way; it leaves the body and goes straight for the soul. The master no longer says to it: You shall think as I do or you shall die; he says: You are free not to think as I do; your life, your goods, everything remains to you; but from this day on, you are a stranger among us. You shall keep your privileges in the city, but they will become useless to you; . . . you shall remain among men, but you shall lose your rights of humanity. When you approach those like you, they shall flee you as being impure; and those who believe in your innocence, even they shall abandon you, for one would flee them in their turn. Go in peace, I leave you your life, but I leave it to you worse than death.[12]

Mill and Tocqueville agree on one thing: that when faced with the opinions of the majority, the intellectual outsider, while free of the fear of physical punishment, is left with two terrible choices: silence or ostracism.

If independent thinkers are forced to face such terrible choices, we cannot expect to come across many of them. Unsurprisingly, Mill laments this state of affairs:

> But the price paid for this sort of intellectual pacification is the sacrifice of the entire moral courage of the human mind. A state of things in which a large portion of the most active and inquiring intellects find it advisable to keep the general principles and grounds of their convictions within their own

breasts, and attempt, in what they address to the public, to fit as much as they can of their own conclusions to premises which they have internally renounced, cannot send forth the open, fearless characters and logical, consistent intellects who once adorned the thinking world.[13]

Conformity is not just a problem for independent characters, like our free spirits, but all citizens. Mill believed conformity stunts the growth of all, insofar as it prevented us from developing the human faculties essential to our happiness or flourishing. "To say that conformity entails unhappiness," writes Zakaras, ". . . means that it causes suffering, but he also means that it involves failure to develop important human faculties and to reach the higher pleasures that attend their exercise." Zakaras then quotes Mill: "To conform to custom, merely as custom, does not educate or develop in him any of the qualities which are the distinctive endowment of a human being. The human faculties of perception, judgment, discriminative feeling, mental activity, and even moral preference, are exercised only in making a choice."[14] We may never reach intellectual or spiritual maturity without taking responsibility for our own thoughts, and this is precisely the threat that conformity poses. A second issue that Mill is raising, however, is how conformity affects truly independent natures, like our free spirits.

Mill is concerned that forced—or, at a minimum, strongly incentivized—conformity robs humanity of characters that can truly move the species forward or in new directions. He does not suggest that great minds are simply less common now than in the past, that democratic society has corrupted the intellect to the point where genius of the highest caliber is no longer possible.[15] He argues instead that there are a great number of powerful minds, but that such minds must be married to a strong character to flourish at all, and this marriage is rare. He rhetorically inquires, "Who can compute what the world loses in the multitude of promising intellects combined with timid characters, who dare not follow out any bold, vigorous, independent train of thought, lest it should land them in something which would admit of being considered irreligious or immoral."[16]

The key, then, is to find individual natures that are both skeptical and strong, stubborn and open-minded, full of feeling but uncorrupted.[17] For Mill, the cultivation of individuality marks the best chance we have of avoiding a society without moral courage, pacified by majority opinion or, in Nietzsche's phrase, "herd" mentality. Individuals with strong moral feeling exist, but are all too often enervated and corrupted without benefitting society through their example. Mill intimates that there are naturally strong temperaments: "Strong impulses are but another name for energy. Energy may be turned to bad uses; but more good may always be made of an energetic nature than of an indolent and impassive one. Those who have most natural feeling are always those whose cultivated feelings may be made the strongest."[18] Much like Nietzsche, Mill observes that "energetic natures" exist and, if they are properly cultivated, that they can become forces for good—or at least moral forces capable of resisting majority tyranny. He further explains what it takes to turn an "energetic nature" into a bona fide character, and we are again reminded of Nietzsche, particularly the latter's discussion of the cultivation of drives: "A person whose desires and impulses are his own—are the expression of his own nature, as it has been developed and modified by his own culture—is said to have a character."[19] A strong, energetic nature that is developed into a genuine character is rare, just like the genuine free spirit is rare. But, again, such humans act as a guide for others, and a truly liberal society will find a place for them and should even cherish them. Mill claims, "In proportion to the development of his individuality, each person becomes more valuable to himself, and is, therefore, capable of being more valuable to others."[20] Mill understands the importance of strong individuals to a healthy society, and he is unequivocal about what the alternative is, or, put differently, what critics of individuality and strong characters must necessarily believe: that a weak and conformist society is the goal we are seeking. "Whoever thinks that individuality of desires and impulses should not be encouraged to unfold itself must maintain that society has no need of strong natures—is not the better for containing many persons who have much character—and that a high general average of energy is not desirable."[21]

By making the stakes so readily apparent, Mill urges us to question the apprehension and insecurity the majority feels when confronted with strong and eccentric characters, when confronted with outsiders. Liberal societies are quick to praise themselves for their openness, their tolerance, and their rights. But Mill shows us that such self-praise often obscures the practical reality of living within them. Liberal political and economic institutions are a necessary, but not a sufficient, condition of a society that is truly free. The Millian test of a free society requires more: it requires both accepting and valuing strong and eccentric characters, it requires embracing outsiders.

Free spirits are likely to bring more benefits than costs to liberal society. Mill did not fear conformity merely because it can stunt spiritual growth; he also feared the natural marriage of conformity and intolerance. Zakaras presents a clear case for the dual danger of conformity: "For Mill, the political dangers of conformity are more immediate. He finds conformity expressed as intolerant ideology; he argues that conformists become active perpetrators of injustice."[22] Put differently, it is a short step from mindlessly adopting the prevailing social orthodoxy to actively suppressing anyone who dares to question it. Ideological conformity does not stay within the bounds of the group, but is "closely linked to intolerance. . . . It results in the common charges of heresy and immorality brought against iconoclastic individuals and dissenting minorities."[23] Conformity is therefore a two-sided threat: on one side, "it involves suppression of self and forfeiture of personal dignity and happiness." On the other, it is "a form of unreflective group identity that creates mistrust and intolerance (and eventually threatens violence against outsiders)."[24] Worse still, these two threats can reinforce one another. Zakaras, citing Mill, concludes that "the first kind of harm can create the second: 'the greatest harm done,' writes Mill, 'is to those who are not heretics, and whose whole mental development is cramped, and their reason cowed, by the fear of heresy' (CW 18:242). The threat alone of exclusion and violence can intimidate people into conformity, can turn them inward against themselves."[25] We might add that the social threat prevents people from developing their natural faculties as well.

What I would like to suggest here is that free spirits—or, for Mill, "energetic natures"—are very important soldiers in the battle against conformity. They act as political foes, whether consciously or not—of those who increase and foment conformity. Their political role might be suitably explained through Adam Smith's metaphoric invisible hand. Just as individuals pursuing their economic self-interest often provide unintended economic benefits to society at large, so too do the spiritual quests of energetic individuals and free spirits benefit society. They provide a model of spiritual strength and independence of mind; through their spiritual strength, they are a check on—and alternative to—fanaticism and ideology; they urge greater skepticism and scrutiny of the prevailing opinions of the day; and they demonstrate the importance of an individual, private sphere of existence where spiritual independence can flourish. I wish to reemphasize the idea that free spirits are a model of freedom of spirit and freedom of thought. This is not a trivial thing, as it seems clear that we need to be *shown* (and reminded often) what genuine freedom of thought is. Despite our liberal "rights" to thought, speech, and expression, true independence of mind is a rarity in our society. Genuinely free thought is in fact quite hard to come by; it is not the norm but the exception. The norm is borrowing thoughts others have generated, and if we are honest, we are all guilty of this from time to time. It takes hard work to form one's own opinions and to actualize independence of mind—it is a goal we ought to aspire to, not something that we automatically possess once we are provided with a corresponding "right."

A sensible way to illuminate this role of free spirits is to contrast them with fanatics. The free spirit is a direct opponent of the fanatic, perhaps a polar opposite. Fanaticism in liberal societies comes in many forms, and fanatical positions are taken by persons on both sides of the political divide. Although the following list is not exhaustive, I put forward as examples of fanaticism groups such as theocrats, white nationalists, social justice warriors, ideological egalitarians (equality as a value above all other values), environmentalists, and technological progressives (those who place unblinking faith in the positive results of technological progress). For all of these groups, it is not the *content* of their ideologies that define their fanaticism, but the *fervor* and *dogmatism* they bring to their cause. Indeed, powerful arguments can and have been made for all of these positions, but a defining practice of the fanatic is to leave aside the capacity for argumentation as they fight for their cause. In place of moderate, sober, liberal debate, the fanatic's tactics are marked instead by mania, lack of proportion, and coercive attempts to convert.

What may first appear as manifestations of strength—that is, the fanatic's open signs of power, both as intellectual and social demonstrations of force—are on futher inspection manifestations of weakness, particularly spiriual weakness. Bernard Reginster aptly demonstrates this as he contrasts the free spirit with the fanatic. Reginster concludes that

> the fanatic is essentially too *weak* to develop a rich, complex personality, and his lack of truthfulness remains important to Nietzsche's critique only insofar as it is a symptom of his weakness. Conversely, we admire the free spirit not primarily for his truthfulness, but for the strength that makes it possible. And we value that strength not simply because it makes

truthfulness possible, but because it is a necessary condition of human greatness.[26]

The fanatic is incapable of human greatness because he is too weak to resist the prevailing traditions, his history, and the values of his time. Leaving human greatness aside, the fanatic is too weak for genuine liberal freedom because he is too weak for spiritual liberation or self-realization. Alternatively, the free spirit is a model of spiritual strength, and one who is able to enter a quest of spiritual liberation and self-realization that is necessary for both enjoying liberal freedom and achieving human greatness. The free spirits teach others, by showing them an example, about the possibility of increasing the quality of their spiritual lives.

Our contemporary liberal societies may have a special need for models such as our free spirits. Along with fanaticism, conformity threatens liberal politics on both sides of the Atlantic.[27] Mill believed conformity was the mark of the age: "In this age, the mere example of non-conformity, the mere refusal to bend the knee to custom, is itself a service. Precisely because the tyranny of opinion is such as to make eccentricity a reproach, it is desirable, in order to break through that tyranny, that people should be eccentric.... That so few now dare to be eccentric marks the chief danger of the time."[28] Regarding the United States, Tocqueville observes, "I do not know any country where, in general, less independence of mind and genuine freedom of discussion reign than in America.... In America the majority draws a formidable circle around thought. Inside those limits, the writer is free; but unhappiness awaits him if he dares to leave them."[29] Indeed, genuine deliberation is perpetually threatened by the power of mass media, public opinion, and political partisanship. True independence of spirit, and the strength to guard it, is something quite rare and, ipso facto, leaves a powerful impression on others. In a democratic age in which sailing with the prevailing winds is commonplace, those who sail against them become even more essential.[30]

These activities of free spirits seem increasingly important in contemporary liberal regimes, where partisan politics and mass media wield enormous influence. In an era when majority opinion finds no lack of mediums for its expansion and dominance, free spirits set an example of operating outside the fray. They thereby provide some balance against majority opinion. They check the dual threat of conformity so clearly presented by Mill. As well, they provide an alternative to the extreme busyness of political activity, representing a way of life that at once provides a check on the encroachment of political life into one's spiritual life and that has potential to benefit the political climate. It would be stretching too far to suggest that free spirits act for this latter reason, but the mere presence of free spirits in political life—visible for others to observe—contributes to the improvement of politics in liberal democracies. What is more, how a society treats free spirits—or outsiders in general—is a true test of how liberal that society is.

Aesthetic Perspective and Spiritual Fullness

A second question regarding the free spirit's relation to liberal society is what he may get out of it. The answer is fairly simple: at least in theory, liberal societies guarantee the necessary freedom—in the form of civil liberties—for the free spirits to "hover fearlessly" over the various conventions of society. In other words, liberal societies leave free spirits free enough to face the "terrible" truths of existence on their own terms and in their own way. This liberal freedom, however, seems to only operate negatively. Being free *from* societal conventions allows for detachment, but it doesn't provide a positive spiritual orientation. We are concerned not only with negative freedom but also spiritual fullness; recall that our definition of spiritual freedom contains a concern for spiritual fullness. Hence, we return to one of our principal questions: In the absence of belief in any "untruths"—namely, the claims of religion and science to answers regarding the fundamental existential, epistemic, and moral questions—how is the free spirit to evade despair and find a way to value and affirm life? Without attachments to political life and community, how does the free spirit achieve spiritual fullness?

The answer, I endeavor to show, is that spiritual freedom opens the way to choosing an aesthetic perspective. To return to section 34 of *Human, All Too Human*, spiritual freedom allows one to "live among men and with oneself as in nature, without praising, blaming, contending, gazing contentedly, as though at a spectacle." Why does the free spirit not praise, blame, or contend? Because, unlike the men who do these things, the free spirit rejects the traditional, moral evaluations by which things are measured to be praiseworthy, blameworthy, or contentious. The absence of such concerns leaves one free to approach life "gazing contentedly, as though at a spectacle." That is, the free spirit looks at life as though at a spectacle; she treats life as an aesthetic phenomenon. An aesthetic perspective can be the positive orientation of the free spirit. Liberated from the burdens of moral perspective, the free spirit chooses an aesthetic perspective, a perspective in which she is able to affirm life. Liberal freedom allows for this choice, and ipso facto is important to free spirits. We must now understand how this choice can lead to fullness.

What does it mean to choose an aesthetic perspective? Nietzsche has a lot to say about aesthetics, though he does not explicitly use the phrase aesthetic perspective. In what follows I hope to clarify what I mean by aesthetic perspective and to identify some differences between my way of looking at Nietzsche's views on aesthetics and other scholarly interpretations. From the beginning of his writings to the end, Nietzsche argues that the whole of existence should be treated as an "aesthetic phenomenon." Only as such can existence be "eternally justified,"[31] or become the object of our affirmation.[32] What Nietzsche precisely means by this will be examined below, but let us begin with a basic definition of an aesthetic perspective. Put simply, taking an aesthetic perspective is the act of treating the whole of existence as an aesthetic phenomenon.[33] I partially choose "aesthetic perspective" in order to avoid confusion with previous scholarly work on Nietzsche's "aestheticism." Alexander Nehamas examined Nietzsche's "aestheticism" in his seminal *Nietzsche: Life as Literature* in 1985. Nehamas's idea is, roughly speaking, that Nietzsche engages the world "as if it were a literary text. And he arrives at many of his views of human beings by generalizing them to ideas and principles that apply almost intuitively to the literary situation, to the creation and interpretation of literary texts and characters."[34] The world is treated as a work of art, open to as many interpretations as there are interpretations of literary texts and other works of art. Nehamas's view of Nietzsche interpreting the world as art or text has met with serious challenges, but remains a powerful view.[35] The scholarly discussion surrounding "aestheticism" focuses primarily on interpretation, and examining Nietzschean interpretation is not my primary objective. Nor am I interested in building on the analogy of world as literary text. Instead, I am concerned with Nietzsche's emphasis on an aesthetic perspective as a means to justify or affirm existence itself.[36] While the task of using an aesthetic perspective to affirm life may include the activity of interpreting the world as art, I will focus more on the role of an aesthetic perspective in helping one to achieve spiritual fullness. As we will see, spiritual fullness is related to Nietzsche's idea of affirming existence. Yet, to be clear, Nietzsche nowhere discusses or defends spiritual fullness as such.

Nietzsche first treats existence aesthetically in *The Birth of Tragedy*. I will quote the passage at length and offer three interpretations, which together provide a clear idea of what Nietzsche is getting at. In section 5 he writes:

> We may assume that we are merely images and artistic projections for the true author, and that we have our highest dignity in our significance as works of art—for it is only as an *aesthetic phenomenon* that existence and the world are eternally *justified*—while of course our consciousness of our own significance hardly differs from that which the soldiers painted on canvas have of the battle represented on it.[37]

Here we see Nietzsche's idea of aesthetic justification of existence. We do not live to carry out the will of God, gaining our eternal reward in another life; nor do we merely exist to serve Nature through our role in preserving the species. Our "highest dignity"—the justification for existence and the world—is "in our significance as works of art." Yet our consciousness of this significance is hidden from us, "because as knowing beings we are not one and identical with the being which, as the sole author and spectator of this comedy of art, prepares a perpetual entertainment for itself."[38] We can, from time to time, participate or share in this aesthetic spectacle as cocreators, "only insofar as the genius in the act of artistic creation coalesces with this primordial artist of the world, does he know anything of the eternal essence of art."[39]

The statement "it is only as an aesthetic phenomenon that existence and the world are eternally justified" is one of Nietzsche's most quoted passages, and I want to analyze it from a few different angles to see what it can mean. In the last paragraph, I engaged in a first possible interpretation, what we might call a metaphysical approach to aesthetic justification. It is evident that there remains a "metaphysical need,"[40] as Nietzsche called it, present in these statements. At this time, he was still captivated by Schopenhauer's idea of a unitary and primordial will; he was, as he claims in his "Attempt at Self-Criticism," the new preface to *Birth of Tragedy* written fourteen years later, "the disciple of a still 'unknown God' "; he was speaking with "a *strange* voice."[41] The later Nietzsche takes pains, at least at times, to repudiate metaphysics, so how can we take any of these early statements seriously? One way is to simply say that Nietzsche was something of a believer when he wrote *Birth of Tragedy*, but later lost that belief, rendering the metaphysical approach to aesthetic justification a dead relic of the past.

But a second interpretation, one that takes into account Nietzsche's Lutheran roots, may be more helpful. We should note that Nietzsche's father was a Lutheran pastor, and Nietzsche was expected to follow in his footsteps. The evidence suggests that Nietzsche expected to do the same until his late adolescence, when he began to question his Christian upbringing.[42] In any case, Nietzsche's idea of treating existence aesthetically might be interpreted as a modification of the Lutheran doctrine of "justification by faith." Through one's faith that Jesus died for our sins on the cross the unrighteous sinner can become righteous; he can become "right with God." A sort of eternal salvation, or a solution to the problem of theodicy, is what Nietzsche has in mind when he claims, "It is only as an aesthetic phenomenon that existence and the world are eternally justified." Elsewhere in his writings, of course, Nietzsche jettisons the idea of eternal salvation in the religious sense, but he seems to suggest that by treating existence aesthetically one can become "right with existence"; that is, one can affirm and value existence in this way, finding a sort of existential harmony and spiritual fullness, and "save" oneself from the dangerous disease of nihilism—the belief that one's life, and the whole of existence, have no meaning, purpose, or intrinsic value. Looked at in this way, we can see how Nietzsche's concern with justification relates to other religious ideas of spiritual fullness or fulfillment, albeit without the belief in a higher power.

There is a third interpretation of this important statement, which comes through Daniel Came's suggestion that when Nietzsche talks about aesthetic justification he means the achievement of an affective attachment to the world. Came argues that "Nietzsche spent most of his productive life trying to identify the foundational conditions that invite love of life and protect against world-denying pessimism."[43] It is with this goal in mind that Nietzsche speaks of aesthetic justification: "It is my general contention that when Nietzsche speaks of the aesthetic justifying life, he does not mean that it shows us that life is *actually* justified, but rather that it educes an affectively positive attitude towards life that is *epistemically neutral*."[44] In other words, without any moral judgment on life—seeing life as something "essentially amoral"—one can still achieve a love and affirmation of life and an attachment to existence through an aesthetic perspective. That is, one can achieve a necessary condition of spiritual fullness through an aesthetic perspective. Recall that spiritual fullness requires an attachment to something, to some source of meaning greater than ourselves. For a free spirit this attachment comes through treating existence aesthetically—an aesthetic perspective imbues existence with value. In addition, the argument here claims that free spirits are uniquely capable of finding this value and affirming life through an aesthetic perspective. Indeed, free spirits endeavor to face the moral and epistemic truths without despair, to turn instead to an aesthetic perspective to find life's value.

All three interpretations arrive, albeit along different paths, at the same basic conclusion: treating life as an aesthetic phenomenon is way of coming to value and affirm life. In other words, an aesthetic perspective is a means for a free spirit to achieve spiritual fullness. It has now become clearer why an aesthetic perspective is important, but we may also ask what it means to take an aesthetic perspective, or to have an aesthetic experience. Often, aesthetic experience is thought to include a sensory response, and something that is aesthetically beautiful is thought to be pleasurable to the senses. But there is also a strong intellectual component to aesthetic experience; aesthetic engagement is at once sensory and intellectual, corporeal and spiritual. In other words, we should resist the temptation to equate aesthetic experience with hedonism. The thinkers that will be highlighted here emphasize the intellectual orientation of aesthetic experience. Nietzsche, and, as we will see later, also Nabokov, Thoreau, and Goethe, are not typical hedonists and sensualists, yet they seek aesthetic engagement with the world.

With this idea of aesthetic engagement as sensual and spiritual in mind, we may also ask what it exactly means to have an aesthetic perspective, rather than, say, a scientific one. I hope a simple example of a snowy mountain peak will illustrate this point. When hiking in the woods with a snowy mountain in view, I might say to a friend that it appears as though "the mountain's soft cap of snow keeps it warm during the winter." My friend is a botanist and doesn't care much for my interpretation, because he is coming from a scientific perspective. He responds with something like, "No, the snow is frozen precipitation that typically gathers at higher elevations, and as it melts it feeds the rivers and streams that irrigate the valleys and meadows where trees, plants, and grasses can then grow." Which interpretation is correct? The answer is that both can be considered correct; it is not the case that one interpretation is right and the other wrong, but rather that the interpretations stem from distinct perspectives. From these distinct perspectives, they can both be right. "The mountain's soft cap of snow keeps it warm in the winter" is an interpretation that arises out of an aesthetic perspective of the view of the mountain. From this perspective, the mountain is seen as a whole, as a unified phenomenon. It is also viewed with some degree of aesthetic distance.[45] The botanist's interpretation, on the other hand, is more in line with what we may call a reductionist, scientific perspective, which views the mountain not as a whole but a collection of parts, each playing a specific biological role. The question about which perspective is better, then, depends on the attitudes and interests of the people involved; it depends on what a particular situation calls for. Scientific perspective is clearly better if one wishes to learn about the snow's ecological function, but if one seeks to enjoy the beauty of the momentary glimpse of a snowy mountain peak, an aesthetic perspective is clearly superior. And Nietzsche does argue, as I do here, that it is an aesthetic perspective that leads to life affirmation, to spiritual fullness.[46]

Art, of course, plays an important role in facilitating an aesthetic perspective, which helps us to face the "terrible" truths. In pithy fashion, Nietzsche remarks, "The truth is ugly. We have art, so that we do not perish from the truth."[47] Nietzsche returns to the subject of art in his later works, albeit without the metaphysical overtones we saw in *The Birth of Tragedy*. He continues his argument that art—understood broadly as the engagement of aesthetic sensibilities, and as encompassing both artistic creation and the enjoyment of created art by participants and spectators—is of paramount importance in treating existence as an aesthetic phenomenon. It is most clearly evident in the aphorism "Our ultimate gratitude to art" in *The Gay Science*. Here Nietzsche claims that "as an aesthetic phenomenon existence is still *bearable* for us, and art furnishes us with eyes and hands and above all the good conscience to be *able* to turn ourselves into such a phenomenon."[48] We should note the striking difference from his earlier formulation that emerges: existence is made "bearable" aesthetically, not "justified." Existence as an aesthetic phenomenon is not given metaphysical or cosmic significance, but it is made bearable, with an intimation that existence is also made *valuable*. This passage also shows the role of art in transforming ourselves, our lives, into an aesthetic phenomenon. Art provides us with the tools to engage with our lives as an artist with his creation, transforming our lives into a creation that engages our aesthetic sensibilities and responds to our artistic input.

Art is needed for the free spirits to face what they consider the "terrible" truths of existence; art makes this task not only bearable but joyful. Nietzsche wants to show that we are able to realize the value and idealization of existence through art: "We need all exuberant, floating, dancing, mocking, childish, and blissful art lest we lose the *freedom above things* that our ideal demands of us." The "ideal" that Nietzsche describes here reminds us of the "free, fearless hovering" that the free spirit regards as the "most desirable condition." Art is a medium by which free spirits are brought back to the freedom of an aesthetic perspective. Living with the knowledge of the "terrible" truths of existence can leave one cold and detached from life, but the moments of bliss that can be reached through an aesthetic perspective make life, at the very least, "bearable."[49]

We can find an illuminating example of this in a position taken by novelist Vladimir Nabokov. When facing critics of his controversial novel *Lolita* in the 1950s, he writes a defense that seems fitting for a free spirit. He defends himself accordingly: "There are gentle souls who would pronounce *Lolita* meaningless because it does not teach them anything.... For me a work of fiction exists only insofar as it affords me what I shall bluntly call aesthetic bliss, that is a sense of being somehow, somewhere, connected with other states of being where art (curiosity, tenderness, kindness, ecstasy) is the norm."[50] Art, and creating art, is for Nabokov good for its own sake. More importantly for the argument here, Nabakov views his work of art as liberated from morality, from the putative need to teach a moral lesson. This is not to suggest that art cannot contain moral lessons, but the "aesthetic bliss" that comes to Nabokov seems to flow out of a "free, fearless hovering" over traditional moral lessons. Nietzsche expresses the need for art in a similar way: "At times we need a rest from ourselves by looking upon, by looking *down* upon, ourselves and, from an artistic distance, laughing *over* ourselves or weeping *over* ourselves."[51]

We may also profitably consider Nietzsche's famous doctrine of the eternal recurrence and what it might mean for an aesthetic perspective. Briefly put, eternal recurrence is the idea that states of affairs, being as they are at any moment, will return or recur an infinite number of times, and that the whole series of momentary states of affairs will recur as well. He first introduces this idea in the aphorism "The Greatest Weight" and wonders what this idea might mean to the individual who believes it. He asks whether, if a demon told you, "This life as you now live it and have lived it, you will have to live once more and innumerable times more; and there will be nothing new in it," you would be able affirm such an existence; to give it significance and value through your own affirmation. Nietzsche continues, "The question in each and every thing, 'Do you desire this once more and innumerable times more?' would lie upon your actions as the greatest weight. Or how well disposed would you have to become to yourself and to life to *crave nothing more fervently* than this ultimate eternal confirmation and seal?"[52] One may wonder whether, through the doctrine of eternal recurrence, one is forced, in a sense, to will all of eternity if one wills one moment.[53] For each moment is tied to all events past, present, and future. To will one moment is to will every set of finite combinations of causes that led to that moment, to will everything that ever has or will ever exist. This also requires willing all bad things that happen along with the good, that is, staring the "terrible" truths of existence in the face, and willing them to happen again. Such willing is difficult, even terrifying, but the free spirit ought to be able to will it nonetheless.[54]

For our purposes, we wish to understand how the eternal recurrence may help us to understand Nietzsche's engagement with existence as an aesthetic phenomenon. I want to highlight two ways in which the eternal recurrence and aesthetic perspective might be related: firstly, through art—or more particularly through "aesthetic distance"—and, secondly, through one's attitude toward time. Let us address the role of art—art as the model for life—first.

Nietzsche returns to the eternal recurrence in *Beyond Good and Evil*, and here he reveals its aesthetic character:

> The ideal of the most high-spirited, alive, and world-affirming human being who has not only come to terms and learned to get along with whatever was and is, but who wants to have *what was and is* repeated into all eternity, shouting insatiably *da capo*—not only to himself but to the whole play and spectacle, and not only to a spectacle but at bottom to him who needs precisely this spectacle—and who makes it necessary because again and again he needs himself—and makes himself necessary.[55]

Willing the eternal recurrence of all events presupposes the "aesthetic distance" we need to look down on ourselves as at a spectacle. Through this doctrine we are able to treat the whole of existence as a spectacle, that is, as an aesthetic phenomenon, and to be grateful for it. As Michael Gillespie remarks, "It is this absolute affirmation of the whole that is essential to the eternal recurrence. Such an affirmation, however, is not just a passive acceptance, a mere saying of the word 'yes,' but a willing, and as such it is also a taking on of absolute responsibility for the whole, for everything that has been and will be."[56] The free spirit needs aesthetic distance and an artistic role to be grateful for existence, to affirm life in the face of the terrible truth that life has no cosmic or metaphysical significance.[57]

There is a further link between the notion of eternal recurrence and aesthetic perspective in the way the theory impacts one's attitude towards time. In short, eternal recurrence focuses one's view on the present moment. As Kathleen Higgins explains, the present moment is "unique," because "in this model the past and future collapse into one another."[58] If time recurs eternally, past and future are ultimately one and the same, although one may at least utilize "past" and "future" as relative designations. Therefore, "the present moment is the only moment in time that stands out from the swirl of recurrence. Moreover, it is a moment of privileged significance because it is the only moment in which we are actively involved in time."[59] Yet Nietzsche is not advocating a sort of light-hearted, "forget the past," seize the day philosophy. Instead, the idea of eternal recurrence emphasizes the present moment as it is "causally connected to all other moments. It is the point at which the causal streams of past and present converge."[60] The lesson of the idea of the eternal recurrence is not to lose oneself in the moment. It is to recognize the importance each moment has in affecting past and future. This knowledge of recurring time, then, gives the present moment a certain weight and importance that slogans like "carpe diem" do not.[61]

The question we are interested in here is, How might this attitude towards time, privileging the present moment, be linked to an aesthetic perspective? There is a sense in which taking an aesthetic perspective privileges the present moment, as well. Leslie Paul Thiele claims that "one lives aesthetically not to arrive at an end called the self-as-art, but because only life lived aesthetically yields its fullest realization at every moment."[62] We discussed earlier the role of art in transforming ourselves. In similar fashion, art allows us to transform the present moment, to focus our artistic energies on the present moment. Thiele offers a stirring passage from Henry David Thoreau's *Walden* to support this claim, and it bears repeating here. Thoreau writes:

> It is something to be able to paint a particular picture, or to carve a statue, and so to make a few objects beautiful; but it is far more glorious to carve and paint the very atmosphere and medium through which we look, which morally we can do. To affect the quality of the day, that is the highest of arts.

> Every man is tasked to make his life, even in its details, worthy
> of the contemplation of his most elevated and critical hour.[63]

Thoreau's attitude is closely mirrored by Nietzsche in the aphorism "What one should learn from artists." He begins the aphorism with the question, "How can we make things beautiful, attractive, and desirable for us when they are not?" We ought to look to artists, for "we want to be the poets of our life—first of all in the smallest most everyday matters."[64]

We see the same attitude towards aesthetic perspective throughout the writings of Emerson. As Zakaras claims, "His observations—the snow, the light and sky—are expressions of wonder, and as such unhinged from the logic of practice or use. . . . Emerson's receptivity enables a new kind of relation to the world, a different kind of seeing. I will call such receptivity *aesthetic*, though the word is not Emerson's, and though Emerson's writing on beauty is never fully separable from his writing on ethics and spirituality."[65] Moreover, Zakaras shows that Emerson saw the intimate connection between individuality and aesthetic receptivity:

> But there is something *individual* in the aesthetic response,
> too. . . . Aesthetic receptivity brings us into contact with
> something that is *ours* and nobody else's. . . . Newness is a
> part of what Emerson tries to capture in describing moments
> of aesthetic receptivity: "But go into the forest, and you shall
> find all new and undescribed. The screaming of the wild geese
> flying by night; the thin note of the companionable titmouse,
> in the winter day; . . . The man who stands on the seashore,
> or who rambles in the wood, seems to be the first man that
> ever stood on the shore, or entered a grove, his sensations
> and his world are so novel and strange." To see the world
> aesthetically, for Emerson, is to see it as though for the first
> time. It is to discover a relation to the world unmediated by
> others, and unmediated by the purposeful instrumentality that
> colors most of everyday living. It is to receive the irreducible
> uniqueness of the world as it presents itself to us—and only
> us—in this particular moment.[66]

Aesthetic perspective is individuating, and arrives along with the sensations of new experiences and of living in the moment. Here Emerson is in profound agreement with Nietzsche and Thoreau, and it is notable that our exemplar free spirits all arrive at a similar conclusion regarding the importance of aesthetic experiences.

Returning to the relationship of aesthetic perspective and time, there is a sense in which living aesthetically is akin to living in the moment, but also to willing the moment. We may not wish to will every moment, for many terrible moments inevitably occur in one's life. Nevertheless, if we will the present moment we do, in a sense, agree to will all the moments that led to the present moment, the bad moments included. If willing one moment requires the willing of eternal recurrence of events, then living aesthetically may be crucial to such willing. For an aesthetic perspective calls for one to will the moment, which does in a sense mean to will all of the causes that led to that moment. The realization that the present moment depends on all other moments in time, that is, accepting the idea of eternal recurrence, involves taking a broader view of the present moment by interpretively placing it in its larger context. Through placing the present moment in its larger context, one interpretively creates "aesthetic" distance from the present moment; one takes an aesthetic perspective. Viewed this way we may better understand why Nietzsche included the word "eternal" when he said "it is only as an *aesthetic phenomenon* that existence and the world are *eternally* justified" (italics mine). Willing the eternal recurrence of time creates and requires aesthetic distance. This seems to be what Nietzsche has in mind when he connects aesthetic perspective to an "eternal" justification of existence.

The preceding discussion should not be regarded as an exhaustive or precise account of the eternal recurrence, but rather as a possible interpretation of the relationship between eternal recurrence and aesthetic perspective. How seriously Nietzsche took the idea of eternal recurrence— that is, whether he truly thought events did recur over and over again in the same precise way—is an open question among Nietzsche scholars, and it is not my intention to resolve this debate here.[67] Furthermore, what the implications of the eternal recurrence are is likewise a topic that has sparked debate and spawned multiple interpretations.[68] The above discussion is only meant to suggest that the eternal recurrence has implications for how we understand aesthetic perspective. First, willing the eternal recurrence presupposes the aesthetic distance necessary to engage the world as a spectacle, as an aesthetic phenomenon. According to Nietzsche, he who wills the eternal recurrence affirms the "play and spectacle" of life. He treats life as an aesthetic phenomenon.[69] Secondly, embracing the idea of eternal recurrence shapes one's attitude toward time, emphasizing the present moment in an attempt to yield life's "fullest realization at every moment."

The relationship between aesthetic perspective and spiritual fullness has now become clear. We observe a positive orientation for the free spirit, and our investigation of this ethical ideal is nearly complete. It is a propitious moment, then, to review the conclusions at which we have arrived: the free spirit is a skeptic who seeks above all to be free of illusions about the world. He is able to face the "terrible truths" of existence without falling into despair due to his cheerful temperament and to his ability to view a world without rational meaning as a cause for wonder rather than crushing doubt, as an invitation to create meaning rather than as a terrifying abyss. The free spirit affirms life, creates value in it, and finds an attachment to it—that is, he achieves spiritual fullness—through an aesthetic perspective, as opposed to traditional moral perspectives such as communal or religious doctrines or belief in human progress of some sort. A truly liberal society supports the free spirit's ability to do all of these things.

In the end, spiritual freedom proves to be a natural ally with liberalism. The desire to safeguard one's soul, focus on one's inner life, and remain stubbornly independent, is not only enabled by liberal society, but benefits that society as well. Free spirits, or the pursuit of spiritual freedom in general, should not only be tolerated but embraced by contemporary liberal democracies. This discovery may indeed have the potential to change the attitude that society has toward nonconformists, outcasts, or all those who fall outside of the mainstream of politics or culture (this is not to suggest that all outsiders are free spirits—they must meet the criteria laid out here). We might embrace the outsider, especially those outsiders that possess the spiritual freedom to check some of the chronic problems that ail liberal democratic societies.

This chapter has addressed the relationship of spiritual freedom to liberal society, and the practical effects of free spirits as they live in society. The next two chapters continue exploring the importance of spiritual freedom to liberal political order, but they shift the focus to individual autonomy. Liberalism requires the idea of autonomous individuals, and critics of liberalism are wont to question this idea. The heart of these critiques is skepticism about individual autonomy, both its possibility and its desirability. The ideal of the free spirit has important implications for both of these questions.

Chapter 5

The Possibility of Autonomy

The Progressive Critique

He alone is free who lives with free consent under the entire guidance of reason.

—Baruch Spinoza

That to secure these rights, Governments are instituted among Men, deriving their just powers from the consent of the governed . . .

—Thomas Jefferson

The liberal state is predicated on the idea of the individual. Not surprisingly, the origins of the nation-state coincide with the origins of liberalism. The Treaty of Westphalia, which established the state system in 1648, is followed three years later by Thomas Hobbes's *Leviathan*, published in 1651. In *Leviathan*, Hobbes makes the first philosophical argument for a social compact, for the idea that humans in a prepolitical state can unite and consent to form a government. For Hobbes, and his liberal successor John Locke, former justifications for political authority—such as the divine right of kings or of patriarchal authority generally—could no longer convince. Such justifications were refuted both theoretically, by the advance of modern science and philosophy, and practically, by the failure of those political authorities to prevent wars and guarantee security for citizens. The new justification for political authority was to come through individuals; the individual citizen was now the foundational unit of political theorizing. Thus, the liberal state does not exist without the individual citizen, and the goal of the liberal state is the freedom of the individual.

The liberal republic envisioned by Baruch Spinoza, for example, placed liberation from authority and independence of mind at the top of political goals, calling them the *summum bonum* and *finis ultimus*. Citizens in Spinoza's liberal republic would be free of superstitions and religious authority, and the spirituality of each citizen would consist in "the desire each human being naturally feels to continue existing as a human being, that is, as a being who lives 'full of his own sense of things.'"[1] Mirroring the free spirit, Spinoza's liberal citizen will feel as many felt living in the Dutch Republic of 1670, "where nothing is esteemed dearer or more precious than freedom."[2] Thus, for Spinoza the goal of the best political regime was the production of citizens that were much like free spirits or at least shared some characteristics—in terms of freedom of spirit and independence of mind, if not solitude and aesthetic perspective.

Nietzsche, by contrast, thought of his free spirits as few in number, and we can't be sure that he would suggest that politics be ordered with the protection of free spirits as the ultimate goal.[3] Yet, as we recall from our earlier discussion, Nietzsche does argue that the state must allow these few to "step a little aside" from the obligations of politics and community. Nietzsche wants the state to protect the strongest individuals by not sacrificing their needs to meet the needs of weaker individuals. By protecting individuals simply—that is, all individuals protected through basic liberal rights—we might infer that a liberal state could work for free spirits, even if that is not Nietzsche's claim or preferred political regime. It is important, however, to be clear that Nietzsche does not advocate for liberalism or the liberal state, throughout his discussion of the free spirit or in his writings generally.[4] Moreover, Nietzsche is concerned that liberal culture may be damaging to great and rare souls, free spirits included. Nevertheless, I argue that liberal political order has a place for free spirits and spiritual freedom, and in turn free spirits and spiritual freedom are beneficial to liberal politics.

The position taken here is somewhere in the middle, sitting between Nietzsche and Spinoza. This discussion does not take the free spirit to be as rare and exceptional as Nietzsche does, but it also does not expect or wish for something like a republic of free spirits, or at least a politics ordered by this ultimate goal.[5] The aim of this project is more humble, attempting to expose the desirability of free spirits for our contemporary liberal democracies. Free spirits must be allowed, as Nietzsche implores, to "step a little aside."⁶ In other words, spiritual freedom must be understood and protected through political freedom. Indeed, the idea of the free spirit justifies, in an important sense, liberal regimes as they exist today.

How might this conclusion differ, however, from other theoretical justifications for a liberal political order? In other words, what import does this conclusion have for liberal political theory? Let us look at a prominent narrative in political theory about the origins of liberal government. Liberalism is predicated on the idea that individuals must consent to form a government under which they will live. From liberal theory emerges a need to locate a position, in space or time, that is separate from extant government or social organization. Efforts to locate such a position, outside of government, from which individuals can consent to initiate government has led to theories of a "state of nature," or a "veil of ignorance." These theories are necessary to ground individual rights philosophically. That is, we must be able to conceive of some state prior to the formation of government where individual rights are located if we are to believe that individuals can be autonomous of government.

Critics of liberalism seek to undermine these "origin stories" of individual rights by refuting such theories or thought experiments. They doubt the possibility of an autonomous individual. My argument here is that the very existence of free spirits *demonstrates* individual autonomy and the need for basic individual rights without recourse to a presocial state or hypothetical veil of ignorance. I will suggest that a justification of individual rights can be found even if we take the criticisms of these "origin stories" seriously. I will do so by addressing two basic challenges, in the next two chapters, levied by critics of individual autonomy. The first, addressed in this chapter, is whether it is possible, the second, addressed in the following chapter, is whether it is desirable.

The Origins of Liberal Government

The first challenge to individual autonomy that the free spirit informs surrounds the question of the very possibility of autonomy. Many political theorists have doubted the notion that the individual can be treated as a discrete unit of analysis. They have asserted that the individual is but a part of the social whole, a social whole that is prior—and therefore irreducible—to individuals, or a social whole that is the natural and necessary end of the individual. If one canvasses the history of Western political thought, a view that society—or the state—is of greater importance than the individual will emerge in various forms. To be reminded of some well-known examples: society is prior to the individual (Aristotle); the individual reaches his highest potential and fulfillment in the state (Plato); the individual realizes the full expression of the ethical life only as a member of the state (Hegel); and the individual experiences true freedom only when he dissolves his particular will into the general will of the state (Rousseau). These views may differ in regards to the timing at which an individual is absorbed into the state—Plato, Hegel, and Rousseau all see the individual achieving their highest fulfillment as a member of the state over time, while Aristotle claims that the individual is never separated, temporally, from society to begin with—but all these various theories assert that separating the individual from society is impossible. I will not recount the details of these arguments here, but it is important to acknowledge the influence they have had on progressives and communitarians, both of the recent past and today.

The placement of society above the individual has a long history in political theory, constituting something closer to the rule than the exception. John Dewey, the early intellectual heavyweight of the progressive movement, starts from the premise that individuals cannot be separated from society, made evident in his summary of the theory of the "social organism" in *The Ethics of Democracy*:

> ... that theory that men are not isolated non-social atoms, but are men only when in intrinsic relations to men.... Society in its unified and structural character is the fact of the case.... Society, as a real whole, is the normal order, and the mass as an aggregate of isolated units is the fiction. If this be the case, and if democracy be a form of society, it not only does have, but must have, a common will; for it is this unity of will which makes it an organism. A state represents men so far as they have become organically related to one another, or are possessed of unity or purpose and interest.[7]

In words that echo Hegel and Rousseau, Dewey asserts the idea that men "are men only when in intrinsic relations to men." Only through interactions with other men are individual men capable of understanding themselves, a view that is carried on by more recent communitarians.

In *Reconstructing Public Philosophy*, William Sullivan encapsulates the communitarian position on the individual's relation to society:

> Self-fulfillment and even the working out of personal identity and a sense of orientation in the world depend upon a communal enterprise. This shared process is the civic life, and its root is involvement with others: other generations, other sorts of persons whose differences are significant because they contribute to the whole upon which our particular sense of self depends. . . . Outside a linguistic community of shared practices, there would be biological *homo sapiens* as a logical abstraction, but there could not be human beings. This is the meaning of the Greek and medieval dictum that the political community is ontologically *prior* to the individual. The *polis* is, literally, that which makes man, as human being, possible.[8]

Sullivan adopts the classical republican thesis that the individual is but a part of the larger political community, that is, the individual does not exist outside of community. In Aristotle's famous phrasing, "It is clear, then, that the city exists by nature and is prior to the individual. For if no individual is self-sufficient when isolated, he will be like other parts in relation to their whole."[9]

As we progress, we will note similar statements in progressives from Dewey to Herbert Croly and Charles Merriam, and in communitarians from Sullivan to Sandel, MacIntyre, and Taylor. Whatsoever their theoretical differences, the most prominent progressive and communitarian thinkers agree on the basic premise that the individual cannot be separated from society. Instead, the individual is a part of the social whole. Their theoretical differences notwithstanding, we might collapse these theories into one category: theories that treat the state as a "social organism." Those who view the state as a living "organism" naturally view the life of the individual as an organic ingredient of the state, as a means to the growth and maintenance of the state. If the state is a social organism, the individual becomes an organic part of the larger living whole. The agency individuals would need to consent to liberal government is ruled out by the fact of their being something akin to biological parts of the larger social body. Not all the aforementioned thinkers utilize such biological language, but they all—in some way or other—view the individual as a part of the social whole, a part that cannot be detached or separated.

Liberalism, as defined here, departs from progressivism and communitarianism at the very outset of theorizing. Liberalism begins with autonomous individuals; it begins with the idea that individuals possess an essential freedom or autonomy that cannot be infringed upon without justification. Liberalism thus denies the conception of state as primarily a "social organism." Dewey was keenly aware of the difference in starting point, and he juxtaposes the theory of state as a "social organism" with the theory of state as a "social contract":

> The essence of the "Social contract" theory is not the idea of the formulation of a contract; it is the idea that men are mere individuals, without any social relations until they form a contract. The method by which they get out of their individualistic condition is not the important matter; rather this is the fact, that they are in an individualistic condition out of which they have to be got. The notion, in short, which lay in the minds of those who proposed this theory was that men in their natural state are non-social units, are a mere multitude; and that some artifice must be devised to constitute them into political society.[10]

According to Dewey, the social contract is the basis of liberalism, and it rests on the faulty assumption that "men in their natural state are non-social units." What Dewey is aiming his criticism at, implicitly, is the "state of nature" at the foundation of liberal theorizing, a criticism that is echoed by others.

The concept of a state of nature hardly needs introduction to those familiar with the history of Western political thought. Modern liberalism begins with Hobbes's argument that human life in the state of nature was "solitary, poor, nasty, brutish, and short." Rights of the individual were first established by appeal to the right of self-preservation. Hobbes begins liberal "rights talk" by placing the right to self-preservation above all else.[11] The individual's need to preserve his material/physical existence trumps the pursuit of virtue or duties towards other men encouraged in ancient and medieval political philosophy. Once individual right is placed above virtue or duty in modern political philosophy, the individual is placed above—or at least before—the political community. John Locke also presupposes the right of self-preservation, using a paradigm very similar to Hobbes's state of nature to justify the preeminence of this right.[12] Liberty promises that each and every person may do what *he* deems necessary for his preservation, that other men or governments "cannot hinder him from using the power left him, according as his judgment and reason shall dictate to him."[13]

Thus, to have liberty is to be free to act according to your own reason in the interest of self-preservation. We have this liberty in the state of nature, but, as both Hobbes and Locke warn us, protection of this liberty is hardly robust in such a state. The state of nature is dangerous and unforgiving, so individuals consented to a social compact that, through political institutions, would alleviate the dangers of the state of nature. Hobbes's and Locke's respective versions of the social compact contain important differences, but, in both, alleviation of the dangers in the state of nature is the goal.[14] Notably, Hobbes's social compact is the more illiberal solution of the two insofar as men give away their natural liberties in order to leave the state of nature. In this way, Hobbes's civil state requires more than just consent. In chapter 17 of *Leviathan*, he states:

> This is more than consent, or concord; it is a real unity of them all, in one and the same person, made by covenant of every man with every man, in such manner as if every man should say to every man *I authorize and give up my right of governing myself to this man, or to this assembly of men.*"[15]

Hobbes begins with individuals in a position where they may consent to government, but once government is formed the individual and his natural liberty are no longer placed above or protected by government power. Hobbes begins from a liberal standpoint but ends with an illiberal solution.

The more liberal Locke, by contrast, seeks to create a government that respects the natural liberties of citizens, and allows them to govern themselves. Government is the institution of natural laws that already exist in the state of nature, where each person has executive power to enforce them. For Locke, government is the institutionalization of individual freedom, not the reduction or extermination of it. Through the social compact we have justification for the creation of government. As individuals, we consent to a government that guarantees to protect our "natural rights"—rights that exist in a state of nature—in a way that they cannot be protected in the state of nature.[16]

In both Hobbes and Locke, the social contract begins with the idea of consent, arising amongst individuals in an assumed state of nature.

Progressive theorists are wont to make the state of nature their target. A number of progressive political scientists in the late nineteenth century, trained in the German schools, jettisoned the idea. Francis Lieber, who had studied in Berlin under Johann Fichte and Georg Wilhelm Friedrich Hegel before advancing German political thought in 1830s America, categorically rejects the concept. As Charles Merriam states, "In Lieber's opinion, the 'state of nature' has no basis in fact. Man is essentially a social creature, and hence no artificial means for bringing him into society need be devised."[17] Moreover, for Lieber, the state is the "natural condition of man, because essential to the full development of his faculties."[18] Merriam claims that this new German school of political science had ushered in a new era, based on history rather than natural right:

> The individualistic ideas of the "natural right" school of political theory, indorsed in the Revolution, are discredited and repudiated. The notion that political society and government are based upon a contract between independent individuals and that such a contract is the sole source of political obligation, is regarded as no longer tenable.[19]

John Burgess, another descendent of the German school, comes to a similar conclusion, arguing that social contract theory assumes that "the idea of the state with all its attributes is consciously present in the minds of individuals proposing to constitute the state, and that the disposition to obey law is universally established."[20] That is, the requisite conditions for a social contract exist only where individuals have a preexisting understanding of, and obedience to, ordered society. Burgess thinks that these conditions do not exist in a state of nature. Only through living socially—that is, through the emergence and later inculcation of social norms and rules—can a group of individuals be prepared to enter into a social contract. If this is true, it follows that the social contract cannot describe the origination of a state. Rather, the social contract could, at most, be the institutionalization of an already existing social order. Again, the idea of isolated individuals constituting political society is declared a myth. Social contract theory based on natural right is, by extension, rejected as a foundation for liberal government.

Partly in response to criticism surrounding the state of nature, another thought experiment was created to "originate" liberal government. A little over three hundred years after Hobbes's *Leviathan*, John Rawls attempted to elude the critics of the state of nature while retaining rights-based liberalism. He did this by imagining individuals in what he called an "original position." The original position is

> a device of representation: it models, first, what we regard (here and now) as fair conditions for the terms of social cooperation to be agreed to . . . ; and second, it models what we regard (here and now) as reasonable restrictions on reasons that may be used in arguing for principles of justice to regulate the basic structure.[21]

The original position allows for decisions about the terms of social cooperation, and about how to form a just society, in a fair and impartial way. It does this by ensuring that those in the original position are ignorant about basic facts about themselves. Individuals have no knowledge of their particular abilities, desires, or of their relative position in the social order. This lack of knowledge is what Rawls calls the "veil of ignorance," and his thought experiment requires that each individual wear this veil when deciding upon basic political terms.

Specifically, individuals in an "original position," wearing a "veil of ignorance," must decide on principles of justice, that is, on the distribution of rights, positions, and resources in the society they are forming. For Rawls, the key to the formation of a just society is that those doing the forming are equal in a highly abstract way, they are equal because of their common ignorance regarding basic facts about themselves.[22] It is this lack of self-knowledge that makes the thought experiment work, specifically the fact that in the original position "no one knows his place in society, his class position or social status; nor does he know his fortune in the distribution of natural assets and abilities, his intelligence and strength, and the like."[23] This ignorance regarding basic facts renders the principles of justice chosen by persons in the original position fair. Moreover, it renders those principles legitimate, as every reasonable person ought to be willing to offer their consent to them.

Rawls's original position offers an alternative method by which to ground and legitimate liberal political order in consent. While it differs from the state of nature theorizing of Hobbes and Locke, it remains a version of a liberal social contract. As such, it requires individual autonomy, both for the representatives in the original position and the citizens that accept and heed the principles of justice chosen by those representatives.

It requires citizens who can reflect upon their own preferred ends as well as share concern for the ends of others. Rawls's novel and provocative suggestion, furthermore, is that autonomous, reflective citizens attempt to agree on political principles and terms of social cooperation from a position of near total equality. The purpose of the social contract is not to leave the dangerous state of nature, but to create a just and fair society of "free and equal persons."

Does the original position successfully evade the attacks that have been launched at the state of nature? To some extent, the answer to this question requires a thorough explanation of the debate between Rawls and his critics surrounding the nature of the original position. Recovering this debate is unnecessary for our purposes here and would be cumbersome for the reader, but a brief summary of it will provide us with important context. Partially in response to this debate, Rawls's description of the original position changed between the publication of *A Theory of Justice* and his later work *Political Liberalism*. In the latter, Rawls explains that the original position is a thought experiment and not an actual metaphysical "position"; a thought experiment that is compatible with differing conceptions of the good life. Moreover, Rawls stresses that there is a social component—of social cooperation and reciprocity—in the original position as well, because in such a state we think not only of ourselves but of the rights of others. In short, Rawls elaborated his position over time in order to rebut many of the criticisms levied by the likes of communitarians and progressives.

Nevertheless, Rawls's original position still requires a conception of individual autonomy. Even if Rawls includes some social understanding of the self in the original position, the person doing the thinking and ultimately choosing the principles of justice *must* be an individual, abstracted from any human group. And this individual must be autonomous to the extent that he or she can voluntarily choose such principles. It is here that the attack on the idea of individual autonomy resurfaces, challenging the notion that political theorizing can begin with the individual. Progressives see the self as socially embedded, and therefore the individual self is incapable of imagining the abstracted self that is necessary for the Rawlsian thought experiment to work. They aim their critique not only at the idea of a political founding via social contract, but at the idea of contracts, entered into by private individuals, as a basis for political life in general. Just as the idea of independent citizens forming a contract out of the state of nature is rejected, so is the idea of free and equal persons in an original position.

In short, both versions of the social contract—that of Hobbes/Locke and that of Rawls—are contested and rejected by progressives. The reason the social contract is rejected is fairly straightforward. There is no such person as an independent citizen or an autonomous individual. Individuals never exist in a prepolitical state, and individuals are not independent or autonomous enough to truly reflect on their ends and others ends, and to choose rationally how best to take both into account in a political framework. Real human beings—not abstract, imaginary equals in an original position—are not autonomous relative to their life situation (social position, natural gifts, familial roles, cultural identity, etc.), or so the argument goes. Michael Sandel, for example, argues that "the liberal attempt to construe all obligation in terms [of voluntary contract] . . . fails to capture those loyalties and responsibilities whose moral force consists partly in the fact that living by them is inseparable from understanding ourselves as the particular persons we are—as members of this family or city or nation or people, as bearers of that history, as citizens of this republic."[24]

For Sandel, an autonomous individual, one who can imagine herself in an "original position" or is able to enter into a social contract, is impossible. We cannot separate ourselves from who we are, and who we are is determined by attachments that we have not chosen. Here Sandel echoes the general idea of the state as a social organism. Sandel goes further, however, as he attacks the "voluntarist self-image," or "unencumbered self," inherent in liberalism. He claims that the

> predicament of liberal democracy in contemporary America may be traced to a deficiency in the voluntarist self-image that underlies it. The sense of disempowerment that afflicts citizens of the procedural republic may reflect the loss of agency that results when liberty is detached from self-government and located in the will of an independent self, unencumbered by moral and communal ties it has not chosen. Such a self, liberated though it be from the burden of identities it has not chosen, entitled though it be to the range of rights assured by the welfare state, may nonetheless find itself overwhelmed as it turns to face the world on its own resources.[25]

Sandel here asserts that the voluntarist self-image is "deficient" and leads to a sense of disempowerment. Liberal citizens are "afflicted" by a loss of agency when liberty is "detached from self-government and located in the will of an independent self." More will be discussed about the "deficiency" of the unencumbered self in the next chapter, but for our purposes here let us conclude that progressive critiques of liberalism are aimed at the impossibility of autonomous individuals entering into a social contract. Individuals cannot be shown to possess "natural rights," nor can they sensibly be placed in a "state of nature" or "original position." Consequently, another philosophical justification of legitimate government must be found.

Progressives find this foundation in a philosophy of history (History with a capital "H"), in the Hegelian idea of history as a rational process and of the modern, rational, democratic state as the "end of history." Along with the idea of History—the never-ending march of social progress—the rational state became the only legitimate concern of political science. "It was the idea of the state, itself, which gave meaning to [political science's] existence and legitimacy to its method. . . . As a result, political science could be established as an applied science of the rational state."[26] Political science and theory, then, is concerned with the progress of the modern, democratic, rational state. The legitimacy of government, of the state, is proved by the continuity of its role in social progress, of improving society. For progressives, there need not be a narrative of state origins, because the state is the result of rational History and social progress. Thus, the debate over legitimate government is the debate between natural right and History.[27]

Yet this debate is also a debate about whether political theory ought to treat the individual as the basic unit, or whether the state—as a social organism—is the sole political unit worthy of analysis. Perhaps the more fundamental question is not whether a presocial state of nature actually existed, but whether it is sensible to treat the individual as the discrete unit at the foundation of political order. In other words, is it possible to begin with autonomous individuals and to build political society up from there? Does an autonomous individual exist? While we may not expect to settle this debate here, the conception of the free spirit does, at a minimum, urge us to return to this fundamental question.

A Practicable Sense of Autonomy

The free spirit presents a version of an autonomous individual. I will here argue that the autonomy of a free spirit is real and practicable and that this sense of autonomy can be helpful in theorizing about liberalism.

Let us take a look at how, exactly, a free spirit is autonomous. Recent scholarship on Nietzsche's free spirit has delved into this very issue. We may recall from chapter 2 that, while Nietzsche believes much of our behavior and character formation is determined by subconscious drives and the external environment, there remains some potential for individual agency in developing one's self. The discussion of the free spirit in *Human, All Too Human* begins to lay out a sense of spiritual autonomy, but it is in *Daybreak* (or *Dawn*) that Nietzsche directly engages with this idea. Nietzsche argues for a limited conception of autonomy, one that is both practicable and developmental. His famous gardening metaphor in *Daybreak* 560, entitled "What we are at liberty to do," provides an initial portrait of this autonomy:

> One can dispose of one's drives like a gardener and, though few know it, cultivate the shoots of anger, pity, curiosity, vanity as productively and profitably as a beautiful fruit tree on a trellis; one can do it with the good or bad taste of a gardener and, as it were, in the French or English or Dutch or Chinese fashion; one can also let nature rule and only attend to a little embellishment and tidying-up here and there; one can, finally, without paying any attention to them at all, let the plants grow up and fight their fight out among themselves—indeed, one can take delight in such a wilderness, and desire precisely this delight, though it gives one some trouble, too. All this we are at liberty to do: but how many know we are at liberty to do it? Do the majority not *believe* in *themselves* as in complete *fully-developed facts*?[28]

The purpose of the gardening metaphor is to establish the self as something that grows and develops, not something that is an established fact. Moreover, just as what grows in a garden is a product of natural processes and natural potentialities, the self also must work with the material it is given. There is no creation of one's self ex nihilo; self-creation or character formation is a matter of modifying what nature and environment present to us. Yet, there must be some autonomous agent at work here, some "one" who is deciding how to cultivate, or not cultivate, the drives. Paul Franco comes to a similar conclusion about the gardening metaphor. He claims that Nietzsche "insists that the way we think about things and evaluate them can have a profound effect on our actions. This does not mean, however, that there isn't an awful lot about ourselves that is given or natural or even undeniable. That is the point of the gardening and artistic metaphors. . . . Our liberty extends only to arranging, cultivating, nourishing, and composing what is already there. This creative activity is powerfully circumscribed by the natural facts that make-up our being, but we are still far from being 'fully developed facts' prior to this activity."[29]

The individual autonomy necessary for this creative activity is not univocal in Nietzsche's writings, however, including seemingly contradictory positions taken in *Daybreak*. For example, in section 109 he suggests that struggles among the drives are where the action of human behavior truly lies, and that the intellect is merely a "blind instrument of another drive which is a rival of the drive whose vehemence is tormenting us."[30] He finishes the same aphorism by claiming that, in the struggle between drives, "our intellect is going to have to take sides." Perhaps we may interpret the "intellect" as possessing the individual agency to cultivate or not cultivate the drives that are determined by nature, but even in such a case, section 109 hardly reads as a ringing endorsement of individual autonomy. Likewise, Nietzsche casts great suspicion towards the notion of free will, claiming it is both an error—the result of "human pride" and "feeling of power" (*Daybeak* 128)—and the cause of inaccurate and harmful moral evaluations, leading to a belief in evil and the creation of "bad conscience" (*Daybreak* 148). We must be able to account for such contradictory statements, and we are able to do so once we comprehend Nietzsche's notion of self-cultivation and his understanding of free will.

The gardening metaphor shows us a way to understand how an individual is autonomous enough to self-cultivate. Again, such cultivation is quite limited in scope. Our subconscious drives incessantly act upon us (*Daybreak* 120); we do not will them into existence. However, the very act of thinking is an autonomous act capable of cultivating drives. Rebecca Bamford argues, "Thinking is explicitly identified as a form of cultivation activity in *D* 382. The warning in this aphorism is thus concerned with what happens if a thinker does not engage in cultivation: conclusions will sprout anyway, regardless of whether the thinker wants them to or not."[31] The drives act upon us whether we like it or not, but it is also true that they are *our* drives. The gardening metaphor shows us that "Nietzsche is claiming that we are free to engage in *cultivating drives*, and he suggests that the drives we are to cultivate are *our own* drives. He is also clear that *knowing* about our freedom to cultivate really does matter significantly to being able to exercise our drive-cultivation freedom. . . . This aphorism helps to clarify Nietzsche's view of freedom as developmental."[32] This is the limited sense in which we are free: we can become cognizant of our drives, we can cultivate or choose not to cultivate our drives, and thereby we develop an autonomous self.

We can see this further when we explore Nietzsche's views on free will. Early in *Beyond Good and Evil*, Nietzsche mocks the idea of free will in the metaphysical sense, but he likewise mocks the easy decision to assert its opposite, that is, unfree will:

> The desire for "freedom of the will" in the superlative metaphysical sense, which still holds sway, unfortunately, in the minds of the half-educated; the desire to bear the entire and ultimate responsibility for one's actions oneself, and to absolve God, the world, ancestors, chance, and society involves nothing less than to be precisely this *causa sui* and . . . to pull oneself up into existence by the hair, out of the swamps of nothingness. Suppose someone were thus to see through the boorish simplicity of this celebrated concept of "free will" and put it out of his head altogether, I beg of him to carry his "enlightenment" a step further, and also put out of his head the contrary of this monstrous conception of "free will": I mean "unfree will," which amounts to a misuse of cause and effect.[33]

To understand freedom and autonomy in Nietzsche's sense, we must return to the discussion of drives. The self is developed through the arrangement of drives—one cannot choose drives, only how to arrange them and which drives to cultivate, which to suppress—and these drives are not rational but rather are products of the affects.[34] Autonomy, for Nietzsche, is not unencumbered choice; it is mastery over one's drives. Ken Gemes summarizes what constitutes an autonomous individual, master of a free will, with a genuine self: "To have a genuine self is to have an enduring coordinated hierarchy of drives. Most humans fail to have such a hierarchy; hence they are not sovereign individuals. Rather they are a jumble of drives with no coherent order."[35] The idea here is that the more control one has over one's drives, the more autonomous of external forces one becomes.

Simon May reaches similar conclusions. May also views Nietzsche's account of autonomy as an account of the mastery of drives. "The more *effectively* the drives are ordered into a hierarchy—the more control the self has over itself and over the circumstances with which it is faced—the more it is autonomous."[36] To be sure, it is hardly obvious how mastering one's drives, by ordering them into a hierarchy, applies to the question of whether one's will is free. It becomes clearer if we think of free will not as free choice, but instead as *feeling* free to act according to our own needs and wants. He who has mastered his drives "gets to know what he wants and needs in order to flourish—and is conscious of possessing the strength and discipline to do what it takes to fulfill those needs and wants. Willing is then free."[37] Willing is free because what one wills is aligned with one's needs and wants. A free will is free in the sense that one who possesses it feels free to act; it is not that he is free to "will" the action into existence. The conclusion is that "successful hierarchy is therefore not the result of something else called 'free will'; it is free will."[38] In the end, what does autonomy for a free spirit look like? May offers a concise account:

> Now let us say that this, roughly, is Nietzsche's picture of the maximally free, autonomous self—the self he most values: such a self has the maximum number and diversity of drives, each of them maximally powerful and with its sustained yes's and no's, organized into a clear and aesthetically pleasing hierarchy by an organizing idea or single taste, which has the commanding strength to commit the individual to her chosen courses—i.e. to "promise herself." Such a self is "free"; it can commit itself unflinchingly.[39]

The free spirit is free in the sense of being in control of herself, particularly by having organized her drives into a clear and aesthetically pleasing hierarchy. Again, autonomy or freedom is likened to self-command and self-control, not unconstrained choice or agency.

How does this view of autonomy square with the view of autonomy proffered by liberalism? Again, liberalism is predicated on the idea of an autonomous individual, one capable of authorizing and legitimizing governmental authority through consent. Our understanding of liberal political order is shaped by our understanding of the liberal self. We ought to know something about ourselves as individuals before accepting the task of forming a theoretical framework for a political regime. What exactly constitutes a liberal self is a matter of long debate, but it is clearly a necessary one if we are to more fully understand liberalism. John Christman and Joel Anderson remark, "Since liberalism is centrally a view about the extent of legitimate interference with the wishes of the individual, it is not surprising that debates over liberalism have centered on the nature of the self."[40] Beginning here, I will replace the term "liberal self" with "autonomous individual," for that is, more precisely, with what we are concerned. Let us hear from Christman and Anderson:

> Liberalism can be characterized in a number of ways, a point addressed in several of the chapters here, but it generally involves the approach to the justification of political power emerging from the social contract tradition of the European Enlightenment, where *the authority of the state is seen to rest exclusively on the will of a free and independent citizen.* . . . Central to the specification of justice in this tradition are the interests and choices of the independent, self-governing citizen, whose voice lends legitimacy to the power structures that enact and constitute justice in this sense.[41]

The autonomous individual is necessary to legitimate and maintain liberal political order, and individual autonomy has been explored from many angles in the liberal school of thought.

Put simply, individual autonomy is understood as the capacity "to be one's own person, to be directed by considerations, desires, conditions, and characteristics that are not simply imposed externally upon one."[42] This quite broad definition invites various refinements, and the concept of autonomy has spawned numerous related debates. The first debate surrounds the question of how many different types of autonomy we ought to pay attention to. At the high end, some commentators have argued there are five salient types. Rainer Forst argues that "five different conceptions of individual autonomy have to be distinguished: *moral, ethical, legal, political,* and *social* autonomy. All of these play a certain role in the concept of political liberty, yet none of them should become—as is so often the case—paramount and dominant at the expense of the others."[43] Additionally, theorists distinguish between "basic" autonomy and "ideal" autonomy, and between "authenticity" conditions and "competency" conditions of autonomy. Others have distinguished between personal autonomy and "local" autonomy, which deals with particular, "local," aspects of the person in question.

Summarizing all of these debates is impossible here, so we must narrow our focus to the conceptions of autonomy that can be illuminated by our discussion of the free spirit. Fortunately, we can limit our focus to the debate over "moral" and "personal" autonomy, which is the distinction that is of highest import for liberalism, and the distinction that theorists of autonomy spend the most time discussing. We are concerned with the idea of the free spirit and how it impacts political liberty; hence Forst's inclusion of legal autonomy can be excluded without consequence. Furthermore, political and moral autonomy deal with relations between and among persons and are closely intertwined, so much so that most theorists of autonomy often keep them together. Finally, social autonomy, according to Forst, refers to an arrangement of societal conditions conducive to maintaining the other four dimensions of autonomy, and therefore need not be addressed here, where our focus is on autonomy and liberal political order.[44]

We are left, then, with personal and moral autonomy. We will examine this debate and how the autonomy of the free spirit aligns with it. First, let us turn to Jeremy Waldron for a summary of the distinction between moral and personal autonomy:

> Modern philosophers distinguish between *personal* autonomy and *moral* autonomy. Talk of personal autonomy evokes the image of a person in charge of his life, not just following his desires but choosing which of his desires to follow. It is not an immoral idea, but it has relatively little to do with morality. Those who value it do not value it as part of the moral enterprise of reconciling one person's interest with another's; instead, they see it as a particular way of understanding what each person's interest consists in. Moral autonomy, by contrast, is associated specifically with the relation between one person's pursuit of his own ends and others' pursuit of theirs. This is particularly true of its Kantian manifestations. A person is autonomous in the moral sense when he is not guided just by his own conception of happiness, but by a universalized concern for the ends of all rational persons.[45]

Personal autonomy involves pursuit of one's own ends, and it comes with no moral obligation. It does require self-reflection and self-understanding, as Waldron intimates with his claim that personal autonomy requires "not just following his desires but choosing which of his desires to follow." Self-knowledge is required, as is being in charge of one's life, that is, being in charge of one's will. Put simply, we might say that one is personally autonomous when she knows herself and is in charge of her will. We might also here note that this sense of autonomy is nearly a parallel to the sense that Nietzsche describes.

Moral autonomy, by contrast, requires consideration of the ends of others and their pursuit of those ends. Moreover, it requires consideration of the "relation" between one's ends and the ends of others. Often, we find that we cannot pursue our own conception of happiness without considering the happiness of others. For example, I can hardly enjoy my beach vacation if my wife has contracted a tropical bug that keeps her bedridden throughout the trip's duration. But my wife's well-being is of particular importance to me, in a way that the well-being of others is not. This sort of concern is not what Waldron has in mind. Indeed, it is not particular concern I ought to have for my fellow citizens, but as Waldron claims, a "universalized concern for the ends of all rational persons." I believe a sensible way to interpret this claim is to acknowledge that, as a morally autonomous person, I am concerned with my fellow citizens' ability to *pursue* their own ends. I do not necessarily concern myself with direct assistance in facilitating those ends, nor with how those ends may affect me personally, but I respect those ends and I ensure that neither I nor anything I am connected to (e.g., a political body) could be responsible for preventing others' pursuit of them.

Liberalism treats both personal and moral autonomy as essential. Firstly, liberal political order requires independent, self-governing citizens that choose their own ends; that is, it requires citizens who are personally autonomous.[46] Secondly, the peaceful maintenance of a liberal political order depends upon the respect that citizens extend to each other regarding the pursuit of their own ends. Hence, liberalism also demands moral autonomy from its citizens. A simple recipe for liberal freedom based on individual autonomy can be seen in Kant's principle of freedom: "Each may seek his happiness in the way that seems good to him, provided he does not infringe upon that freedom of others to strive for a like end which can coexist with the freedom of everyone."[47] One is personally autonomous while seeking happiness in the way that seems good to him, and morally autonomous as he does not infringe on the freedom of others to do the same. In this passage, we see a marriage of personal and moral autonomy, a marriage necessary for citizens in a liberal political order.

We might ask whether the free spirit is autonomous in this combined sense. A subject worthy of consideration here is Nietzsche's notion of a "sovereign individual," a human type of Nietzsche's that also touches on the issue of autonomy. Nietzsche introduces the sovereign individual in the second essay of the *Genealogy of Morals*, and it is best to quote him at length. After suggesting that the morality of custom and society are a means to cultivation of individuals with the right to make promises, Nietzsche writes:

> Then we discover that the ripest fruit is the *sovereign individual*, like only to himself, liberated again from morality of custom, autonomous and supramoral (for "autonomous" and "moral" are mutually exclusive), in short, the man who has his own, independent, protracted will and the *right to make promises*— and in him a proud consciousness, quivering in every muscle, of *what* has at length been achieved and become flesh in him, a consciousness of his own power and freedom, a sensation of mankind come to completion. This emancipated individual, with the actual *right* to make promises, this master of a *free* will, this sovereign man . . .[48]

The reader will note the striking similarity between Nietzsche's description of the sovereign individual and his descriptions of the free spirit. In addition, two remarkable claims are present in this passage: the first is that, according to Nietzsche, autonomy and morality are "mutually exclusive"; second, that only the sovereign individual who is master of a free will has the right to make promises.

It should be fairly clear that the sovereign individual/free spirit is autonomous in the sense of personal autonomy. Recall Waldron's definition: ". . . personal autonomy evokes the image of a person in charge of his life, not just following his desires but choosing which of his desires to follow." Certainly the free spirit is autonomous in this sense. Christopher Janaway proffers a description of the sovereign individual that evinces personal autonomy more transparently than does May's account:

> We might be able to conceive of something like the following as an approximation to Nietzsche's sovereign individual: someone who is conscious of the strength and consistency of his or her own character over time; who creatively affirms and embraces him- or herself as valuable, and who values his or her actions because of the degree to which they are in character; who welcomes the limitation and discipline of internal and external

nature as the true conditions of action and creation, but whose evaluations arise from a sense of who he or she is, rather than from conformity to some external or generic code of values.[49]

Again, we see Nietzsche's sovereign individual as someone in charge of his character and able to choose which desires to follow, where choosing is understood as a product of his drives, which he has organized into a hierarchy. In this sense, then, he is also in charge of his action and creation; that is, he possesses a free will. Moreover, the sovereign individual's evaluations arise from a sense of who he is, not from external—conventional or traditional—codes of values.

It is clear, then, that Nietzsche had an account of personal autonomy, and that his sovereign individual ought to be seen as autonomous in the personal sense. Nietzsche suggests, as well, that the free spirit possesses the same autonomy as the sovereign individual, evidenced by similar remarks he makes about autonomy and free will when discussing the free spirit.[50] The autonomy of the liberal self, however, is associated with both personal and moral autonomy. Only autonomy in this combined sense qualifies as the individual autonomy necessary for liberalism. Can the Nietzschean account of autonomy be reconciled with moral autonomy as well? We remember from Waldron's definition that moral autonomy is associated with the "relation between one person's pursuit of his own ends and others' pursuit of theirs." A person who is morally autonomous must be guided "not just by his own conception of happiness, but by a universalized concern for the ends of all rational persons."[51] On this definition, it would be hard to reconcile Nietzsche's conception of an autonomous individual with moral autonomy. Perhaps the anti-liberal Nietzsche stops short of arguing for moral autonomy. After all, moral autonomy is at odds with personal autonomy—"'autonomous' and 'moral' are mutually exclusive"—although Nietzsche himself did not employ this precise distinction between moral and personal. Part of the answer to this dilemma is that Nietzsche was concerned primarily with the distinction between strong wills and weak wills.[52] Indeed, his conception of "free will" seems more appropriately a conception of a strong will—with its capacity for self-command—rather than a free will in the traditional sense. Nietzsche focuses more on self-mastery than freedom of choice. Yet, after digging deeper into this idea of strong versus weak wills, we might discover a point of reconciliation.

Strong wills can rule over weak wills, perhaps ought to rule over weak wills, in Nietzsche's inegalitarian view:

This emancipated individual, with the actual *right* to make promises, this master of a *free* will, this sovereign man—how should he not be aware of his superiority over all those who lack the right to make promises and stand as their own guarantors, of how much trust, how much fear, how much reverence he arouses—he "*deserves*" all three—and of how this mastery over himself also necessarily gives him mastery over circumstances, over nature, and over all more short-willed and unreliable creatures?[53]

On Nietzsche's account, only some individuals—the sovereign individuals—are capable of personal autonomy.[54] Those capable of autonomy should not be constrained by those too weak to achieve it. Yet this is something that moral autonomy seems to require. What results is a large gap between those few who possess a true character and those who don't. Gemes remarks, "The sovereign individual, who has a unified, independent, protracted will counts as having a genuine character, being a person. Modern man, who is at the mercy of a menagerie of competing forces, internal and external, has no such character."[55] Thus, the modern liberal may not meet the standards of Nietzsche's sovereign individual. Nietzsche's account seems to reject the view that the majority of liberal individuals can be autonomous, and he appears unconcerned with this problem, which is unsurprising given his anti-liberal leanings.

It may be that Nietzsche's account of the sovereign individual is simply incompatible with liberal autonomy. And it is certainly a stretch to hold up the sovereign individual as a model of liberal autonomy. But it is also not so clear that personal and moral autonomy can be as easily decoupled as they appear to be in the sovereign individual. We should recall that in Nietzsche's description, he claims that only a sovereign individual has "the right to make promises."[56] This aspect of the sovereign individual intimates a concern with moral autonomy, as it is defined by modern liberals, to some degree. The ability to make and keep promises certainly has a moral dimension, thus it blurs the line between personal and moral autonomy. Moreover, the ability to promise is also essential to the idea of liberal government, authorized and legitimized by individual consent.

Making a promise involves at least two people: the person making the promise and the person receiving it. There are a few ways we may evaluate the action of promise-making, but all contain a moral component. For the sovereign individual to make and keep a promise, she must either harbor a concern for the particular person or group to whom she is making the promise or she must harbor a concern "for the ends of all rational persons," insofar as trust in relations is necessary for a rational, well-functioning society. One might object, however, by claiming that Nietzsche doesn't seem to be thinking about the function of promises in society, or of concern with other persons, when he is describing the sovereign individual. He seems much more focused on demonstrating that the sovereign individual, uniquely, has "the right to make promises." Thus, the lesson is not the importance of promise-making but rather the demonstration of strength on the part of the sovereign individual. She alone has the strength and self-command to make promises.

But this objection cannot overcome the fact that promise-making always contains a concern for others, that is, a moral concern. The sovereign individual, in order to be autonomous, must be recognized by others as autonomous. He wants to be seen as one with the right to make promises; his self-mastery should be recognized by others: "The 'free' man, the possessor of a protracted and unbreakable will, also possesses his *measure of value*; looking out upon others from himself, he honors or he despises; and just as he is bound to honor his peers, the strong and reliable (those with the *right* to make promises) . . ."[57] Indeed, the sovereign individual seeks out his peers and measures himself against them. He considers himself in relation to others, both his peers and his inferiors, which we might qualify as a moral concern. He wants others to understand that he has mastery over himself and his drives.

The moral concern present in Nietzsche's sovereign individual does not precisely match the concern for "the ends of all rational persons" required by Waldron's definition of moral autonomy. The free spirit or sovereign individual, therefore, is not entirely autonomous in the combined sense of autonomy that we marked out earlier. He is surely personally autonomous, but his moral autonomy may not extend as far as the liberal definition. Nevertheless, the focus on promise-making is an important one for individual autonomy and its relationship to liberalism. Its importance surrounds the idea of being responsible, or for taking ownership, of one's actions, and it is tied to the idea of self-authorization necessary for liberal consent. It is essential to the idea of a social contract, a theme that will be discussed in the next section.

To conclude, the free spirit is autonomous, albeit in a limited sense. I would also suggest again that we see a *practicable* sense of autonomy being offered by the free spirit. It is an autonomy that is developmental rather than established, something to work towards rather than something given. It points in the direction of self-governance, or to the capacity to govern ourselves to the extent that we can become aware of our drives and the struggles among them. I call it practicable because it is the practice of achieving self-development and self-mastery (which is fleeting and must be earned over and over again) that characterizes individual autonomy. In contrast to a sense of autonomy that regards the individual as metaphysically free, unburdened by physical reality or unconscious impulses and thereby free to make a fully unconstrained choice (we may think of Kant), the sense of autonomy described here is one that individuals must practice, moment after moment, day after day. It is autonomy that must be continually earned. The capacity for self-governance that comes with it is important for our understanding of liberalism, it provides the foundation for a government based in consent. Individual autonomy bolsters the case for a social contract, and spiritual freedom provides a new way to think about the social contract. We turn to this theme now.

An Inverted Social Contract

To review, liberalism requires the idea of an autonomous individual. We see this in early liberals like Locke and later liberals like Rawls. We also observe a common or conventional understanding of liberalism being focused on the individual. For instance, the *Wikipedia* entry on Liberalism begins, "Liberalism (from the Latin *liberalis*, "of freedom; worthy of a free man, gentlemanlike, courteous, generous") is the belief in the importance of individual freedom."[58] The *Stanford Encyclopedia of Philosophy* has this to say: "Liberalism is, of course, usually associated with individualist analyses of society. 'Human beings in society,' Mill claimed, 'have no properties but those which are derived from, and which may be resolved into, the laws of the nature of individual men.'"[59] In short, liberal freedom is individual freedom. Hence, any political philosophy that undermines the idea of individual autonomy cannot be liberal.

Liberal theorists, however, have not been able to simply refute the insight that individuals are ineluctably social beings. Critics have forcefully questioned the possibility of autonomy. I contend that the free spirit enters the debate and scores a point for liberal theory. The existence of the free spirit points to the existence of the autonomous individual. Thus, it further points to the possibility of a social contract, one that guarantees rights against government overreach and is consented to by individuals qua individuals, even if state of nature or Rawlsian "original position" theorizing are jettisoned. Debunking the idea of natural right (regardless of whether critics have truly done this) does not prove that the autonomous individual is a fiction, or that rights for individuals need not be claimed and protected. The free spirit is brought into the world as part of the social order—just as progressives claim—but, through her own efforts, emerges *out of society*. She is an individual that has liberated herself in crucial ways from the social state, from the "social organism." She *becomes*, to an extent sufficient to satisfy the criteria of autonomy, an individual. Thus, the assertion that a social state is the normal order, and that "the mass as an aggregate of isolated units is the fiction," may be true at the outset of life, but need not be at the end. We can base liberal freedom on the individual even if we doubt that humans are fundamentally isolated or that individuals "preexist" society.

The free spirit is a product of the social order, but liberates herself from that order as she matures. Naturally, any person born and raised in society, who has been socialized through a common language and common practices, is bound to share some of the thinking of that society. She is bound, as well, to grow up sharing the values of the society in which she was reared. The relationship of the individual to society is the same for all persons at the beginning of life; it is a relationship of dependence and strong identification with social norms. The free spirit, however, gradually liberates herself from society over time, gradually decreasing her dependence on, and identification with, society. As she seeks spiritual fullness, the free spirit breaks away from the common practices and values that were given to her. Again, we should recall that the free spirit may retain attachments to people and things of her choosing, but strong attachments to society, and membership in the political community, will not be the source of her spiritual fulfillment.

The sequence of the social contract could, then, be inverted. Rather than forming relations between isolated individuals and constituting them into political society, the social contract might be viewed as an agreement amongst individuals already in society—but liberated from the social order and therefore capable of autonomous consent—that some individual rights, guaranteed against the political order, should be put in place. The free spirit represents an autonomous individual, albeit one who *emerges out* of the social order. If we take the free spirit seriously, liberalism doesn't require an imaginary "veil of ignorance," or a proof of "natural man," to justify individual political rights. By acknowledging the possibility of a free spirit, we also acknowledge the possibility of treating the individual as the foundational unit of political theory. In other words, the bedrock of liberal political theory—the autonomous individual—remains possible without justification through a presocial state of nature or an original position.

The critics may likely reply, however, that liberal theory treats *all* individuals as autonomous, not only those who may be considered free spirits. Merely introducing the free spirit as an example of an autonomous individual is not enough to "save" the origin story of liberal political order. Despite the extent to which the criticism is legitimate—insofar as we think of model free spirits as uncommon, and spiritual freedom as an uncommon aspiration—it can be powerfully countered through two arguments. First, even if we imagine spiritual freedom to be an aim of the few, we might argue that demonstrating the autonomy of *any* individuals is enough for liberal theory. As discussed earlier, a Millian test of liberal democracy would question whether both political institutions and civil society within a given state are able to accommodate free spirits. If free spirits are autonomous individuals, a society that accommodates them is liberal and one that does not is illiberal. For Mill, at least, the existence of any autonomous individuals and an evaluation of the institutions and civil society they exist within is enough to determine how liberal a state is, as discussed in chapter 4. Furthermore, if we consider spiritual freedom to exist on a spectrum, with individuals embodying the characteristics of a free spirit in greater or lesser degrees, we possess a conception of spiritual freedom capacious enough to strongly support liberal theory and individual autonomy. If spiritual freedom is a choice-worthy goal for all individuals—as I believe it is—we have reason to adopt and appreciate the liberal values that facilitate its pursuit. Despite the fact that many, perhaps even most, individuals will not achieve the same depth of spiritual freedom as our model free spirits, protecting the space for such a quest remains an important concern of a liberal society.

Non-free spirits, those who view their selves as socially embedded, or those who have not yet achieved individual autonomy, are free in a liberal regime to think of themselves in these ways. Freedom of association allows for individuals to treat themselves, first and foremost, as members of a community or social group. Liberalism *does not require* that each individual think of herself as autonomous. It does not, therefore, threaten the freedom of others to think of themselves in terms of their roles in the state, and in their roles in their communities. But it *does require* that individuals be treated as individuals, and that those who wish to identify with some group do so within the confines of a political order that guarantees protection for those who do not seek group identification. A liberal political order can accommodate the spiritual goals of all; the ideal state of progressive reformers *cannot* accommodate autonomous individuals like the free spirit. Only a political order that allows individuals to remain autonomous—that curtails in fundamental ways the obligations that society can place on them—can be considered liberal.

A second argument to consider as we think about an inverted social contract is the following. Even if the inverted social contract does not justify liberal government, it at least supplements the existing "origin" stories that make such an attempt. It accomplishes this by reaffirming the original contract once one has become autonomous. We might pair the idea of "tacit consent" with the inverted social contract to strengthen the liberal case. The idea of "tacit consent," traced to Locke's second treatise and borrowed by later social contract theorists, establishes a basis of consent, albeit a consent that is less deliberate than consent that is shown explicitly.[60] It is unpractical, of course, to expect deliberate and explicit consent for all members of a territory before creating government, and early social contract theorists like Locke were well aware of this. John Bennett clearly explains how Locke uses the idea of tacit consent to alleviate this problem:

> Locke wants to say that everyone who has come on the territory of a given government has tacitly consented to obey its laws. How can he justify this? To answer this question we must understand what tacit consent is and when it can be given. "Tacit" means the same as "silent," and tacit consent is simply consent given without words. If I ask my class, "Who will agree to prepare a report on Locke's theory of tacit consent?" and someone raises his hand, he has thereby agreed to prepare the report (provided he understood what was said and that raising his hand was a conventional way of agreeing, in the circumstances). Consent may also be given without any action whatsoever on the part of the person agreeing; for instance, I might say to the class, "Does anyone object to altering the syllabus for the course by deleting topic 7?" and if no one responds in any way then everyone has agreed to the deletion (provided he understood and was able to make a response in the situation, that is, was not paralyzed). This is the sort of tacit consent Locke has in mind. It is not mysterious or unusual.[61]

We consent to things tacitly all the time, and by remaining in a particular territory, under its particular civil government, we grant our tacit consent to that government. If tacit consent provides a tool through which a beginning to liberal government may be achieved, it does so in a way that may not be ultimately satisfying, especially to critics of liberalism. We may want individuals to grant their consent more explicitly as well.

Tacit or silent consent may, however, be followed by explicit consent given by autonomous individuals later on, reaffirming the liberal social contract. To use an analogy from Catholicism, "tacit consent" is a sort of "Baptism" while the inverted social contract is a sort of "Confirmation." In the Catholic Church, and most other Christian denominations, the sacrament of Baptism performs the function of incorporating a child (usually an infant) into the church. In the standard case, the choice to perform the sacrament is made by the parents and the church, not by the individual child. Simply by being born into a Christian family, the child is made a member of the church. Much like the tacit consent that enters one into the social contract, an individual enters the church through baptism. The purpose of the sacrament of Confirmation, on the other hand, is for the church member, who was baptized as a child, to reaffirm or confirm their membership in the church as an adult. To receive the sacrament, they must be at an "age of discretion" according to Catholic doctrine, or an age appropriate for individual consent.[62] Thus, each individual "confirms" their membership in the church as an adult. Analogously, a liberal political order relies on tacit consent to "baptize" individuals into political society, but we can think of individuals "confirming" the liberal social contract after realizing their autonomy. In this sense, then, we might consider the inverted social contract as a supplement to the original social contract, buttressing the original contract and the notion of liberal freedom.

Regardless of what novel ways we may approach the social contract in light of our knowledge of spiritual freedom, the crucial takeaway is that the existence of autonomous individuals has not been refuted. Critics of liberalism continue to assert that no individual is or can be autonomous. Yet the picture of the free spirit provided here demonstrates the possibility of treating individuals as autonomous. It proves the assertion of the socially embedded self—without the potential for individual autonomy—wrong, at least for some individuals, and suggests that we ought to be satisfied with the fundamental liberal institutions of free speech, assembly, and association, partly because they prevent the imposition of oppressive constraints on free spirits. After all, the existence of communal or common values, collective deliberation, and social action is not threatened by liberal political order. Instead, individuals are protected from being coerced into participating in such things. The liberal does not deny the existence or even the importance these things, she merely denies the obligation to participate in them.[63] For the free spirit specifically, we can infer that she will likely opt out of such participation in order to secure her autonomy. She does this because, as we discuss in the next chapter, individual autonomy is not only possible, it is desirable as well.

Chapter 6

The Desirability of Autonomy
The Communitarian Critique

> I ended up deciding that . . . my individual salvation would only come from a collective salvation of some sort. My true sense of self would only come if I had some sense of community.
>
> —Barack Obama

> Loneliness is the poverty of self; solitude is the richness of self.
>
> —May Sarton

The history of politics and of political thought is not especially kind to outsiders. Undoubtedly, the free spirit is an outsider. In fact, the free spirit *desires* to be an outsider, believing that detachment from society is *necessary* for her spiritual pursuits. Yet throughout history we see both actions and arguments aimed at remedying the problem of outsiders: we observe reeducation efforts in fascist and communist regimes, philosophical arguments for ostracism of rare or too great individuals,[1] banishment[2] or exile,[3] or, in more recent times, claims that such person are "lost" or even "pathological." In addition, the idea that humans seek conformity rather than difference is well documented, from political philosophers like Tocqueville to contemporary psychological researchers. None of these actions or arguments should come as a great surprise to us, and together they evince the possibility that a free spirit is simply lost in the wilderness, too stubborn or incapable of finding her way back to human society. We can concede that humans are social beings to some degree, without conceding the stronger claim that each individual is but a part of the social whole. Thus, we require an argument about the desirability of spiritual freedom: can such a life of detachment truly lead to spiritual fullness?

This question brings us to a second narrative in political theory, a narrative that doubts the desirability of individual autonomy. In this chapter, we will question this desirability and address the concerns of communitarian critics of individual autonomy. Communitarians have repeatedly argued that the notion of individual autonomy obscures the socially embedded nature of identity and value. In light of this argument, "calls have been made to reconfigure the idea of autonomy in ways that take more direct account of the social nature of the self and the relational dynamics that define the value structure of most people."[4] Where questions of value and identity are concerned, according to communitarians, we cannot sensibly speak of an autonomous individual. If we try, we are guilty of advocating "hyper-individualism," of trying to assert the existence of individual identity and value creation where none is possible.[5] Values and attachments are essential to our understanding of spiritual fullness, so communitarians can also be said to imply that spiritual fullness and individual autonomy are incompatible. In different but overlapping ways, thinkers such as Charles Taylor, Michael Sandel, Alasdair MacIntyre, and Patrick Deneen identify a central problem in the liberal order: the spiritual emptiness of the liberal individual.

As we shall see, communitarians do not attack liberal democracy on the basis of political injustice, legislative or executive inefficacy, or the threat of diminishing economic prosperity. The concern is not for liberal order itself, but rather the individuals that live within it. The liberal individual is variously "lost," "disempowered," "atomized," "lacking meaning," or "lacking narrative unity." A return to community is required for individuals to recover their identities and a sense of meaning or purpose. These thinkers charge liberalism with the disintegration of the connections between ourselves and the things that might bring us spiritual fullness, things like religion, community, and traditional values. For Deneen, this is precisely liberalism's aim: "The loosening of social bonds in nearly every aspect of life—familial, neighborly, communal, religious, even national—reflects the advancing logic of liberalism and is the source of its deepest instability."[8] The idea seems to be that liberalism disconnects individuals from sources of meaning, sources that offer a place for our attachments and provide a sense of identity. Barack Obama put it quite simply when reflecting on his own life, stating that "I ended up deciding that . . . my individual salvation would only come from a collective salvation of some sort. My true sense of self would only come if I had some sense of community."[9] Indeed, the idea of collective salvation is not reserved for academics or intellectuals, but is rather a driving force at the deepest level of politics. This critique is one we must take seriously if we wish the free spirit to be a choice-worthy ideal.

Autonomous and Spiritually Empty

The communitarian challenge to liberalism focuses on the absence of attachments. Recall our definition of spiritual fullness, it requires some sort of attachment. Thus, prima facie, it appears that this challenge may have some merit. Communitarians, however, have very specific ideas of where this attachment should be located; meaningful attachments, they emphasize, come from engagement with the political community. We return to the question, Is it possible for the individual in liberal democratic societies to achieve spiritual fullness? Communitarians do not think so. They may not all proffer the same reasons for why the liberal individual is inevitably an unfinished or unfulfilled human project, but all of their theories suggest that the liberal political order must be modified, if not overturned, for spiritual fullness to be possible. That is, liberalism must either be somehow modified to reflect the importance of community to the constitution of individual identity and thereby to meaningful attachments, or it must be overturned and replaced by a political order that is organized around the importance of community.

The liberal tradition emphasizes certain foundational principles. Among these are individual liberty, guaranteed by individual rights, and the political virtue of toleration as the preferred ends of political order. Moreover, liberalism places the individual in a position prior to political community. The liberal self has a very limited scope of obligation to community. John Rawls follows Kant's argument that there are "natural duties" we owe other persons as persons. These duties obtain regardless of what political regime a person lives under. For the liberal self, only such natural duties are obligatory, that is, they are duties one has whether one has consented to them or not. One may, as a liberal citizen, incur other duties and obligations, but only on the condition that they are voluntary. All particular obligations to others—that is, those that are not universally applicable to all other humans—can only be founded in consent. Therefore, particular obligations to others in the same political community cannot be coerced or forced upon the liberal self; they must be freely chosen. This renders the liberal citizen largely independent of political society. As Rawls acknowledges, "There is, I believe, no political obligation, strictly speaking, for citizens generally."[10]

The autonomous, liberal citizen has little obligation to the political community, unless she decides to enter into some obligations willingly. Underlying this state-citizen relationship is the assumption that the state's proper role does not include the provision of spiritual guidance. In other words, guiding the pursuit of spiritual fullness for each citizen—through, for example, inculcation of communal values—is not deemed a proper state function. A liberal state will allow citizens to pursue spiritual fullness privately. Citizens are free to associate with others in order to achieve this goal if they so choose, but there is no compulsion to locate the source of spiritual fullness in the political community.

Communitarians view this fact of liberalism as resulting in the "atomization" of society. Taylor lumps all liberal theories into this category. Taylor uses the term "atomism" often to describe liberalism, as he does in his essay of the same name:

> The term "atomism" is used loosely to characterize the doctrines of social contract theory which arose in the seventeenth century and also successor doctrines which may not have made use of the notion of social contract but which inherited a vision of society as in some sense constituted by individuals for the fulfillment of ends which were primarily individual.[11]

Atomistic liberal theories place the ends of individuals above the ends of society and community. Deneen echoes Taylor's view, arguing that liberalism is not so much about rights as it is a transformation of human life and the world:

> Liberalism is thus not merely, as is often portrayed, a narrowly political project of constitutional government and juridical defense of rights. Rather, it seeks to transform all of human life and the world. Its two revolutions—its anthropological individualism and the voluntarist conception of choice, and its insistence on the human separation from and opposition

to nature—created its distinctive and new understanding of liberty as the most extensive possible expansion of the human sphere of autonomous activity.[12]

At its core, liberalism promises to liberate individuals from previous constraints of society and nature, thereby extending as much as possible the "human sphere of autonomous activity." As we shall see, communitarians believe that this relationship of individual to society at once misinterprets the basic values that we hold and is an obstacle for creating the meaningful attachments that can lead to spiritual fullness. Instead, the political community—or the state—is essential to citizens' pursuit of spiritual fullness.

Communitarians, and progressives as well, are unconcerned about treating individuals as autonomous units partly because they imagine a state that has a role to play in nearly every aspect of a human life. Their idea of the state is not merely "institutional" or "procedural," as they make clear with their definition of the state as a social organism. The notion of a social organism describes the "natural" origins of the state, but the functions of the state extend even further, to the spiritual life of the individual. Membership in the state makes spiritual fulfillment possible for the individual. Dewey invokes Plato as he discusses the spiritual role of the state:

> Nothing could be more aside from the mark than to say that the Platonic ideal subordinates and sacrifices the individual to the state. It does, indeed, hold that the individual can be what he ought to be, can become what, in idea, he is, only as a member of a *spiritual organism*, called by Plato the state, and, in losing his own individual will, acquiring that of this larger reality. But this is not loss of selfhood or personality, it is its realization. The individual is not sacrificed; he is brought to reality in the state.[13]

The state, then, is not only a social organism but a spiritual organism. It has a central role to play in the spiritual life of its citizens.

This spiritual role of the state is not confined to the Platonic republic and its aristocratic structure. It extends to the liberal democratic state as well. According to Dewey, "Democracy is a form of government only because it is a form of moral and spiritual association."[14] The progressive/communitarian ideal of the state recognizes no natural limit to the state, because, according to Theodore Woolsey, the state "is as truly natural as rights are."[15] It follows, then, that the power of the state "may reach as far as the nature and needs of man reach, including intellectual and aesthetic wants of the individual, and the religious and moral nature of its citizens."[16] In a state so empowered—and, as Woolsey asserts, a state made capable—to satisfy all of these human needs and longings, one would find it hard to convince others of the need for the individual to have protected freedoms *from* the state.[17]

What follows from this line of thinking is that the state and political community are justified in taking a guiding, perhaps even paternal, role in shaping the spiritual lives of citizens. Spiritual fulfillment requires attachment to some source of meaning, and membership in the political community can provide this. If political community is dissolved, or if the state is thought to be merely a set of institutions, rather than a social and spiritual organism, citizens' search for meaning becomes a much more difficult quest. According to Sandel, the tenets of liberal political order destroy this meaning, and liberal citizens thereby suffer from a lack of meaningful attachments. They become lost in a world without an anchor. In the past, membership in the state, in the political community, provided the anchor and the source of attachment, but the liberal political order destroyed this. To hear Sandel again, "With the loss of community came an acute sense of dislocation. In an impersonal world, men and women groped for bearings."[18] It is no surprise, then, that Sandel prescribes a return to strong political community as a cure for the ills that liberal democracy has wrought. But we must ask what, precisely, is the source of these ills? If liberalism succeeds in founding legitimate government, protecting basic rights, upholding contracts, and providing a form of procedural justice, what does it lack? Why does it leave men and women "groping for bearings"?

To answer these questions we need to delve more deeply into the idea of community. All of us live somewhere and with some others, with the exception of those very few who decide to take leave of any place where humans live together.[19] Simply being part of a grouping of humans may have certain pitfalls for free spirits. Community, however, is a technical philosophical concept, not simply association with others. Communitarians are often inclusive in their descriptions of community, identifying both micro and macro communities. Communities can be particular organized groups—religious congregations, ethnic groups, groups united by local history, and so on—and community can be used to describe civil society as a whole. Going back to Aristotle's *Politics*, civil society is described also as a "community," where there existed a common ethos and a shared set of norms around which citizens collectively sought the good life. Thus, communitarians mean to include many different types of community as they discuss the role of community, from local communities to American civil society.[20]

Communities come in various shapes and sizes, but regardless of a community's characteristics, membership plays a spiritual role. As I have already argued, free spirits can and do choose to associate with others, they can and do have friends. But the notion of membership in a community entails more than association or cooperation; it is also a source of identification and attachment. The idea of community overlaps, but cannot be wholly included in, the realm of politics, for a community is comprised of a grouping of persons that cannot be separated by partisan divisions or the outcome of an election. Indeed, one's political activities do not determine whether one is considered to be a member of the larger community. Community is linked, in its most basic sense, to geographical space, to a location where a group of people live. Moreover, a "community of place also has an affective component—it refers to the place one calls 'home,' often the place where one is born and bred."[21] Community is not, however, limited only to geographic space. Many religious and ethnic groups consider themselves part of communities that cross oceans, national boundaries, and disconnected space, but these widely dispersed groups are still considered communities. According to communitarians, there exist

> communities of memory, or groups of strangers who share a morally-significant history. . . . Besides tying us to the past, such communities turn us towards the future—members strive to realize the ideals and aspirations embedded in past experiences of those communities, seeing their efforts as being, in part, contributions to a common good. They provide a source of meaning and hope in people's lives.[22]

Community, then, is a broad concept that can be applied to groups from local organizations to transnational religious and ethnic groups, and that provides a sense of attachment, meaning, and hope.

The emphasis on memory, history, shared meaning, and hope distinguishes the sphere of community from the sphere of politics we examined earlier; it further distinguishes it from what we might call political cooperation. Philosopher Josiah Royce explains the difference between community and political cooperation:

> Men do not form a community, in our present restricted sense of that word, merely in so far as the men cooperate. They form a community . . . when they not only cooperate, but accompany this cooperation with that ideal extension of the lives of individuals whereby each cooperating member says: "This activity which we perform together, this work of ours, its past, its future, its sequence, its order, its sense—all these enter in to my life, and are the life of my own self writ large."[23]

Clearly, community membership is more involved and complex than political membership, and we begin to see how it might lead to spiritual fullness. Communities provide us with a narrative, a meaningful story to which we can attach. We therefore need community if we are to achieve spiritual fullness through meaningful attachment, and liberalism threatens our ability to do this.

Community, Narrative, and Meaning

The self that liberalism engenders is incomplete, lacking an identity and stripped of meaningful attachments to the world. Genuine individual identity is substantially constructed out of the social, historical, and political roles given to us. When we identify ourselves in these roles, the loyalties and responsibilities we have to them are infused with "moral force." Yet what if one simply chooses not to recognize the alleged "moral force" of these particular loyalties and obligations, or more radically still rejects the historical and political roles themselves?[24] Why will this detached individual be spiritually empty? It is because, according to Sandel, human beings require narrative, a story about who they are, why they are here, and how they should live. Liberalism threatens to enervate or potentially eliminate the natural human capacity for narrative by allowing individuals to reject their own traditions and historical roles. He remarks:

> There is a growing danger that, individually and collectively, we will find ourselves slipping into a fragmented, storyless condition. The loss of the capacity for narrative would amount

to the ultimate disempowering of the human subject, for without narrative there is no continuity between present and past, and therefore no responsibility, and therefore no possibility of acting together to govern ourselves. *Since human beings are storytelling beings*, we are bound to rebel against the drift to storylessness.²⁵

We must recover our meaningful narrative, according to Sandel, by once again recognizing and reaffirming the social, historical, and political roles given to us.

MacIntyre likewise emphasizes the importance of narrative for a full spiritual life. MacIntyre's theory of virtue ethics is his self-proclaimed attempt to put us on a path out of what he deems are the "new dark ages" of morality. Before discussing this attempt, some comments about MacIntyre's identification as a communitarian are necessary. MacIntyre is undoubtedly a critic of liberalism, but he rejects the label communitarian rather directly in the preface of *After Virtue*:

> Let me turn now to a very different criticism, that of those defenders of liberal and individualist modernity who frame their objections in terms of the liberalism versus communitarian debate, supposing me to be a communitarian, something I have never been. I see no value in community as such—many types of community are nastily oppressive—and the values of community, as understood by the American spokespersons of contemporary communitarianism, such as Amitai Etzioni, are compatible with and supportive of the values of the liberalism that I reject.²⁶

MacIntyre is clear that he does not regard community as an unalloyed good, and his desire to reinvigorate the virtues in modern society is focused not on community involvement but rather a true pursuit of the human good.

Nevertheless, I believe that MacIntyre might still be plausibly categorized as communitarian, at least in the sense of making community the place within which we discover the good. MacIntyre argues that liberal modernity is marked by a disappearance of the belief in a natural human good, that is, an objective good that we can reason about in order to reach its truth. It has been replaced with subjective morality with a focus on a person's "values," which cannot be argued about. The consequences of this disappearance are that it has become impossible to provide morality with a rational justification and that morality has ceased to have a coherent relation to human nature. He concludes that Nietzschean nihilism and an empty moral pluralism are the inevitable, and extremely undesirable, products of modern liberalism.[27] MacIntyre's prescription for this liberal malady is a return to Aristotelian virtue. His theory of virtue consists of three stages of temporal development: the first outlines how individuals acquire virtues for themselves; the second stage examines how virtues fit in a whole, unified life; the third shows how virtue "relates the life of the individual to that of his or her community."[28]

Concerning the role of the virtues in a whole human life, MacIntyre rhetorically implores, "Is it rationally justifiable to conceive of each human life as a unity, so that we may try to specify each such life as having its good and so that we may understand the virtues as having their function in enabling an individual to make of his or her life one kind of unity rather than another?"[29] In other words, MacIntyre is arguing that human virtues, while good in themselves, also must work together to form a whole virtuous life; they each have a function and collectively they provide a life with "narrative unity." When we see that lives have "narrative unity"—that life itself is a story with a beginning and end—we can evaluate the virtue of a whole life. Not only can we see the good of individual virtues, but the good of a whole life. MacIntyre claims that unity of an individual life is "the unity of a narrative embodied in a single life. . . . To ask 'What is the good for me?' is to ask how best I might live out that unity and bring it to completion."[30] Indeed, MacIntyre echoes Sandel's claim about the storytelling nature of man: "A central thesis then begins to emerge: man is in his actions and practice, as well as in his fictions, essentially a story-telling animal."[31] The second stage of moral development ceases when one's virtues are arranged in such a way that they may bring about the good, the narrative unity, of one's life.

The third stage begins when one realizes that "I am never able to seek for the good or exercise the virtues only *qua* individual. . . . It is not just that different individuals live in different social circumstances; it is also that we all approach our own circumstances as bearers of a particular social identity."[32] It is via this third stage that we might place MacIntyre alongside other communitarians. For MacIntyre, no individual is truly able to reach the good without direct involvement with others in the community. We cannot reason about the human good without this direct connection. As he argues in his work, *Dependent Rational Animals*, "Rational enquiry about my practical beliefs, relationships, and commitments is therefore not something that *I* undertake by attempting to separate myself from the whole set of my beliefs, relationships, and commitments and to form them from some external standpoint. It is something that *we* undertake from within *our* shared mode of practice by asking, when we have good reason to do so, what the strongest and soundest objections are to this or that particular belief or concept that we have up to this point taken for granted."[33] We can only rationally pursue the good in concert with others; there is no "external standpoint"—which we might liken to the detachment sought by the free spirit—from which we might rationally evaluate what is good for us. He continues, "It is not only for the achievement of our common good that we are dependent on the other members of our communities, but we depend too on some particular others to achieve most of our individual goods."[34]

It is impossible for us to achieve our individual good, and to achieve a life of narrative unity, without interaction with other members of the community and without their recognition: "For it is only on the basis of this recognition that we can ensure that our deliberations really are the deliberations of the community, rather than an adversarial exercise of dialectical skill by individuals with opposing views, in which the outcome of the argument may be to undermine someone's standing as a member of the community or even the whole notion of mutual recognition. Here too there is a limitation placed on rational criticism and enquiry."[35] To do this, communal standards provide the parameters—and delineate the limitations—of each individual's rational criticism and enquiry about the good. Our deliberations are oriented towards the good while we deliberate within these limits and while we seek to share our conception of the good with other community members. This is the path towards a regeneration of the virtues: "When recurrently the tradition of the virtues is regenerated, it is always in everyday life, it is always through the engagement by plain persons in a variety of practices, including those of making and sustaining families and households, schools, clinics, and local forms of political community."[36]

Ultimately, MacIntyre's aim is not explicitly the return of community and communal values, but the regeneration of the ethics of virtue. His critique of liberalism does not aim at its individualism per se, but the emptiness of the liberal moral universe. Nevertheless, the project requires the return of community, albeit community of a specific type. As he puts it in the preface of *After Virtue*:

> My own critique of liberalism derives from a judgment that the best type of human life, that in which the tradition of the virtues is most adequately embodied, is lived by those engaged in constructing and sustaining forms of community directed towards the shared achievement of those common goods without which the ultimate human good cannot be achieved. Liberal political societies are characteristically committed to denying any place for a determinate conception of the human good in their public discourse, let alone allowing that their common life should be grounded in such a conception. On the dominant liberal view, government is to be neutral as between rival conceptions of the human good, yet in fact what liberalism promotes is a kind of institutional order that is inimical to the construction and sustaining of the types of communal relationship required for the best kind of human life.[37]

However MacIntyre views his own opposition to liberalism, it is clear that a return to "communal relationships" is required for his moral project to succeed. It is also clear that he considers the individual, extricated and separated from the communities that allow for narrative unity and a pursuit of genuine human goods, to be morally deficient and spiritually empty.

Let us return to the idea of "narrative unity," which is the way in which individuals develop morally and cultivate the virtues necessary to achieve the good. The "narrative unity" or wholeness of one's life must include the story of one's social, historical, and political background. MacIntyre uses language nearly identical to Sandel to illustrate this fact: "I am someone's son or daughter, someone else's cousin or uncle; I am a citizen of this or that city, a member of this or that guild or profession; I belong to this clan, that tribe, this nation. Hence what is good for me has to be the good for one who inhabits these roles."[38] For MacIntyre as for Sandel, the self is empty, stripped of meaningful narrative, without the social, historical, and political content such roles provide. The idea of the autonomous individual, with its emphasis on voluntarism, wrongly locates these roles in the realm of choice, as open to acceptance or rejection, and therefore misses the essential nature of humans as storytelling beings.

There seem to be many reasons why we may be skeptical of these arguments, particularly of the idea that all human beings require a meaningful narrative for life. First of all, it is far from obvious that a life with less or no narrative unity—we can imagine a life filled rather with events and moments rather than identities and social roles—is ipso facto less meaningful or without meaning. Many people find the moments in which they transcend their everyday roles or identities—their narrative unity—to be the most meaningful or satisfying of all. Aesthetic perspective, or aesthetic receptivity, that we see championed by our free spirits calls precisely for this transcendence or detachment. Secondly, one may even question what the implications of the claim that all human beings require a meaningful narrative would be for a person with a physical disability that impairs their long-term memory, and inhibits memories of the narrative variety.[39] Is it impossible for this person's life to have meaning? Meaning may be found in isolated events just as much as in a "whole, unified" life. Why place so much emphasis on the latter? A second contentious point raised by MacIntyre is that the good is inextricably tied to the idea of narrative unity. Many humans are forced to live relatively horrible lives due to external constraints largely outside of their control. If an understanding of one's narrative unity is required to answer the question "What is the good for me?" it follows that humans whose narratives approach horror stories are somehow supposed to discover their own specific good by delving deeper into this narrative, an activity that in all probability is likely to cause more horror.

It may also be the case that "narrative unity" is more closely tied to memory and autonomy than the attachments we have to other human beings. Nietzsche was concerned with the idea of life having a coherent narrative (recall his famous proclamation "You shall become the person you are"[40]), but this concern was articulated in a way that emphasized individual autonomy rather than connection to an external human good. David Owen argues that the first essay of *On the Genealogy of Morals* implicitly points out "that to experience oneself as valuable (autonomous) requires that one experience one's self as unified." An autonomous individual's "response to the question 'who are you?' would consist in simply referring to his place in society or recounting the narrative of his life."[41] For Nietzsche, individuals are historical, and autonomous action requires having knowledge, or memory, of one's history. Yet this requires no further connection to the greater human community; it requires first and foremost a connection to one's past. In short, the phrase "You shall become the person you are" may be "read as proposing a narrative account of the self in which one is always already becoming what one is simply because the narrative which constitutes 'what one is' is always already ongoing."[42] A more thorough theoretical unpacking of this idea is out of place here, but recall our earlier discussion of Nietzsche's "sovereign individual," who embodies the autonomy created by a unified self. Here, it is sufficient to note that Nietzsche's concern for "narrative unity" is of a much weaker or procedural sort than that of MacIntyre (or Sandel), who brings a substantive account of human goods into the narrative picture.

Returning to our theme of outsiders, we might also imagine greater numbers of people who feel that finding the good *requires* a departure from the story of their lives and the social roles they inhabit. Put differently, people who find themselves in this position must *change* their story, replacing the familial, traditional, and communal roles they've been given with something better. Indeed, they may seek to leave the roles that MacIntyre describes above—that is, they may seek to change their narrative drastically in order to shed these roles—as they seek to find the good. In such a case, following a free spirit's quest for liberation from tradition, society, and history seems like a sensible decision. Naturally, such a quest bears no contradiction to the historical, narrative self that Nietzsche describes, yet such wholesale abandonment of previous social roles does conflict with the concept of narrative put forth by the likes of Sandel and MacIntyre.

Despite these criticisms of the idea of narrative unity, MacIntyre and Sandel are not alone in advocating its importance. Taylor may be better described as a theorist of modernity than a theorist of liberalism, but his version of modernity dovetails with the version of liberalism presented by MacIntyre and Sandel. He too asserts the importance and inescapability of understanding our lives in narrative form.[43] What the modern man must do, according to Taylor, is live within a framework that supplies meaning to his life. This is peculiar to the modern, secular age in which religious and philosophic moral structures built around ideas of good and evil are weakening and no longer have a hold on most people. Taylor claims that "the [ancient and medieval] existential predicament in which one fears condemnation is quite different from the [modern] one where one fears, above all, meaninglessness."[44] Thus a framework of meaning is necessary if we are to overcome our greatest fear, but also to ground one's identity: "To know who I am is a species of knowing where I stand. My identity is defined by the commitments and identifications which provide my frame or horizon."[45]

All frameworks of meaning must, according to Taylor, come from social, historical, and political commitments to which all individuals are inextricably attached. Taylor contrasts the "disengaged self" with the "strong evaluator." The former is the self of liberal modernity, an atomistic person who is "metaphysically independent of society."[46] This person seeks a framework of meaning to supply standards of living but has nowhere to go to find these standards. We must get such standards outside ourselves lest any evaluation of our lives become merely subjective preference. A "strong evaluator" recognizes this, utilizing a "vocabulary of worth" to undergird his standards of living. This "vocabulary of worth" comes from the "horizon of evaluations"—or frameworks—rooted in history, community, and society.[47] We may recall the very similar argument made by MacIntyre, that communal standards provide the material and the limits for our rational enquiries into the good. Taylor endeavors to show that, without the standards and evaluations that membership in a larger human community offers to the individual, he or she will be lost at sea, meandering through life without a framework of meaning. In other words, communal values are necessary for any meaningful attachment to life, and therefore for spiritual fullness.

Taylor does suggest, however, that it is possible for "some superman of disengaged objectification" to live without a framework.[48] But he quickly adds that such a person who lives outside of society, detached from society's evaluations and standards, is "pathological," has an "identity crisis," and is incapable of realizing her full human potential.[49] It should be readily apparent that the free spirit described here falls under this category. For Taylor, it appears our free spirit would be "pathological," exhibiting an ill-conceived notion of spiritual freedom in an obsessive and compulsive manner that diminishes his potential and worth. In addition, the free spirit would lack any meaningful sense of attachment or identity. Meaningful attachment can *only* be found if one seeks it in political society, community, and tradition.

The reservations about the spiritual health of the modern, liberal individual held by communitarians vary, yet all point to the same basic conclusion: the spiritual malaise of liberal modernity is due to the separation and detachment of the individual from community and the treatment of the individual as a sort of spiritual "atom." Individual autonomy undermines the pursuit of spiritual fullness, and therefore ought to be jettisoned.[50] Whether or not individual autonomy is possible, these arguments certainly endeavor to show that it is undesirable.

Autonomous and Spiritually Full

I think we have shown that the free spirit successfully rebuts the challenge that autonomy cannot be desirable. Free spirits do not seek spiritual fullness through community membership, or through the adoption of communal values. As we discussed earlier, a free spirit is reared in society and therefore ineluctably shares common values early on in life. And she may continue to hold some of these values later in life, provided she has independently arrived at the recognition of their merit. Nevertheless, communal values are for the free spirit something to be suspicious of and, often, to avoid. A free spirit's skeptical attitude leads her to detach from community in search of spiritual freedom and, ultimately, the spiritually fulfilling qualities of an aesthetic perspective. In our definition of community there was a mention of its "affective component," the importance of affective attachment one has to the community, to the place one calls "home." We know from our discussion of aesthetic perspective, and from our interpretation of Nietzsche's famous passage about treating life and existence as an aesthetic phenomenon, that treating life aesthetically can produce in free spirits an affective attachment to one's own existence, attachment that may help one achieve spiritual fullness.

The crucial difference is this: while the communitarian highlights affective attachment to community, the free spirit affective attachment to life and existence. Both indicate the need to have positive feelings for and an attachment to something, but the scope of that something is very different. In both there is a search for some meaning in life or, in the language I am using here, a pursuit of spiritual fullness.

Indeed, much of the communitarian argument for greater communal attachment is predicated on its affective component, the idea that the individual feels somehow empty or incomplete when detached from community. Moreover, communitarians deny the possibility of spiritual fullness *without* community. We can see, however, that free spirits may seek the same thing—spiritual fullness—outside of community, they create an affective attachment to existence, engendering love of life and the world, through an aesthetic perspective. We have identified, then, a mutual goal of spiritual fullness, albeit a goal arrived at by very different methods. For communitarians, community is the place of spiritual fullness, the place of affective attachment to others and the place to find life's meaning. For free spirits, the community that communitarians advocate is an obstacle to spiritual fullness.

Let us briefly return to the question of why community is an obstacle to achieving spiritual freedom. Freedom of spirit is a necessary condition of aesthetic perspective, and aesthetic perspective is essential for a free spirit's spiritual fullness. Hence, if freedom of spirit is threatened by community, so is spiritual fullness. The reason that adoption of communal sources of meaning is impossible for the free spirit can be easily gleaned from our earlier discussion. Amy Mullin aptly summarizes the logic when she states that "free spirits are not characterized by values that they have in common, but are instead identified by their ability to shake loose of contemporary value judgments and to interpret differently."[51] Indeed, a free spirit is only free if he has liberated himself from the meaning provided by community. If eventual adoption of any communal meaning did occur, it would only occur after the initial process of liberation was followed by a process of reasoning, a process that led to the free spirit concluding that such meaning is worth esteeming.[52]

What does the free spirit value so highly that community seems less valuable by comparison? While it may be overly simplistic to attribute the free spirit's way of life to the pursuit of one value, we can surmise that the characteristics of the free spirit—such as solitude, skepticism, autonomy, and detachment—all follow in some way from a very strong evaluation of self-knowledge and of knowledge gained by oneself, through experience and experimentation. Mullin claims that

> free spirits take it upon themselves to decide what and whether and how to assimilate the new to the old. They refuse to be dictated to by tradition, authority, or the power of habit, and are resolutely experimental. The free spirit is immoral because he is determined to depend upon himself in all things, and not upon a tradition.[53]

The experimental free spirit is determined to see things anew, to seek out new perspectives. In most cases, tradition and community are incompatible with newness, and with the curious drive to experiment. The determination to rely only on oneself while pursuing knowledge is not merely idle curiosity. Rather, disregard of communal meaning is necessary for the free spirit to avoid oppression; such communal values are oppressive in themselves, insofar as they inhibit an individual's pursuit of spiritual freedom.

We might use Nietzsche as an example. He found oppressive communal values in the Christian morality of his time, which enervated the wills of great individuals and were an illness to healthy souls. In fact, he found himself infected with the values of this age: "I am, no less than Wagner, a child of this time; that is, a decadent."[54] Yet Nietzsche found a way, he claims in *Ecce Homo*, to throw off the values of his time and the illness they brought with them. In "Why I am so wise," he explains—

while describing himself—that the free spirit "instinctively . . . collects from everything he sees, hears, lives through, *his* sum: he is a principle of selection, he discards much. He is always in his own company, whether he associates with books, human beings, or landscapes."[55] By rejecting the values of his time and choosing solitude Nietzsche nursed himself back to health. But, he insists, to do this, the nature of the free spirit was required: a cheerful temperament, to be healthy at bottom. "I took myself in hand, I made myself healthy again: the condition for this—every physiologist would admit it—is *that one be healthy at bottom*."[56]

We can see deeper into this transformation of Nietzsche's with the help of his early notebooks, in which he often kept autobiographical remarks about his development. Daniel Blue uncovers a description of this, of Nietzsche's willful rejection of Christianity and his foreordained calling of becoming a Lutheran minister. This description encapsulates much of the criteria of spiritual freedom we have discussed: the desire to shed communal values; the willingness to leave traditional or conventional roles and worldviews behind, both in theory and practice; the importance of temperament in determining how individuals react to the revaluation of values. During his last couple of years at his Gymnasium (Schulpforte), before enrolling at the University of Bonn, Nietzsche began to consciously leave the Christian faith and even to diagnose the problems that arose from this change. Here is what Blue has to say:

> As he had recognized at Schulpforte, the Christian religion was subtly entwined not only with his vision of the world but with his emotions and the ideals that served as his guides. That childhood resource had now been withdrawn, and he had not yet found a worldview to replace it. The obvious alternative lay in the very ideals that led him to reject religion in the first place, and it might help to define what these were. Nietzsche never argued at this time that Christianity could be proved false—that he had, as it were, some infallible criterion by which to discredit it. His claims always turned on culture and the interpretive structures it imposed. Had he been raised differently, he would have believed differently. That in a nutshell was the insight he had stressed in "Fate and history," and he would foreground it again in a letter he would shortly write to his sister. In both documents, however, he introduced a second factor, one based on character. Knowing that one's

attitudes toward Christianity are a reflection of upbringing, one could accept it anyway, since after all there existed no positive reason to regard it as false; or one could reject it, since there is no positive reason to regard it as true. The choice a person made—and either was theoretically defensible once the effect of environment was recognized—might be logically capricious but was no gratuitous leap of faith. Rather a person's decision would reflect individual character and temperament. It was not that the believers or skeptics possessed superior grounds for their decisions, although Christians might have some implausible claims to defend. Religious belief could not be argued. Human beings made choices based on the kind of person that they were.[57]

For one with the character and temperament of a free spirit, doubting and possibly shedding any sort of communal values is a step towards spiritual health.

The Importance of Liberal Values

In the end, we can see that spiritual freedom aligns with liberal values. Attachment to community is not needed for spiritual fullness. Free-spirited experimentation and the drive to pursue knowledge independently are both good for their own sake and necessary for the free spirit's health. In a society where membership requires adoption of communal values—whether the political structure of that society is communist, fascist, communitarian, or progressive—there is a threat to the health of free spirits. If this is so, can a free spirit live in any type of society that has shared values? It is hard to imagine a "society" of people without some shared values. What is distinctive about liberal political order is that it supports a society within which shared values can be held without being oppressive. Liberal values like liberty, toleration, and privacy can be held collectively without oppressing individuality. Indeed, the health of free spirits may depend on liberal values. One may here object that the free spirit aims to liberate himself from communal values, and in the same breath I argue that shared values may be essential to a free spirit's health. We should not, however, conflate shared values with communal values. Communal values are the result of a public order of standards and evaluations, and are meant to be an alignment of an individual's values with the values of the community. Free spirits may share some values, like the ones mentioned above, if those values increase their ability to liberate themselves from community. Liberty, toleration, and privacy all contribute to the individual's "safe distance" from society.

As a final foray into the healthy partnership of spiritual freedom and liberalism, it is worth returning to our representative free spirits themselves. We can find direct and explicit endorsements of liberal values throughout the works of our chosen free spirits (although such endorsements do not come from Nietzsche). We can, for example, listen to the praise of liberal values from the likes of Emerson, Lewis, and Goethe. Emerson clearly understood the importance of liberal values to individual freedom. Neal Dolan claims that Emerson's political philosophy was concerned with one crucial question: "How does a society go about enshrining, symbolizing, and transmitting counter-traditional liberal values without creating another potentially rigid and repressive tradition?"[58] Dolan argues that Emerson used his poetic gifts to inspire his fellow American citizens "with liberal values such as rational wonder at the cosmos, disciplined work in pursuit of property, a critical attitude toward tradition, suspicion of government, and respect for natural rights, especially the core right to liberty."[59] Moreover, Emerson was a strong advocate for the realm of the "private man," and I believe we can add toleration to his list of liberal values as well. Emerson realized that protection of individual spiritual freedom did not require the abolishment of all shared values, but rather that dynamic, liberal values must be the values that are shared. Like all free spirits, Emerson was a skeptical man, and this skepticism prevented him from ever having "a basis for any coherent set of religious, ethical, or political commitments."[60] In spite of this skepticism, however, Emerson was able to hold and promote liberal values.

Not surprisingly, Emerson avoided any mention of the republican or communitarian values in his political writings, despite their popularity during his time:

> Emerson pointedly refrained from tapping into the available classical-republican concept of democracy precisely because it implied the sacrifice of individuals to the needs of the community or the state. Instead, he richly endorsed the liberal concept of democracy because it contains a check on the potential excesses of democratic communitarianism.[61]

Communal values are directed at the flourishing of the community at the expense of the individual. The liberal values endorsed by Emerson, conversely, are directed at individual liberty and self-reliance. As George Kateb writes, "Emerson's guiding sense [was] that society is a means for the end of individuals, who are themselves ends. [Liberal] democracy is the set of political arrangements that provide the protections and encouragements to become individuals, rather than servants of society."[62] If society is a means for the end of individuals, our free spirits should find themselves in an environment conducive to their own spiritual pursuits. Liberal values are not designed to produce spiritual fullness, but they are designed to allow individuals to achieve spiritual fullness on their own. We may note, as well, that Emerson's identification of "rational wonder at the cosmos" has much in common with the free spirit's valuation of aesthetic perspective. Rational wonder at the cosmos may result in the affective attachment to existence that our free spirit gains through an aesthetic perspective. Again, the complementarity of liberal values and spiritual fullness is evident.

C. S. Lewis approaches liberalism differently than Emerson, but it finds a strong endorsement here as well. Dyer and Watson observe that "Lewis endorsed a version of John Locke's social contract theory to ground political legitimacy, and he adopted a version of John Stuart Mill's harm principle in his approach to questions about the legislation of morality. Although many of Lewis' best-known works contain withering critiques of modern political thought, Lewis never wrote a treatise on politics or offered a sustained vision of a well-functioning political order."[63] True, Lewis never proffered a direct political framework, but this was in keeping with his understanding of liberal values, which are to be desired not because they lead to the most "well-functioning political order," but because they do the most to curtail the potential rise of tyranny and leave space for spiritual freedom. Later on, Dyer and Watson conclude that, "although Lewis never systematically described his political philosophy, he did have a political system of choice, and his thinking, as we have noted, was heavily influenced by a strong belief in the fallen nature of humanity. Lewis was a partisan of classical liberal democracy . . . because it curtailed the likelihood of political tyranny."[64]

Goethe indirectly supported liberal values as well, prefiguring Mill's harm principle in his approach to politics. He relates his views to Eckermann accordingly: "The most sensible thing is always for everyone to carry on his own business, for which he was born and which he has learnt and that he does not hinder others from doing theirs."[65] They may arrive at liberal values from different paths, but all seem to converge around the idea that the adoption and protection of liberal values is the surest path to facilitating spiritual freedom. Free spirits have a shared interest in a society with liberal values, values aimed at protecting individual freedom. This makes good sense, of course, for they also recognize the desirability of autonomy.

Conclusion

Free Spirits or Free Riders?

Perhaps we should conclude by first anticipating a couple of likely and justifiable criticisms. First, won't there be "bad" free spirits? Isn't detaching from social norms dangerous, and won't it lead to antisocial or threatening behavior? Secondly, are not free spirits also free riders? Do they not benefit greatly from a political system to which they contribute very little? If there are not adequate responses to these criticisms, the exposition of spiritual freedom seems a futile exercise. But I think we can rebut both of these criticisms in a convincing manner.

The possibility of dangerous free spirits is not hard to imagine. Indeed, detaching from society could be considered a form of antisocial behavior, and we must be able to distinguish between a free spirit and a sociopath. For example, was Ted Kazinski—the Unabomber—a free spirit? Timothy McVeigh? Do terrorists, who find great fault with societal norms and seek to change them at whatever cost necessary, share the basic characteristics of the free spirit? It seems that many individuals who feel angry, unappreciated, or shunned by society also practice detachment, yet the ultimate consequences of that detachment can be very harmful for society. The problem of "bad" free spirits can be addressed in two ways, one normative and the other institutional. Normatively, I have suggested throughout the argument here that free spirits *choose* detachment in order to pursue spiritual fulfillment. They are "outsiders," not "outcasts." They are not *shunned* by society, but find themselves inclining towards spiritual goals that society cannot provide. Moreover, I have suggested that in seeking affective attachment free spirits are drawn to aesthetic perspective and a sense of wonder, both positive orientations that should not be dangerous, but rather beneficial to society. Put succinctly, the goal of spiritual fullness provides a positive orientation for an individual that mere detachment from society does not. Detachment is practiced *in order* to pursue spiritual fullness; detachment is not simply a negative reaction to society.

Furthermore, liberal institutions are equipped to deal with the possibility of "bad" free spirits. Nowhere in our discussion are free spirits given latitude to harm society; the argument has only been that free spirits should be allowed their spiritual quest. The free spirit can live well within the liberal political order, and liberal institutions can deal with free spirits who go rogue, so to speak. Theoretically, we should recall the liberal harm principle provided by John Stuart Mill: "The only purpose for which power can be rightfully exercised over any member of a civilized community, against his will, is to prevent harm to others."[1] Mill remarks that this is "one very simple principle, as entitled to govern absolutely the dealings of society with the individual in the way of compulsion and control."[2] Certainly, those free spirits who seek to damage society in serious ways ought to be dealt with in the same manner as all criminals. The power of the liberal state can be "rightfully exercised" over any member—free spirits included—who seeks to harm others.

The more difficult allegation to counter, however, is the charge that free spirits are really just free riders, parasites on the healthy body of society. Yet this criticism is softened when we consider that the free spirit's greatest demand is merely for spiritual autonomy. Clearly, the free spirit also demands certain political freedoms, but these are in no way extraordinary. And the free spirit is unlikely to refuse the minimal obligations of a liberal political order. Political obligations such as voting, paying taxes, and showing up for jury duty are well within the limits a free spirit places on political engagement. There is little reason to think that free spirits are likely to be more parasitical on the practical provisions of a political system than any other citizen is likely to be. The free spirit will shun political activism, occupying political roles, strong engagement in political and communal discourse, and the like, but she feels the same obligation to provide for her own material necessities as other citizens do. Indeed, her spiritual independence may depend in some measure on whether or not she can provide for her own material necessities, given the entangling of one's will to another when the other is depended upon for basic material needs. Yet any type of political obligation that substantially threatens spiritual freedom is cause for political disobedience. The free spirit's spiritual fullness requires political and communal detachment and an aesthetic perspective. If political overreach threatens this spiritual fullness, then the free spirit is justified, I believe, in opposing political authority. A liberal political order ensures that such opposition is highly unlikely, or at least much less likely than in illiberal regimes. In a basic sense, society owes the free spirit very little, and the free spirit owes society a minimum of obedience.

Perhaps more importantly, there is a positive role that free spirits play in society, that of a bulwark against spiritual and political oppression. In extreme cases, such oppression may take the form of political propaganda, which free spirits will clearly resist, internally at the very least. In modern liberal democracies, the power of public opinion can also result in spiritual oppression. Free spirits are consistently resistant to public opinion and the putative authority it can possess, and this provides a check on would be political oppressors. Many political thinkers, such as Hume, Tocqueville, and Mill, have cautioned liberal societies about the dangers of public opinion. Modern liberal societies are often not, in practice, as tolerant of freedom of thought as they are in theory. Tocqueville warned of the democratic "tyranny of the majority"; Hume worried that a politics of opinion would be run by parties running on extreme, and especially abstract, speculative principles that were in reality merely prejudices. And we can return to Mill's view of public opinion: "Protection against the tyranny of the magistrate is not enough; there needs protection also against the tyranny of the prevailing opinion and feeling, against the tendency of society to impose . . . its own ideas and practices as rules of conduct on those who dissent from them."[3]

These warnings should not fall on deaf ears, as thoughtful liberal citizens are all too accustomed to these problems. The putative authority of public opinion in liberal societies—on virtually all topics of human concern, from politics to religion to natural science—poses a severe threat to the intellectual freedom these societies are, at least in theory, designed to protect. Resistance to public opinion is the responsibility and choice of individual citizens; it is not a function of government to liberate citizens from such authority, nor could it plausibly do so without contradicting its own role in protecting intellectual and spiritual freedom.

Some protection from public opinion seems necessary. As Mill claims, "There is a limit to the legitimate interference of collective opinion with individual independence; and to find that limit, and maintain it against encroachment, is as indispensable to a good condition of human affairs as protection against political despotism."[4] Yet how is one to find and measure the "legitimate interference of collective opinion with individual independence?" This seems a tall task, for it is extremely difficult to pinpoint the quantity of "interference" collective opinion has on an individual's independence. Indeed, given different individuals with different resistances to "interference," a given quantity of "interference" may abolish the independence of one individual while hardly affecting another. We do not, however, need such precision in our measurement of collective "interference" in order to judge political regimes on the basis of their protection of intellectual freedom and individual independence. Freedom of speech, press, and assembly are reliable measuring sticks for the openness of a political regime. They indicate how free a regime is in theory, but none of these can be used to measure the "interference of collective opinion with individual independence" described above. It is enough, however, to acknowledge that some interference exists and to look for the influence of public opinion in liberal regimes and to search for ways to mitigate it.

The free spirits have a role to play in this battle. Free spirits demonstrate how intellectual and spiritual freedom in theory—that is, freedom of thought protected through political rights—also becomes intellectual and spiritual freedom in practice. Skepticism is a powerful way to destabilize, and thereby mitigate the influence of, the authority of public opinion, because skeptical citizens, like our free spirits, tend to be wary of not just political party propaganda but dogmatic theories of politics, science, and religion in general. Indeed, the way free spirits live, in practice rather than theory, provides an alternative to the extremes of public opinion. British political philosopher John Gray distinguishes between liberalism as a practice and liberalism as dogma, and he argues that the practice of liberalism is the much more resilient of the two. Gray argues that the skeptic (which he calls the "political Pyrrhonist") is suited to the liberal project because "he will not engage in the vain project of constructing a liberal doctrine," but will instead "protect the historical inheritance of liberal practice from the excesses of an inordinate liberal ideology."[5]

The free-spirited skeptic will focus on liberal practices without seeking to establish a liberal doctrine, much like the Emersonian vision of liberal values discussed earlier, where the values chosen will be those that can be held without becoming dogmatic and oppressive. In both cases, the free spirit acts as a sort of role model for spiritual freedom. By remaining steadfastly resistant to traditional values, political party lines, and public opinion, free spirits exemplify the possibilities of spiritual independence in a liberal political order. It is one thing to acknowledge the existence of freedom of thought, with freedom of speech, press, and assembly as its guarantor, but it is quite another to truly exercise this freedom. As Søren Kierkegaard observed, "Aren't people absurd! They never use the freedoms they do have but demand those they don't have; they have freedom of thought, they demand freedom of speech."[6] Free spirits are a model for others in liberal societies to think critically about their freedoms and to practice them as well.

Through their solitude, skepticism, and resistance to social and political pressures, free spirits serve as a constant reminder of spiritual freedom for other citizens. Free spirits *demonstrate* the independence of mind necessary to combat ideology and popular opinion. They cleanse the air, so to speak, surrounding political and social discourse. They bring balance to conversations about how to live by providing a genuine alternative to the ethics of the ubiquitous political community. In today's modern democracies, aggregated political will, representative government on a huge scale, mass marketing, political polling, and mass media combine to make the individual increasingly insignificant. Correspondingly, varied individual viewpoints become increasingly scarce, diluting and enervating political and social discourse. Free spirits certainly cannot stem such a tide on their own, but they play a positive role by demonstrating spiritual independence in the midst of such a storm.

Summing Up

Our study of spiritual freedom has left us with three principal conclusions. First, spiritual freedom is a desirable category of liberal freedom that should be understood and protected. Free spirits seek detachment from politics in order to pursue more spiritual goals, and they should be allowed to do so without fear of persecution. Second, despite the apparently apolitical nature of free spirits, their political detachment is good for society in several ways, notably for loosening the knot of ideology and weakening fanaticism, and for demonstrating independence of mind. Third, and finally, spiritual freedom bolsters the case of liberalism in two ways: it shows that liberalism is superior to other forms of political order in its ability to accommodate outsiders, that is, to accommodate free spirits; and spiritual freedom provides us with a different way of thinking about, and a "proof" of, the individual autonomy and individual consent that is required by liberal democracy. Let us say a little more about each of these conclusions.

The conception of spiritual freedom described in this book adds to our understanding of freedom generally. It is not enough to speak only of political/civil and economic liberties. The yearning for freedom runs deeper than that, even if at times this yearning seems mysterious or primordial. The greatest difficulty in attempting to discuss spiritual freedom, which I experienced while writing about it, is to distill it into a concept. In an effort to overcome this difficulty, I focused on the free spirit as an embodiment of spiritual freedom. Through the free spirit we begin to conceptualize a sense of freedom that has heretofore been neglected in the literature on freedom, yet seems quite prevalent in human society. We already possess a sophisticated vocabulary for talking about other sorts of freedom. Political and civil liberties can be discussed through legal and constitutional rights; economic liberties through property rights, tax structure, and opportunity. I have endeavored to provide the means by which we may discuss spiritual freedom as well.

It is important to note that spiritual freedom is not to be regarded as a more central or more important sense of freedom that must be enhanced at the expense of, or in competition with, political and economic freedoms. Instead, we should consider spiritual freedom as a special category of liberal freedom, in the same way that political, economic, and religious freedom can be seen as categories of liberal freedom. Moreover, the concept of spiritual freedom developed here does not require new institutional forms for its protection. Our extant liberal institutions and constitutionally guaranteed rights (particularly to speech, expression, religious exercise, etc.) already provide such protection. Rather than encourage institutional change, this discussion of spiritual freedom aims to bolster the case for liberal political order, and to defend it from contemporary critics. I contend that liberals today should be further concerned with the growth of bureaucratic and technocratic rule. If we only talk about freedom in terms of institutions and civil liberties, we tend towards technocratic rule in these areas. Protecting freedom becomes of matter of getting these practical questions "right," and who better to solve the practical problems of freedom than bureaucratic and technocratic experts. An enriched understanding of our liberal freedom, one that contains a spiritual aspect, a human longing for freedom, may help to prevent or at least slow the descent into what Weber called the "rational" modern state.

The free spirit's implications for liberal political theory and for politics extend further yet. The free spirit offers new insights into the possibility of individual autonomy. I have shown that free-spirited individuals can be largely autonomous relative to the political, social, traditional, and historical roles into which they are born and raised. This argument may not, and does not intend, to debunk all challenges to individual autonomy. Nonetheless, the existence of the free spirit does debunk the claim that individuals are lost without attachment to community or to the "social organism," suffering from a crisis of identity and spiritual emptiness. The question of whether we can think of individuals as autonomous units—of whether we can embrace a view of individuals as self-governing agents, who are largely independent of their roles within social and political structures—is answered in the affirmative by the free spirit.

Throughout this work we have explored Nietzsche's free spirit, but I have also generated the criteria for a free spirit in a broader sense. I have suggested that free spirits are more numerous and heterogeneous than Nietzsche seemed to think. Nietzsche's various descriptions offer a guide to the free spirit, but it is necessary to parse out the salient characteristics to reach a conception of spiritual freedom. Spiritual freedom is a combination of intellectual freedom and a pursuit of spiritual fullness. It requires some degree of detachment from societal norms, political community, traditions, and customs. Detachment is a result of both a skeptical outlook—at least regarding the more ambitious, dogmatic claims placed on the individual by society—and the desire to find meaning, or affective attachment, elsewhere. I have suggested that free spirits may find affective attachment to existence through an aesthetic perspective, as opposed to a political, scientific, moral, or religious perspective. These criteria are not meant to be exhaustive, but they do provide a starting point for successful conversations about spiritual freedom.

The differences between the free spirit conceptualized in this way and Nietzsche's free spirit should again be iterated. While the two conceptions are largely compatible, Nietzsche believed free spirits to be part of an elite group separated from the mass of society, and he did not discuss the idea of spiritual fullness, at least not directly. Our broader conception of the free spirit, by contrast, allows for a much wider range of eligible individuals. Our conception has an interest in spiritual pursuits, so long as they do not come in the form of unthinking adherence to dogma, mystical intuitions, or religious doctrine; these attachments preclude the possibility of spiritual freedom. Nonetheless, varied pursuits of spiritual fullness in a pluralistic, liberal society are compatible with the broader conception of spiritual freedom.

Again, it would be a difficult empirical task to determine the prevalence, and influence, of free spirits in society. This is partly due to its necessarily loose definition. There are degrees of spiritual freedom found in individuals, and determining which individuals "are" or "are not" free spirits would be a difficult and likely fruitless endeavor. The free spirit as discussed in this work, through Nietzsche's rich descriptions and the examples of Goethe, Hesse, Emerson, Thoreau, and Lewis, provide a model for the free spirit. This model may be aspired to and emulated by others, but we should not think of spiritual freedom as an all or nothing affair, as a case of achieving the title or coming up short. The criteria for a free spirit provided here allow for many eligible individuals, and in many cases individuals may achieve the criteria only partially, and only intermittently.

The goal of quantifying the number of free spirits would likely prove elusive, at least partially due to the fact that they are unlikely to gather in social organizations in the manner of organized religious or political groups.[7] Yet there is little doubt that the growth and strength of the scientific perspective since the enlightenment, particularly in western Europe and North America, has increased the strength of skepticism.[8] Science, with its insistence on verification of claims, promotes skepticism. But science hasn't been able, for many people, to provide what is needed for spiritual fullness or to answer questions about meaning in life and attachment to existence. Exploring such a theme is outside of our purview here, but perhaps spiritual freedom is a concept that could help to show how a scientific worldview could deal with the problem of spiritual emptiness.

Returning to politics and political philosophy, we have not concluded that the production of free spirits should be the end of politics or the basis for the ideal regime. It is not, for example, a call to arms for the advancement of a Spinozan liberal republic, where independence of mind is held up as the ultimate goal for every citizen. The more humble aims of the argument are twofold: to buttress the liberal idea that the individual, treated as an autonomous unit, ought to be the foundation of political theorizing, and to confront the charge levied by progressives and communitarians that individuals are inevitably spiritually empty when detached from political community.

The primary goal should not be to turn all citizens into free spirits, but to allow for free spirits in a liberal society that fosters pluralism. A key component of liberal theory is that political freedom, which protects individual autonomy, must be withheld from no one. Majority choice in democracies does not override this freedom. As Maurizio Viroli remarks, a "law accepted voluntarily by members of the most democratic assembly on earth may very well be an arbitrary law that permits some part of the society to constrain the will of other parts, thus depriving them of their autonomy."[9] To apply this logic to the argument that I have been presenting, if one part of society (e.g., communitarians, progressives) seeks to constrain the will of another part (free spirits) through a majoritarian vote, the former part has still passed an arbitrary law that deprives the latter of their autonomy. Thus, the question of whether or not our liberal political order should protect free spirits does not depend on how ubiquitous free spirits are. I believe a loose definition of spiritual freedom may apply to many citizens in the West, but the strength of the argument does not rely on any sort of quantification. If there are merely a few free spirits, the requirements for their spiritual freedom still ought to be understood and provided for. Liberal political order does this already, and I think liberals should be committed to making sure it continues to do so.

Another goal of this book is to encourage liberal citizens to be more free spirited. On the one hand, the argument calls for tolerance of the free spirit as an exception. On the other, the argument ought to inspire reflection on spiritual freedom amongst liberal citizens. Powerful political parties, mass media, and mass marketing are all strong forces that, in some sense, seek the capture of the spirit. By selling or promoting certain ideologies, beliefs, and lifestyles, these forces ineluctably encroach upon the individual's spiritual freedom. I am not suggesting that all political messages or all marketing campaigns are empty and nefarious, but it seems uncontroversial to suggest that individuals would do well to treat them with skepticism and to avoid wholesale adoption. Similarly, the aforementioned forces together constitute the threat of majority tyranny, and if spiritual freedom were to increase among liberal citizens, the influence of these forces would decrease. One should not need to look further than the history of mass movements in the twentieth century to realize the importance of keeping these forces in check.

Taken together, there is a strong normative thrust to my conclusions. I seek to show a type of human being whose ethical choices—namely, to seek a strong sense of autonomy and to engage the world aesthetically—ought to be taken seriously by political philosophy. A philosophic concern for free spirits should urge us, I believe, towards an accompanying concern for maintaining the institutions of a liberal political order. My argument is meant to serve as a defense of liberalism, insofar as liberalism is understood as a political philosophy predicated on individual autonomy and a political philosophy that seeks to retain as much autonomy for liberal citizens as possible.

Whatever their real political impact, we should recognize that free spirits will not be fulfilled by direct involvement in politics or the seeking of political goals in the traditional sense. The free spirit does not need to be involved with overarching or determinate political goals; he does not seek to force change on the world he inhabits. If one can truly affirm all of existence, one need not search for a means to change it. "In the end one would live among men and with oneself as in nature, without praising, blaming, contending" but would instead be "gazing contentedly, as though at a spectacle, upon many things for which one formerly felt only fear."[10] We are warned that such rare individuals will confound and annoy the great majority of men. "Modern men usually grow extremely impatient when confronted by such natures, which *become* nothing without our being able to say that they *are* nothing."[11] But Nietzsche further reminds modern men that "we must therefore allow certain men their solitude and not be so stupid, as we so often are, as to pity them for it."[12] We allow certain men and women their solitude, granting them a chance to do what Nietzsche feared men of his time were especially unable to do: to say to themselves, with Goethe, that "the best is the profound stillness towards the world in which I live and grow, and win for myself what they cannot take from me with fire and sword."[13]

Notes

Introduction

1. Patrick J. Deneen, *Why Liberalism Failed* (New Haven, CT: Yale University Press, 2018); Edward Luce, *The Retreat of Western Liberalism* (Boston: Atlantic Monthly Press, 2017); Jason Brennan, *Against Democracy* (Princeton, NJ: Princeton University Press, 2016); John Gray, *Post-liberalism: Studies in Political Thought* (New York: Routledge, 2014).

2. Alexander Solzhenitsyn, "A World Split Apart—Commencement Address Delivered at Harvard University, June 8, 1978," OrthodoxyToday, http://www.orthodoxytoday.org/articles/SolzhenitsynHarvard.php.

3. Deneen repeatedly criticizes the materialism of liberalism throughout the book, but here is a pithy summary of his position: "In contrast to ancient theory—which understood liberty to be achieved only through virtuous self-government—modern theory defines liberty as the greatest possible pursuit of satisfaction of the appetites." Deneen, *Why Liberalism Failed*, 48.

4. Solzhenitsyn, "A World Split Apart."

5. I will alternate between masculine and feminine pronouns throughout the work. But whenever the free spirit is mentioned, I am referring to both male and female free spirits.

6. The ancient Greek Pyrrhonian type of skepticism is the best fit for the free spirit, a subject that will be developed further later on.

7. "Meaning," here and elsewhere in this work, is employed in the sense of meaning as significance, or importance. When an individual tries to find meaning in existence, he or she is trying to find the significance or importance that existence has for him or her. Thus, the use of the word "meaning" throughout should be contrasted with communicative meaning, that is, utterances used to communicate with another person. I avoid use of the word "meaning" in cases of communicative meaning, employing other appropriate words instead. For a helpful discussion of the different senses of the word "mean," see A. P. Martinich, "Four

Senses of 'Meaning' in the History of Ideas: Quentin Skinner's Theory of Historical Interpretation," *Journal of the Philosophy of History* 3, no. 3 (2009): 225–45.

8. I emphasize the word "demonstrate" here to draw attention to the fact that mere differences of opinion are not enough to resist the power of social forces. In periods of strong ideological constraints, independence of mind needs to be demonstrated, or shown, in a more robust way than when we witness citizens disagreeing over minor issues. A propensity to be different, to exist outside of the group, to detach oneself in a more complete way—as free spirits do—will be effective at checking social forces. In this way free spirits act as a model for others.

9. See, respectively, Charles Taylor, *The Malaise of Modernity* (Toronto: House of Anansi Press, 1991); Alasdair MacIntyre, *After Virtue: A Study in Moral Theory*, 2nd ed. (Notre Dame, IN: University of Notre Dame Press, 1984); Michael J. Sandel, *Democracy's Discontent: America in Search of a Public Philosophy* (Cambridge, MA: Belknap Press of Harvard University Press, 1996).

10. This is not to say, however, that such a state is permanent. Naturally life consists of periods of joy and suffering. Spiritual fullness is reached, we may say, when on the whole life is considered both desirable and full, that is, not lacking in any significant way.

11. Charles Taylor, *A Secular Age* (Cambridge, MA: Belknap Press of Harvard University Press, 2007), 5.

12. Ibid., 6.

13. Anthony Mottola, trans., *The Spiritual Exercises of St. Ignatius* (Garden City, NY: Image Books, 1964), 129.

14. Ibid., 130.

15. Ignatius, of course, is not a skeptic, and therefore doesn't meet one of the principal criteria of a free spirit. Nevertheless, his description of spiritual fullness is instructive for our purposes here. Moreover, as we will see later in our discussion of C. S. Lewis, there is a humility surrounding our use of reason, engendered by our "fallen nature," that does bring some theists closer to the free spirit model put forward here.

16. Jean-Jacques Rousseau, *The Reveries of the Solitary Walker*, trans. Charles E. Butterworth (Indianapolis: Hackett, 1992), 68–69.

17. Charles Larmore, *The Morals of Modernity* (New York: Cambridge University Press, 1996), 123.

18. Friedrich Nietzsche, *Daybreak*, trans. R. J. Hollingdale (Cambridge: Cambridge University Press, 1982), sec. 510. See also Nietzsche, *The Gay Science*, trans. Walter Kaufmann (New York: Random House, 1974), secs. 5, 214, 266, and 305.

19. We might think, for example, of the character Joseph Knecht in Hermann Hesse, *The Glass Bead Game (Magister Ludi)* (New York: Henry Holt, 1943). Knecht is an exceptionally virtuous man, achieving the highest position in his professional order, becoming a moral leader and authority. Despite his excellence in matters intellectual and moral, Knecht finds himself spiritually empty. At the

conclusion of the novel, Knecht leaves his "virtuous life," so to speak, in order to seek out spiritual fulfillment. Knecht's example will be discussed in Chapter 3.

20. John Dewey, "The Ethics of Democracy," in *The Early Works of John Dewey, 1882–1898*, ed. Jo Ann Boydston, vol. 1, *1882–1888* (Carbondale: Southern Illinois University Press, 1969), 231–32.

21. To avoid confusion I will use the term "liberalism" to denote liberal political philosophy and will use "liberal regime" or "liberal democracy" to refer to an actual liberal political order.

22. The notion of affective attachment, found in psychological literature, will be explained in greater detail later. For our purposes here, however, one should note that affective attachment is a concept used in social psychology to explain the emotional bonds we make with other entities, whether concrete (other humans or groups) or abstract (political ideas or religious beliefs).

Chapter 1

1. Christine Daigle, "The Ethical Ideal of the Free Spirit in *Human, All Too Human*," in *Nietzsche's Free Spirit Philosophy*, ed. Rebecca Bamford (New York: Rowman and Littlefield, 2015), 44.

2. Friedrich Nietzsche, *Human, All Too Human*, trans. R. J. Hollingdale (Cambridge: Cambridge University Press, 1986), sec. 225.

3. Daigle makes a similar observation: "The free spirit, as conceived in this book (HH), is a viable ethical ideal. It may provide us with a tamed version of Nietzsche, one that does not cohere easily with the later more radical Nietzsche, but as far as HH is concerned the free spirit is the phenomenological ethical ideal of authenticity and search for truth that we should all aim for." Daigle, "Ethical Ideal," 44.

4. Amy Mullin, "Nietzsche's Free Spirit," *Journal of the History of Philosophy* 38, no. 3 (2000): 404.

5. Rebecca Bamford, *Nietzsche's Free Spirit Philosophy* (New York: Rowman and Littlefield, 2015).

6. I thank Judd Owen for his suggestion of the descriptor "spiritual seekers."

7. Nietzsche, *Human, All Too Human*, secs. 31–33, respectively.

8. Ibid., sec. 34.

9. Ibid., sec. 32.

10. Ibid., sec. 33.

11. Ibid., sec. 34.

12. Nietzsche does not mean enduring or eternal truth when he employs the term "truth." He does not mean to suggest that there are no logical truths about the world—put differently, he takes Aristotle's principle of noncontradiction for granted—but rather that all transcendental, metaphysical, disembodied, disinterested, categorical, or eternal moral truths are in fact illusions.

13. Brian Leiter, "The Truth Is Terrible," *Journal of Nietzsche Studies* 49, no. 2 (2018): 151–73.

14. Ibid., 1.

15. Ibid., 2.

16. Ibid.

17. Friedrich Nietzsche, "Fate and History: Thoughts," trans. George Stack, in *The Nietzsche Reader*, ed. Keith Ansell Pearson and Duncan Large (Oxford: Blackwell, 2006), 14.

18. For a good summary of the Dionysian perspective—and its contrasting Apollonian perspective, see chapter 2 of Kathleen Marie Higgins, *Nietzsche's "Zarathustra"* (Philadelphia: Temple University Press, 1987).

19. Joshua Foa Dienstag, "Nietzsche's Dionysian Pessimism," *American Political Science Review* 95, no. 4 (2001): 933. I do not wish to delve too deeply into Dionysian pessimism here, but I should acknowledge that a deeper apprehension of Dionysian pessimism does shed light on the temperament of the free spirit. Dienstag's article is the best place to start exploring Nietzschean/Dionysian pessimism. Here is a helpful quote: "In Dionysian pessimism, Nietzsche creates an alternative that is as ruthlessly skeptical toward all ideas of progress as is Schopenhauer's pessimism but does not issue in despair (see Janaway 1998, 25). It looks toward the future, not with the expectation that better things are foreordained, but with a hope founded only on taking joy in the constant processes of transformation and destruction that mark out the human condition" (935). In other words, the experience of human life itself is sufficient to found hope for the future, absent any illusions about a better life in the future.

20. Gordon Bearn proffers a concise explanation for how this may occur: "For those with the courage to live without metaphysics, the discovery that what we care about has no rational foundation is, at the same time, the discovery that what we care about is precious, wonderful." Gordon C. F. Bearn, *Waking to Wonder: Wittgenstein's Existential Investigations* (Albany: State University of New York Press, 1997), 36.

21. Friedrich Nietzsche, *The Will to Power*, trans. Walter Kaufmann (New York: Random House, 1967), sec. 1052.

22. For a similar view, see the exposition of affirmation and the eternal recurrence in Michael Allen Gillespie, "'Slouching toward Bethlehem to Be Born': On the Nature and Meaning of Nietzsche's Superman," *Journal of Nietzsche Studies*, no. 30 (2005): 62.

23. Leiter, "Truth Is Terrible," 154. Examples of our illusory claims to knowledge abound in Nietzsche's works, but for a quick summary of his epistemological skepticism see *The Gay Science*, trans. Walter Kaufmann (New York: Random House, 1974), secs. 110–12, pp. 169–73. That our ordinary beliefs are illusory is only more strongly evidenced by the scientific advances since Nietzsche's time, a point that Leiter mentions as well. For example, our modern understanding of

physics—and the questions raised by quantum mechanics—only take us further away from the belief that the world of our senses is the world as it is in itself.

24. Nietzsche, *Gay Science*, sec. 111.
25. Leiter, "Truth Is Terrible," 154.
26. See, for example, Nietzsche, *Gay Science*, sec. 335. Here Nietzsche searches for the origination of the moral feeling that seeks validation of our actions through universal moral law. He asserts the possibility of judging morality from various perspectives, and criticizes the selfishness of assuming that our own moral judgments must be true and apply to all others: "For it is selfish to experience one's own judgment as a universal law." He continues in the next paragraph, saying "that our opinions about 'good' and 'noble' and great can never be *proved true* by our actions because every action is unknowable."
27. See, for example, Nietzsche, *Gay Science*, sec. 120; *Beyond Good and Evil: Prelude to a Philosophy of the Future*, trans. Walter Kaufmann (New York: Vintage, 1989), sec. 221.
28. Friedrich Nietzsche, *The Anti-Christ*, in *Twilight of the Idols, and The Anti-Christ*, trans. R. J. Hollingdale (New York: Penguin, 1968), sec. 54.
29. For just a few, see Nietzsche, *Gay Science*, sec. 57; *Anti-Christ*, secs. 54 and 55; *Human, All Too Human*, secs. 629 and 630; *Beyond Good and Evil*, secs. 230 and 231.
30. Nietzsche, *Gay Science*, sec. 347.
31. Ibid.
32. Nietzsche, *Anti-Christ*, sec. 32.
33. Nietzsche, *Human, All Too Human*, sec. 225.
34. Jessica N. Berry, *Nietzsche and the Ancient Skeptical Tradition* (New York: Oxford University Press, 2011), 10–11.
35. Nietzsche, *Beyond Good and Evil*, sec. 204.
36. Ibid., sec. 209. In the preceding section, 208, Nietzsche maligns skepticism. But he maligns skepticism as an intellectual "sickness" taking over Europe. It is clear here, as Berry also points out, that he is speaking of modern skepticism, which through its denial of the possibility of knowledge renders modern Europeans weak and sickly.
37. Berry, *Skeptical Tradition*, 16.
38. Sextus Empiricus, *Outlines of Scepticism*, trans. Julia Annas and Jonathan Barnes (Cambridge: Cambridge University Press, 2000), 1–4. Note that the Academics that Sextus identifies look like modern skeptics, asserting that nothing can be known. The difference between ancient skeptical practice and modern philosophical skepticism is recognized by Sextus in his time.
39. Berry, *Skeptical Tradition*, 34.
40. Later in her analysis, Berry recognizes this fact as well: "The Skeptic does not use doubt methodologically to establish any conclusion about the possibility of knowledge. He does not aim to define knowledge, determine its

scope, or elucidate its justification conditions. And he certainly does not aim to demonstrate that knowledge is impossible. Along with everything else, the genuine skeptic suspends judgment on this question as well." Ibid., 91.

41. Tad Brennan, *Ethics and Epistemology in Sextus Empiricus* (New York: Garland, 1999), 21.

42. Berry, *Skeptical Tradition*, 43.

43. Ibid.

44. Brennan, *Ethics and Epistemology*, 17.

45. I will allow myself a conjecture about Nietzsche's aims in a footnote, though attempting to prove it is too tall a task here. Nietzsche clearly thought that, at his point in history, dogmatic metaphysical claims were extremely powerful, to the point that they were internalized by the majority of Europeans. If this be the case, it is not surprising that he at times resorts to both bombastic rhetoric and his own dogmatic claims. Reaching individuals in societies so steeped in dogmatism requires both the use of dogmatism (for that is what such individuals are accustomed to) and the need to be "shocking." In my view, much of Nietzsche's more extreme writings can be understood as responding to these requirements.

46. Berry, *Skeptical Tradition*, 190.

47. To be fair, even Berry stops short of promising to prove Nietzsche is a Pyrrhonist. Instead, she promises to demonstrate that he was heavily influenced by the ancient skeptical tradition. See ibid., 24–25. In my view, she easily clears the bar for the latter, less ambitious hypothesis.

48. Ibid., 62.

49. Ibid., 130–31.

50. Nietzsche, *Beyond Good and Evil*, preface.

51. Ibid. Nietzsche here calls Plato's "invention of the pure spirit and the good as such" the most "dangerous" error, "a dogmatist's error"; hence identifying Plato and his theory of forms as dogmatic.

52. Sextus, *Outlines of Scepticism*, 119.

53. Ibid., 121.

54. Berry, *Skeptical Tradition*, 112.

55. Friedrich Nietzsche, *Twilight of the Idols*, in *Twilight of the Idols, and The Anti-Christ*, "Maxims" 26.

56. Berry, *Skeptical Tradition*, 132.

57. See Daigle, "Ethical Ideal," 33.

58. Nietzsche, *Human, All Too Human*, sec. 34.

59. John Christian Laursen, *The Politics of Skepticism in the Ancients, Montaigne, Hume, and Kant* (Leiden: E. J. Brill, 1992), 16. The idea of being "content to live with appearances" aligns closely with the notion of taking an "aesthetic perspective," which I explore in the next section.

60. Berry, *Skeptical Tradition*, 141.

61. David Keirsey, *Please Understand Me II: Temperament, Character, Intelligence* (Toronto: Prometheus Nemesis, 1998), 20.
62. Ibid., 21.
63. Nietzsche, *Human, All Too Human*, sec. 486. See also *Gay Science*, sec. 290. Near the end of this section comes the phrase, "For one thing is needful: that a human being should *attain* satisfaction with himself, whether it be by means of this or that poetry or art."
64. For these six methods, see Friedrich Nietzsche, *Daybreak*, trans. R. J. Hollingdale (Cambridge: Cambridge University Press, 1982), sec. 109.
65. Ibid., sec. 560. On Nietzsche's use of the gardening metaphor, see Paul Franco, *Nietzsche's Enlightenment: The Free-Spirit Trilogy of the Middle Period* (Chicago: University of Chicago Press, 2011), 81–83.
66. We may also find philosophers in many different walks of life, and we may suspect that Nietzsche would expect free spirits and philosophers in many places in society, not merely in philosophy departments and other places in academia. Evidence of this can be found in the section "On Scholars," in part 2 of, Friedrich Nietzsche, *Thus Spoke Zarathustra*, trans. Walter Kaufmann (New York: Viking Penguin, 1966), p. 124.

Chapter 2

1. What sort of political practice free spirits avoid will be explained in greater detail later. However, practice should be distinguished from theory. Free spirits, as we shall see, may engage in political philosophy while shunning engagement in practical politics.
2. Friedrich Nietzsche, *Beyond Good and Evil: Prelude to a Philosophy of the Future*, trans. Walter Kaufmann (New York: Vintage, 1989), sec. 29.
3. Ibid., sec. 26.
4. Ibid., sec. 44.
5. See, for example, Walter Kaufmann's portrait of Nietzsche in the introduction to Friedrich Nietzsche, *Thus Spoke Zarathustra*, trans. Walter Kaufmann (New York: Viking Penguin, 1966).
6. Leslie Paul Thiele, *Friedrich Nietzsche and the Politics of the Soul* (Princeton, NJ: Princeton University Press, 1990), 28–30.
7. Ibid., 38. Thiele's use of the term "law" is odd in this sentence insofar as a law must be promulgated in order to be law. But the meaning—that the individual seeks to rule himself at all costs, even taking leave of society—should be clear.
8. When Thiele discusses Nietzsche's individualism, he is not speaking specifically about the free spirit, as I am here. My disagreement with Thiele's argument may be at least partially attributed to this difference in object.

9. Julian Young, *Friedrich Nietzsche: A Philosophical Biography* (Cambridge: Cambridge University Press, 2010), 247–49.

10. All commandments taken from Friedrich Nietzsche, *Sämtliche Werke: Kritische Studienausgabe*, ed. Giorgio Colli and Mazzino Montinari (Berlin: Walter de Gruyter, 1986), 8:19 [77]. My translation from the German, with the help of John Graeber. It is hard to know precisely when Nietzsche wrote the ten commandments, but they can be found in his collected works dated 1875–1880. For reference, *Human, All Too Human* was published in 1878, with additions in 1879 and 1880.

11. It also bears noting that Nietzsche was financially supported by many friends during his writing years following his resignation from the University of Basel. Additionally, he maintained correspondence with several close friends throughout these years as an independent writer and philosopher.

12. Christine Daigle, "The Ethical Ideal of the Free Spirit in *Human, All Too Human*," in *Nietzsche's Free Spirit Philosophy*, ed. Rebecca Bamford (New York: Rowman and Littlefield, 2015), 34.

13. Christa Davis Acampora, "Being Unattached: Freedom and Nietzsche's Free Spirits," in Bamford, *Nietzsche's Free Spirit Philosophy*, 189.

14. "Moreover, because of the way in which they hold their attachments, in contrast with the fettered spirits who are addicted to their attachments, free spirits, at least as described here, appear to be able to *love* in ways that a more narrow partiality might not allow. They enjoy 'the greatest experience of human society' (D 205), avoid 'inertia of spirit' (HH 637), and are better prepared for a new *form* of love, namely, what Nietzsche associates with a love of life (GS, Preface to the Second Edition 3). If we recognize these considerations as related (being unstuck makes one available for, being open for, even more attachments of a different sort), then this provides opportunities to appreciate a distinctively affirmative dimension of Nietzsche's sense of independence and how it potentially positively, rather than negatively, impacts our relations with others." Acampora, "Being Unattached," 198.

15. Friedrich Nietzsche, *Human, All Too Human*, trans. R. J. Hollingdale (Cambridge: Cambridge University Press, 1986), sec. 481. This comment should certainly strike a chord with citizens accustomed to contemporary politics. The overload of political media, flooded through 24-hour-a-day news channels and social media, surely has the capacity to "devour a daily tribute from the capital in every citizen's head and heart," and many have noted the "diminution of the capacity" for concentration and application.

16. Friedrich Nietzsche, *The Anit-Christ*, in *Twilight of the Idols, and The Anti-Christ*, trans. R. J. Hollingdale (New York: Penguin, 1968), foreword, p. 126.

17. Nietzsche, *Human, All Too Human*, sec. 481.

18. I am indebted to Bill Glod for this last item on the list.

19. A couple of notable examples are Jason Brennan, *Against Democracy* (Princeton, NJ: Princeton University Press, 2016); and Christopher H. Achen and

Larry M. Bartels, *Democracy for Realists: Why Elections Do Not Produce Responsive Government* (Princeton, NJ: Princeton University Press, 2016).
   20. Brennan, *Against Democracy*, 3.
   21. Ibid., 6.
   22. Ibid., 231–232.
   23. Nietzsche, *Human, All Too Human*, sec. 438.
   24. We can speculate about what regimes would be out of consideration: totalitarian states such as Nazi Germany, Soviet Russia, modern day North Korea, and so on; modern theocracies and even bureaucratic "nanny" states are also candidates for regimes that cannot be reconciled with Nietzsche's call from freedom from politics, depending on the level of control the state possesses and uses.
   25. We may recall Plato's "city in speech," from the *Republic*, or Hegel's ideal state, in the *Philosophy of Right*, as examples of what Nietzsche is here challenging on the grounds of individual freedom.
   26. Nietzsche, *Human, All Too Human*, sec. 235.
   27. This claim should be qualified to an extent. Administrative positions that require constant concern with the current political climate would also seem incompatible with the free spirit's spiritual pursuits. And, as in the case of Goethe, administrative positions so time consuming that they compromise one's spiritual pursuits also seem off the table.
   28. See, for example, Hugo Halferty Drochon, "The Time Is Coming When We Will Relearn Politics," *Journal of Nietzsche Studies*, no. 39 (2010): 80.
   29. Herman W. Siemens, "Agonal Communities of Taste: Law and Community in Nietzsche's Philosophy of Transvaluation," *Journal of Nietzsche Studies*, no. 24 (2002): 83.
   30. For example, Hugo Halferty Drochon, *Nietzsche's Great Politics* (Princeton, NJ: Princeton University Press, 2016). For a recent, broad view of Nietzsche's political thought, see the compilation edited by Herman W. Siemens and Vasti Roodt, *Nietzsche, Power, and Politics: Rethinking Nietzsche's Legacy for Political Thought* (New York: Walter de Gruyter, 2008).
   31. Amy Mullin, "Nietzsche's Free Spirit," *Journal of the History of Philosophy* 38, no. 3 (2000): 404. Italics mine.
   32. Siemens, "Agonal Communities of Taste," 85. Many scholars have noted the special importance of genius to Nietzsche. See also Brian Leiter, "The Truth Is Terrible," *Journal of Nietzsche Studies* 49, no. 2 (2018): 151–73, and his discussion of the "spectacle of genius."
   33. Paul F. Glenn, "The Politics of Truth: Power in Nietzsche's Epistemology," *Political Research Quarterly* 57, no. 4 (2004): 582–83.
   34. The term "epistemologies" is not a common rendering, but we can make sense of Glenn's term as "claims to knowledge" and "worldviews." The struggle to which Glenn refers is the struggle over competing claims to knowledge and competing worldviews.
   35. Ibid., 582.

36. Anthony K. Jensen, "Anti-politicality and Agon in Nietzsche's Philology," in Siemens and Roodt, *Nietzsche, Power, and Politics*, 319.

37. Ibid., 326.

38. Readers should note that the discussion about the new philosopher here also applies to Nietzsche's infamous Übermensch. I choose to focus on the new philosopher, rather than the Übermensch, because the former is much more fully developed in Nietzsche's texts.

39. Jeremy Fortier, "Nietzsche's Political Engagements: On the Relationship between Philosophy and Politics in *The Wanderer and His Shadow*," *Review of Politics* 78, no. 2 (2016): 206.

40. Nietzsche, *Human, All Too Human*, sec. 638. The new philosopher is an intellectual type, like the free spirit, but the new philosopher is willing to take action in the battle over ideas and values.

41. Nietzsche, *Beyond Good and Evil*, sec. 26.

42. We should also note Nietzsche's celebration of Renaissance princes in *The Anti-Christ*. In that work, he does praise certain types of political rule. This does not, however, contradict the idea that the free spirit shuns politics. Rather, Nietzsche seems to be playing the role of new philosopher in *The Anti-Christ*. That work seems to have a culturally transformative purpose. Nietzsche's use of strong rhetoric and forceful expression demonstrate an intention to influence culture, rather than merely thinking through a problem.

43. Richard Schacht, "Nietzsche's Free Spirit," in Bamford, *Nietzsche's Free Spirit Philosophy*, 184.

44. Laurence Lampert, " 'Beyond Good and Evil': Nietzsche's 'Free Spirit' Mask," *International Studies in Philosophy* 16, no. 2 (1984): 47.

45. Laurence Lampert, *Nietzsche's Task: An Interpretation of "Beyond Good and Evil,"* (New Haven, CT: Yale University Press, 2001), 97.

46. Nietzsche, *Beyond Good and Evil*, sec. 44; Mullin, "Nietzsche's Free Spirit"; Peter Berkowitz, *Nietzsche: The Ethics of an Immoralist* (Cambridge, MA: Harvard University Press, 1995).

47. Paul Kirkland, "Nietzsche's Honest Masks: From Truth to Nobility 'Beyond Good and Evil,' " *Review of Politics* 66, no. 4 (2004): 579.

48. Paul Kirkland, *Nietzsche's Noble Aims: Affirming Life, Contesting Modernity* (Lanham, MD: Lexington Books, 2009), 19.

49. Daniel Blue, *The Making of Friedrich Nietzsche: The Quest for Identity, 1844–1869* (New York: Cambridge University Press, 2016), 87–88. For a later commitment to solitude, see Nietzsche, *Beyond Good and Evil*, sec. 44.

50. Numerous examples might be culled to prove this point. For example, "Nietzsche's Essence," from Lou Salomé, *Nietzsche*, trans. Siegfried Mandel (Redding Ridge, CT: Black Swan, 1988); or R. J. Hollingdale, "The Hero as Outsider," in *The Cambridge Companion to Nietzsche*, ed. Bernd Magnus and Kathleen M. Higgins (Cambridge: Cambridge University Press, 1996), 71–89.

51. Nietzsche, *Beyond Good and Evil*, sec. 44.

52. See Schacht, "Nietzsche's Free Spirit," 182–86.

53. Michael Allen Gillespie, "'Slouching toward Bethlehem to Be Born': On the Nature and Meaning of Nietzsche's Superman," *Journal of Nietzsche Studies*, no. 30 (2005): 52.

54. J. Harvey Lomax, *The Paradox of Philosophical Education: Nietzsche's New Nobility and the Eternal Recurrence in "Beyond Good and Evil"* (Lanham, MD: Lexington Books, 2003), 63–64.

55. "Geist? What is Geist to me? What is knowledge to me? I value nothing but impulses—and I could swear that we have this in common. Look through this phase, in which I have lived for several years—look beyond it! Do not deceive yourself about me—surely you *do not think that the "freethinker" is my ideal! I am* . . . Sorry, dearest Lou! F. N." Christopher Middleton, ed. and trans., *Selected Letters of Friedrich Nietzsche* (Chicago: Hackett, 1969), no. 99, p. 189. As mentioned above, this letter must be taken in the context of Nietzsche's loneliness and romantic pursuit of Salomé. It also should be noted that the translation here is "freethinker," which may be an allusion to the "freethinking" liberals that Nietzsche abhorred, mentioned earlier.

56. See Paul Franco, *Nietzsche's Enlightenment: The Free-Spirit Trilogy of the Middle Period* (Chicago: University of Chicago Press, 2011).

57. Nietzsche, *Human, All Too Human*, sec. 626. In this aphorism, Nietzsche presents Goethe as his example.

58. Ibid., sec. 638.

Chapter 3

1. It should be noted that some dispute this claim. Jacob Golomb distinguishes the free spirit par excellence from the free spirit simpliciter, and argues that a free spirit par excellence could not really exist. Jacob Golomb, "Can One Really Become a 'Free Spirit Par Excellence' or an Übermensch?," *Journal of Nietzsche Studies*, no. 32 (2006): 22–40. I cannot attempt to refute Golomb's entire argument here, but suffice it to say that there does not seem to be textual justification for the aforementioned distinction. It seems to me that the free spirit par excellence is simply that, the most excellent free spirit. The modifier *par excellence* is used precisely to signify that something is the best of its kind, not that it is of another kind. Furthermore, I think Nietzsche's discussions of Goethe as a model free spirit in both *Human, All Too Human* and *Twilight of the Idols* strongly suggest that Goethe is what Nietzsche has in mind when he discusses the free spirit par excellence.

2. Johann Peter Eckermann, *Eckermann's Conversations with Goethe*, trans. R. O. Moon (London: Morgan, Laird, 1850), 136–37.

3. See especially Friedrich Nietzsche, *Human, All Too Human*, trans. R. J. Hollingdale (Cambridge: Cambridge University Press, 1986), secs. 625 and 626.

4. Friedrich Nietzsche, *Twilight of the Idols*, in *Twilight of the Idols, and The Anti-Christ*, trans. R. J. Hollingdale (New York: Penguin, 1968), sec. 49.

5. Thomas B. Saine, "The World Goethe Lived In: Germany and Europe, 1750–1830," in *The Cambridge Companion to Goethe*, ed. Lesley Sharpe (Cambridge: Cambridge University Press, 2002), 6–22. "Goethe was attracted mainly by two things: a culturally active circle around the dowager duchess Anna Amalia, who had ruled as regent for some fifteen years and laid the basis for Weimar's rise to the status of a German Athens; and his genuine affection and friendship for the young duke, eight years his junior, whom he somewhat idealistically hoped to be able to mold into a model German ruler" (7).

6. W. Daniel Wilson, "Goethe and the Political World," in Sharpe, *Cambridge Companion to Goethe*, 210.

7. Ibid., 210.

8. Eckermann, *Conversations with Goethe*, 40.

9. Ibid., 143.

10. Ibid., 203.

11. "A widely diffused reputation, a high position in life are good things. But with all my reputation and position I have not brought things further than that I must keep silence at the opinion of others so as not to wound them. This would now in fact be a very bad sport, if I had not with it the advantage, that I learn what others think, but they not what I do." Ibid., 41.

12. 7. Lesley Sharpe, "Goethe and the Weimar Theatre," in *Cambridge Companion to Goethe*, 119.

13. Saine, "World Goethe Lived In," 6.

14. Wilson, "Political World," 208.

15. Goethe remarks, "Above all I only had pleasure in the representation of my inner world, before I knew the outer." Eckermann, *Conversations with Goethe*, 52. In addition, Barker Fairley describes Goethe's lack of an "outer world" in *A Study of Goethe* (London: Oxford University Press, 1950), 216–33. Fairley suggests that it is in the *Sorrows of Young Werther* that the overwhelming power of Goethe's inner world becomes apparent: "We have only to read the letter dated 18 August in which the outer world and even the universe seems to dissolve and disappear in an ocean of feeling to realize how lavishly, how dangerously, introspective a work it is. But any page of it will tell us as much. In its extreme form this sentiment rejects the outer world completely" (216–17).

16. Fairley, *Study of Goethe*, 234.

17. Ibid., 245.

18. Ibid., 246–47.

19. Ibid., 241.

20. Ibid., 259.

21. Ibid.

22. H. B. Nisbet, "Religion and Philosophy," in Sharpe, *Cambridge Companion to Goethe*, 224.

23. Eckermann, *Conversations with Goethe*, 31.

24. Nisbet, "Religion and Philosophy," 247.

25. The influence Nietzsche had on Hesse throughout the latter's life can be found throughout Ralph Freedman, *Hermann Hesse: Pilgrim of Crisis* (New York: Pantheon, 1978).

26. Robert Galbreath, "Herman Hesse and the Politics of Detachment," *Political Theory* 2, no. 1 (1974): 70.

27. Ibid., 66.

28. Freedman, *Herman Hesse*, 189.

29. Ibid., 166.

30. Ibid.

31. Galbreath, "Politics of Detachment," 66–67.

32. Ibid., 67.

33. Hermann Hesse, *The Glass Bead Game (Magister Ludi)* (New York: Henry Holt, 1969), 13.

34. Ibid., 15.

35. Ibid., xvii–xviii

36. Peter Roberts, "Life, Death and Transformation: Education and Incompleteness in Hermann Hesse's *The Glass Bead Game*," *Canadian Journal of Education* 31, no. 3 (2008): 674.

37. For example, "Aside from his great talent for music and for the Glass Bead Game, he was aware of still other forces within himself, a certain inner independence, a self-reliance which by no means barred him or hampered him from serving, but demanded of him that he serve only the highest master. And this strength, this independence, this self-reliance, was not just a trait in his character, it was not just inturned and effective only upon himself; it also affected the outside world." Hesse, *Glass Bead Game*, 135.

38. Ibid., 123.

39. Ibid., 274.

40. To fully disclose Knecht's reasons for leaving his post, it should be noted that Knecht criticized the order for excessive isolation, claiming that it had become narcissistically obsessed with its own goal and had lost sight of its obligations to society as a whole. Nevertheless, these criticisms were secondary to Knecht's primary motivation of spiritual independence, and did not ultimately drive his departure.

41. Ibid., 286–87.

42. Roberts, "Life, Death and Transformation," 673.

43. My purpose is not to examine Hesse's mysticism or his understanding of self-realization, but this summary from Galbreath gives us a sense of Hesse's

position: "'Detachment,' 'non-attachment,' 'desirelessness,' 'equanimity,' and other cognates also refer in mysticism to a process of purgation or self-discipline as a necessary prerequisite to the attainment of higher consciousness. Hesse's knowledge of mysticism and its central role in his later novels suggests the immediate source of his politics of detachment." Galbreath, "Politics of Detachment," 66.

44. Ibid., 71.

45. Keith Ansell-Pearson, "Beyond Selfishness: Epicurean Ethics in Nietzsche and Guyau," in *Nietzsche's Free Spirit Philosophy*, ed. Rebecca Bamford (New York: Rowman and Littlefield, 2015), 61.

46. Justin Buckley Dyer and Micah J. Watson, *C. S. Lewis on Politics and the Natural Law* (New York: Cambridge University Press, 2016), 14.

47. Ibid.

48. Ibid., 4–5.

49. Ibid., 6.

50. Ibid., 85.

51. C. S. Lewis, *That Hideous Strength: A Modern Fairy-Tale for Grown-Ups* (New York: Macmillan, 1979), 109.

52. Ibid., 130.

53. Dyer and Watson, *C. S. Lewis*, 11.

54. Francis Schaeffer, *Back to Freedom and Dignity*, in *The Complete Works of Francis A. Schaeffer* (Westchester, IL: Crossway, 1982), 1:382–83.

55. C. S. Lewis, *The Discarded Image: An Introduction to Medieval and Renaissance Literature* (Cambridge: Cambridge University Press, 1964).

56. Dyer and Watson, *C. S. Lewis*, 30.

57. C. S. Lewis, "Equality," in *Present Concerns* (San Diego: Harcourt Brace Jovanovich, 1986), 17.

58. Dyer and Watson, *C. S. Lewis*, 90.

59. Ibid., 88.

60. Ibid., 111.

61. George Stack, "Emerson and Nietzsche: Fate and Existence," *Nineteenth Century Prose* 19, no. 1 (1992): 1–15. See also chapter 6 of Daniel Blue, *The Making of Friedrich Nietzsche: The Quest for Identity, 1844–1869* (New York: Cambridge University Press, 2016).

62. Which is not to suggest that the ties between Emerson and Nietzsche are not interesting. For those interested, see the following: George Stack, *Nietzsche and Emerson: An Elective Affinity* (Athens: Ohio University Press, 1992); David Mikics, *The Romance of Individualism in Emerson and Nietzsche* (Athens: Ohio University Press, 2003).

63. Bryan-Paul Frost, "Religion, Nature, and Disobedience in the Thought of Ralph Waldo Emerson and Henry David Thoreau," in *History of American Political Thought*, ed. Bryan-Paul Frost and Jeffrey Sikkenga (Lanham, MD: Lexington Press, 2003), 355.

64. Ibid.

65. Mary Oliver, introduction to *The Essential Writings of Ralph Waldo Emerson*, by Ralph Waldo Emerson, ed. Brooks Atkinson (New York: Modern Library, 2000), xii.

66. I will not venture into a thorough description of idealism here, but this passage of Emerson's (from the essay "The Transcendentalist") is an adequate summary: "It is well known to most of my audience that the Idealism of the present day acquired the name of Transcendental from the use of that term by Immanuel Kant, of Konigsberg, who replied to the skeptical philosophy of Locke, which insisted that there was nothing in the intellect which was not previously in the experience of the senses, by showing that there was a very important class of ideas or imperative forms, which did not come by experience, but through which experience was acquired; that these were intuitions of the mind itself; and he denominated them Transcendental forms . . . whatever belongs to that class of intuitive thought is popularly called at the present day Transcendental." Emerson, *Essential Writings*, 86.

67. Ibid., 64.

68. Ibid., 135.

69. Ibid., 331.

70. Ralph Waldo Emerson, *Representative Men* (Boston: Phillips, Sampson, 1850), 170–71.

71. Ibid., 159.

72. Ibid., 156.

73. Emerson, *Essential Writings*, 260.

74. I think a strong case could be made that Emerson did not thoroughly understand the Pyrrhonist variety of skepticism, and therefore turns it into a straw man that can stand in for his attack on an easy or radical skepticism. Such an argument is outside our purview here, however, so I will merely suggest that Emerson's praise of the skeptical, experimental spirit aligns quite closely with Pyrrhonism.

75. Alex Zakaras, *Individuality and Mass Democracy: Mill, Emerson, and the Burdens of Citizenship* (New York: Oxford University Press, 2009), 104.

76. Ibid., 82.

77. Ibid., 110.

78. Emerson, *Essential Writings*, 87.

79. Ibid., 87–88.

80. Ibid., 89–90.

81. Ibid., 134.

82. Ibid.

83. Ibid., 90.

84. Ibid., 136.

85. Ibid., 145.

86. Ibid., 93.

87. Zakaras, *Individuality and Mass Democracy*, 69.

88. Ibid., 53.

89. Frost, "Religion, Nature, and Disobedience," 368.

90. Henry David Thoreau, *Walden and Other Writings*, ed. Brooks Atkinson (New York: Modern Library, 1950), 711.

91. Ibid., 725.

92. Ibid., 719.

93. Ibid., 726.

94. Some scholars would disagree that Thoreau holds society in contempt. For example, Brooks Atkinson claims that "Thoreau was no misanthrope. He required, as he said, 'a broad margin to my life,' so that his thoughts might grow freely. His perceptions were so acute, his understanding of men was so penetrating that he was unhappy in company that misjudged him. A person who was spiritually coarse wounded him grievously. But he was always civil, courteous and kind in his ordinary relationships around town; he had abundant affection for his family and his friends; he was generous with his talents; and in those last ten years of his life, when his private battle with life was won, he overflowed with good will toward good men." Atkinson, introduction to Thoreau, *Walden and Other Writings*. Here we see Thoreau's concern for spiritual freedom over society, but without total solitude. Speaking for myself, I think we also find a tinge of resentment, a bit of contempt for a society that didn't fully embrace him, in his writings. At least, I sense this in Thoreau in a way I do not in Emerson. Yet nothing in the larger argument here rests on the question of whether or not Thoreau was a misanthrope, hence I mention it only in a footnote.

95. Ibid., xx.

96. Ibid., 730–31.

97. Ibid., 650–51.

98. Ibid., 635.

99. Ibid., 659.

100. Ibid., 637.

101. Emerson, *Essential Writings*, 767–68.

102. Ibid., 784.

103. Ibid., 779.

104. George Kateb, "Self-reliance, Politics, and Society," in *A Political Companion to Ralph Waldo Emerson*, ed. Alan M. Levine and Daniel S. Malachuk (Lexington: University Press of Kentucky, 2011), 73.

105. Frost, "Religion, Nature, and Disobedience," 372.

106. Freedman, *Herman Hesse*, 369.

Chapter 4

1. John Stuart Mill, *On Liberty*, ed. Gertrude Himmelfarb (New York: Penguin, 1981), 59.

2. Alex Zakaras, *Individuality and Mass Democracy: Mill, Emerson, and the Burdens of Citizenship* (New York: Oxford University Press, 2009), 135.
3. Gertrude Himmelfarb, introduction to Mill, *On Liberty*, 8.
4. Ibid., 16.
5. Mill, *On Liberty*, 71.
6. Ibid., 125.
7. Ibid., 63.
8. Zakaras, *Individuality and Mass Democracy*, 134.
9. Mill, *On Liberty*, 73.
10. Ibid., 120.
11. Ibid., 94.
12. Alexis de Tocqueville, *Democracy in America*, ed. and trans. Harvey C. Mansfield and Delba Winthrop (Chicago: University of Chicago Press, 2000), 243.
13. Mill, *On Liberty*, 94.
14. Zakaras, *Individuality and Mass Democracy*, 132.
15. There are places where Tocqueville and Nietzsche do argue, on the contrary, that this is the case.
16. Mill, *On Liberty*, 95.
17. Zakaras identifies three intellectual virtues to which Mill thinks all democratic citizens should aspire. They are courage, self-reliance, and skepticism. Zakaras, *Individuality and Mass Democracy*, 159–60.
18. Mill, *On Liberty*, 124.
19. Ibid.
20. Ibid., 127.
21. Ibid., 124–25.
22. Zakaras, *Individuality and Mass Democracy*, 131.
23. Ibid., 129.
24. Ibid., 133.
25. Ibid., 133.
26. Bernard Reginster, "What Is a Free Spirit? Nietzsche on Fanaticism," *Archiv für Geschichte der Philosophie* 85, no. 1 (2003): 82.
27. Of course, fanaticism and conformity are often mutually reinforcing.
28. Mill, *On Liberty*, 132.
29. Tocqueville, *Democracy in America*, 244.
30. We continue to see evidence of an attack on free speech and thought in general today, with emphasis being placed on "trigger warnings" and "safe spaces" for those who may be offended by others' speech. In addition, social media and search engine preferences have led to more and more citizens living in veritable echo chambers, listening and responding only to views they already hold. The strength, and stubbornness, of spiritual freedom appears increasingly valuable.
31. Friedrich Nietzsche, *The Birth of Tragedy*, trans. Walter Kaufmann (Toronto: Random House, 1967), sec. 5.

32. The doctrine of the eternal recurrence. Friedrich Nietzsche, *Beyond Good and Evil: Prelude to a Philosophy of the Future*, trans. Walter Kaufmann (New York: Vintage, 1989), sec. 56.

33. I will also render "whole of existence" as "world." I will use the two interchangeably throughout.

34. Alexander Nehamas, *Nietzsche: Life as Literature* (Cambridge, MA: Harvard University Press, 1985), 3.

35. See Brian Leiter, "Nietzsche and Aestheticism," *Journal of the History of Philosophy* 30, no. 2 (1992): 275–90.

36. Aesthetic perspective allows for aesthetic justification for the world, as opposed to moral justification. Nietzsche, the self-declared "Immoralist," praises aesthetic valuation over moral valuation. See Phillipa Foot, "Nietzsche: The Revaluation of Values," in *Nietzsche: A Collection of Critical Essays*, ed. Robert Solomon (Garden City, NY: Doubleday, 1973), 156–68.

37. Nietzsche, *Birth of Tragedy*, sec. 5.

38. Ibid.

39. Ibid.

40. Friedrich Nietzsche, *The Gay Science*, trans. Walter Kaufmann (New York: Random House, 1974), sec. 347.

41. Nietzsche, *Birth of Tragedy*, sec. 3.

42. Daniel Blue, *The Making of Friedrich Nietzsche: The Quest for Identity, 1844–1869* (New York: Cambridge University Press, 2016). See especially chapters 1–4.

43. Daniel Came, "The Aesthetic Justification of Existence," in *A Companion to Nietzsche*, ed. Keith Ansell Pearson (Oxford: Blackwell, 2006), 60.

44. Ibid., 61.

45. I am indebted to Kathleen Higgins for the wording in this and the preceding sentence. It should be noted, as well, that an aesthetic perspective does not require the use of metaphor, as this particular example uses.

46. This is not to suggest that Nietzsche deems scientific perspective "bad" or even second best. Nietzsche also praises the activity of science throughout his works.

47. Friedrich Nietzsche, *Sämliche Werke: Kritische Studienausgabe*, ed. Giorgio Colli and Mazzino Montinari (Berlin: Walter de Gruyter, 1986), 13:500.

48. Nietzsche, *Gay Science*, sec. 107.

49. Paul Franco considers the role of art described in *Gay Science* 107 to be essential to a free spirit's independence from morality, and to the production of gay science: "Art is indispensable to achieving this standpoint, which, insofar as it floats above morality, can be understood as the quintessence of gay science." Paul Franco *Nietzsche's Enlightenment: The Free-Spirit Trilogy of the Middle Period* (Chicago: University of Chicago Press, 2011), 127. One can see the kinship between Franco's statement here and Nietzsche's early description of the

free spirit as "free, fearless hovering over men, customs, laws and the traditional evaluations of things." Art and aesthetic perspective dislocate us, they can sweep us away from the concerns of everyday life, including the concerns of morality and traditional evaluations.

50. From the afterword to Lolita. See Vladimir Nabokov, *Lolita*, 2nd ed. (New York: Vintage, 1997), 314–15.

51. Nietzsche, *Gay Science*, sec. 107.

52. Ibid., sec. 341.

53. See the "The Drunken Song" in Friedrich Nietzsche, *Thus Spoke Zarathustra*, trans. Walter Kaufmann (New York: Viking Penguin, 1966), sec. 8, p. 323. Here Zarathustra asks, "Have you ever said Yes to a single joy? O my friends, then you said Yes to *all* woe. All things are entangled, ensnared, enamored; if ever you wanted one thing twice, if ever you said, 'You please me, happiness! Abide, moment!' then you wanted *all* back."

54. See Michael Allen Gillespie, " 'Slouching toward Bethlehem to Be Born': On the Nature and Meaning of Nietzsche's Superman," *Journal of Nietzsche Studies*, no. 30 (2005): 61–64, for a striking exposition of what it takes to will the eternal recurrence.

55. Nietzsche, *Beyond Good and Evil*, sec. 56.

56. Gillespie, "Slouching," 62.

57. Nietzsche, *Birth of Tragedy*, sec. 15. And again in *Gay Science*, sec. 107.

58. Kathleen Marie Higgins, *Nietzsche's Zarathustra* (Philadelphia: Temple University Press, 1987), 175.

59. Ibid.

60. Ibid., 177.

61. For a fuller discussion of how one might interpret the eternal recurrence, see chapter 6 of Higgins, *Nietzsche's Zarathustra*, 159–201.

62. Leslie Paul Thiele, *Friedrich Nietzsche and the Politics of the Soul: A Study of Heroic Individualism* (Princeton, NJ: Princeton University Press, 1990), 137.

63. Quoted from Thoreau's *Walden*, "What I Live For," in Thiele, *Politics of the Soul*, 136.

64. Nietzsche, *Gay Science*, sec. 299.

65. Zakaras, *Individuality and Mass Democracy*, 66.

66. Ibid., 67. The Emerson quote that Zakaras cites is from *Emerson: Essays and Lectures*, ed. Joel Porte (New York: Library of America, 1983).

67. For my part, I agree with Nehamas, who claims that while we cannot say for sure whether Nietzsche believed in the eternal recurrence as a true cosmological theory, we can at least be pretty sure that he was not confident enough in his ability to prove it that he saw it as fit for publication. It was Nietzsche's sister, Elizabeth Förster-Nietzsche, who included sketches of a proof in *The Will to Power*, which she published after Nietzsche's death. *The Will to Power* was constructed from a collection of Nietzsche's notes. These notes were organized and

published by Förster-Nietzsche and Nietzsche's friend Heinrich Köselitz, so one can only speculate as to how well the ideas in this book do justice to what Nietzsche himself would have expressed, or whether Nietzsche would have attempted to publish these notes at all. See Nehamas, *Nietzsche*, ch. 5, for a thorough discussion.

68. To cite only a few: Arthur Danto, *Nietzsche as Philosopher* (New York: Columbia University Press, 1965), 203–9; Karl Löwith, *Nietzsche's Philosophy of the Eternal Recurrence of the Same*, trans. J. Harvey Lomax (Berkeley: University of California Press, 1997); Tracy B. Strong, *Friedrich Nietzsche and the Politics of Transfiguration* (Berkeley: University of California Press, 1975), 260–93; Arnold Zuboff, "Nietzsche and Eternal Recurrence," in Solomon, *Nietzsche*, 348–57.

69. Nietzsche, *Beyond Good and Evil*, sec. 56.

Chapter 5

1. Aaron L. Herold, "Spinoza's Liberal Republicanism and the Challenge of Revealed Religion," *Political Research Quarterly* 67, no. 2 (2014): 246.

2. Baruch Spinoza, *Theological-Political Treatise*, trans. Samuel Shirley (Indianapolis: Hackett, 1998), 3.

3. Nietzsche argues, "Moreover, if the purpose of all politics really is to make life endurable for as many as possible, then these as-many-as-possible are entitled to determine what they understand by an endurable life." Friedrich Nietzsche, *Human, All Too Human*, trans. R. J. Hollingdale (Cambridge: Cambridge University Press, 1986), sec. 438.

4. Nietzsche speaks harshly of liberalism throughout his works. For example, Friedrich Nietzsche, *Beyond Good and Evil: Prelude to a Philosophy of the Future*, trans. Walter Kaufmann (New York: Vintage, 1989), sec. 252; *Daybreak*, trans. R. J. Hollingdale (Cambridge: Cambridge University Press, 1982), sec. 197. See, for example, Bruce Detwiler, *Nietzsche and the Politics of Aristocratic Radicalism* (Chicago: University of Chicago Press, 1990); Daniel Conway, *Nietzsche and the Political* (London: Routledge, 1996), ch. 7. Some scholars have noted, as well, that liberalism never penetrated as deeply into German political thought as it did in the rest of western Europe. Stephen R. C. Hicks, *Explaining Postmodernism: Skepticism and Socialism from Rousseau to Foucault*, expanded ed. (Roscoe, IL: Ockham's Razor, 2011), 105.

5. Even Spinoza, however, did not *expect* a regime to be capable of producing only liberal, free-spirited citizens. He believed that the "common people" would likely never overcome superstition and the "emotional attitudes" that make free-thinking impossible. Spinoza, *Theological-Political Treatise*, preface, p. 8. Nevertheless, Spinoza still made a republic that respects free-thinking persons the aim of politics. Ibid., ch. 20, pp. 231–32, 234.

6. Nietzsche, *Human, All Too Human*, sec. 481.

7. John Dewey, "The Ethics of Democracy," in *The Early Works of John Dewey, 1882–1898–*, ed. Jo Ann Boydston, vol. 1, *1882–1888* (Carbondale: Southern Illinois University Press, 1969), 238–39.

8. William M. Sullivan, *Reconstructing Public Philosophy* (Berkeley: University of California Press, 1982), 158, 173.

9. Aristotle, *Politics*, trans. Peter L. Phillips Simpson (Chapel Hill: University of North Carolina Press, 1997), 1253a24–27.

10. Dewey, "Ethics of Democracy," 241.

11. Hobbes's claim is that "the Right of Nature, which writers commonly call *jus naturale*, is the liberty each man hath to use his own power, as he will himself, for the preservation of his own nature, that is to say, of his own life." Thomas Hobbes, *Leviathan*, ed. Edwin Curley (Cambridge, MA: Hackett, 1994), 79.

12. In his chapter entitled "The State of Nature," Locke argues that the law of nature, which all men apprehend through their reason, instructs us that "every one, as he is bound to preserve himself, and not to quit his station willfully." John Locke, *Two Treatises of Government*, ed. Peter Laslett (Cambridge: Cambridge University Press, 1988), 271.

13. Hobbes, *Leviathan*, 79.

14. It is true, of course, that Locke does not share Hobbes's dire description of the state of nature. Locke argues that the law of nature exists in a prepolitical state, and he believes that nature, once labor is applied to it, is bountiful rather than scarce. Nonetheless, Locke argues for a civil government as a "remedy for the inconveniences of the state of nature." Locke (1988), 276.

15. Ibid., 109.

16. This brief summary does not, admittedly, encompass the logic of, or the debates surrounding, the concept of the state of nature. Nor does it mention other thinkers, notably Hume, Rousseau, and Montesquieu, who bring different conceptions of the state of nature to the fore. For my purposes here, however, I mean only to remind the reader that the state of nature portrayed by early liberals positioned the individual—or at least individual families—as prior to the formation of society.

17. Charles E. Merriam, *A History of American Political Theories* (New York: Macmillan, 1903), 307.

18. John G. Gunnell, *The Descent of Political Theory: The Genealogy of an American Vocation* (Chicago: University of Chicago Press, 1993), 27.

19. Ibid.

20. John W. Burgess, *Political Science and Comparative Constitutional Law* (Boston: Ginn, 1891), 62.

21. John Rawls, *Justice as Fairness: A Restatement* (Cambridge: Belknap Press of Harvard University Press, 2003), 85.

22. It should be noted that as Rawls continued to develop his theory of justice—and, as critics argued, that even persons in the original position could

not unreservedly be considered impartial—persons behind the veil of ignorance were considered to have different stores of "knowledge."

23. John Rawls, *A Theory of Justice*, rev. ed. (Cambridge: Harvard University Press, 1999), 118.

24. Michael J. Sandel, *Democracy's Discontent: America in Search of a Public Philosophy* (Cambridge, MA: Belknap Press of Harvard University Press, 1996), 14.

25. Ibid., 203.

26. John Marini, "Progressivism, Modern Political Science, and the Transformation of American Constitutionalism," in *The Progressive Revolution in Politics and Political Science: Transforming the American Regime*, ed. John Marini and Ken Masugi (Lanham, MD: Rowman and Littlefield, 2005), 234.

27. For a brief discussion of this debate, see James Ceasar, *Nature and History in American Political Development* (Cambridge, MA: Harvard University Press, 2006), 70–81. Other camps close to and, in some cases, overlapping with progressives are "reform" liberals or "contemporary" liberals. These camps view the state as the essential mechanism for providing liberal rights to individuals, but these rights include a whole host of rights that classical liberals reject (e.g., right to work, right to healthcare, right to education). They add many positive rights to the liberal platform. While these camps may reject the idea that they begin with the state—arguing instead that the state is there to provide positive rights for the individual—the practical outcome is hardly different. The state, and the study of the application of state power, is the overriding concern of these camps as well.

28. Nietzsche, *Daybreak*, sec. 560.

29. Paul Franco, *Nietzsche's Enlightenment: The Free-Spirit Trilogy of the Middle Period* (Chicago: University of Chicago Press, 2011), 81.

30. Nietzsche, *Daybreak*, sec. 109.

31. Rebecca Bamford, "Health and Self-cultivation in *Dawn*" in *Nietzsche's Free Spirit Philosophy*, ed. Rebecca Bamford (New York: Rowman and Littlefield, 2015), 90. Bamford refers to Nietzsche's *Daybreak*, sec. 382, in the quoted passage.

32. Bamford, "Health and Self-cultivation in Dawn," 91.

33. Nietzsche, *Beyond Good and Evil*, sec. 21.

34. See *Daybreak*, sec. 115, for Nietzsche's enumeration of drives and their affects. As well, Christopher Janaway asks and answers the question, "What is an affect? At times Nietzsche talks simply of 'inclinations and aversions,' 'pro and contra,' or 'for and against.' . . . Affects are, at the very least, ways in which we *feel*." Christopher Janaway, "Autonomy, Affect, and the Self in Nietzsche's Project of Genealogy," in *Nietzsche on Freedom and Autonomy*, ed. Ken Gemes and Simon May (New York: Oxford University Press, 2009), 52.

35. Ken Gemes, "Nietzsche on Free Will, Autonomy, and the Sovereign Individual," in Gemes and May, *Nietzsche on Freedom and Autonomy*, 46.

36. Simon May, "Nihilism and the Free Self," in Gemes and May, *Nietzsche on Freedom and Autonomy*, 90.

37. Ibid., 91.
38. Ibid.
39. Ibid., 94.
40. From the introduction to John Christman and Joel Anderson, eds., *Autonomy and the Challenges to Liberalism: New Essays* (New York: Cambridge University Press, 2005), 9.
41. Ibid., 3–4. Italics mine.
42. John Christman, "Autonomy in Moral and Political Philosophy," in *Stanford Encyclopedia of Philosophy*, ed. Edward N. Zalta, Spring 2011 ed., http://plato.stanford.edu/archives/spr2011/entries/autonomy-moral/.
43. Rainer Forst, "Political Liberty: Integrating Five Conceptions of Autonomy," in Christman and Anderson, *Autonomy*, 229.
44. Ibid., 237.
45. Jeremy Waldron, "Moral Autonomy and Personal Autonomy," in Christman and Anderson, *Autonomy*, 307.
46. Recall, as well, that liberal political power is legitimated by a social contract agreed upon by independent, self-governing citizens. The end of liberal government, as it were, must be *chosen* by autonomous individuals.
47. Immanuel Kant, *Practical Philosophy*, trans. and ed. Mary J. Gregor (Cambridge: Cambridge University Press, 1996), 291.
48. Friedrich Nietzsche, *The Genealogy of Morals*, in *The Genealogy of Morals, [and] Ecce Homo*, trans. Walter Kaufmann (New York: Vintage, 1967), second essay, sec. 2.
49. Janaway, "Autonomy, Affect, and the Self," 62.
50. Friedrich Nietzsche, *The Gay Science*, trans. Walter Kaufmann (New York: Random House, 1974), sec. 347.
51. Waldron, "Moral Autonomy and Personal Autonomy," in Christman and Anderson, *Autonomy*, 307.
52. In *Beyond Good and Evil*, sec. 21, Nietzsche asserts, "In real life it is only a matter of strong and weak wills."
53. Nietzsche, *Genealogy of Morals*, second essay, sec. 2.
54. As Gemes remarks, "[Nietzsche] then seeks to unsettle his audience with the uncanny idea that autonomy and free will are achievements of great difficulty, achievements which they themselves have by no means attained." Gemes, "Nietzsche on Free Will," 38–39.
55. Ibid., 38.
56. Nietzsche, *Genealogy of Morals*, second essay, sec. 2.
57. Ibid.
58. *Wikipedia*, "Liberalism," last modified 20 January 2019, https://en.wikipedia.org/wiki/Liberalism.
59. Gerald Gaus, Shane D. Courtland, and David Schmidtz, "Liberalism," in *Stanford Encyclopedia of Philosophy*, ed. Edward N. Zalta, Spring 2018 ed., https://plato.stanford.edu/archives/spr2018/entries/liberalism/.

60. From *Second Treatise*: "And to this I say, that every Man, that hath any Possession, or Enjoyment, of any part of the Dominions of any Government, doth thereby give his *tacit Consent*, and is as far forth obliged to Obedience to the Laws of that Government, during such Enjoyment, as any one under it." John Locke, *Two Treatises of Government*, ed. Peter Laslett (Cambridge: Cambridge University Press, 1988), 348.

61. John G. Bennett, "A Note on Locke's Theory of Tacit Consent," *Philosophical Review* 88, no. 2 (1979): 227.

62. Catholic Church, "The Sacraments of Christian Initiation," in *Compendium of the Catechism of the Catholic Church* (Vatican: Libreria Editrice Vaticana, 2005). Code of Canon Law 989 applies specifically to the sacrament of Confession, but it stipulates the "age of discretion," which is also necessary for Confirmation. For the Sacrament of Confirmation, Catholic law currently holds that this must be at least age seven, though the sacrament is usually taken in the early to late teen years (thirteen to sixteen). This is, of course, significantly earlier than the age of eighteen required for legal adulthood. One could argue that the age limit of church law does not adequately constitute an "age of discretion" (an argument to which I am sympathetic), but the example still holds for the analogy here, because the goal is a consensual reaffirmation of faith and church membership.

63. Will Kymlicka provides a good argument for why the communitarian "social thesis" ultimately fails in Will Kymlicka, *Contemporary Political Philosophy: An Introduction* (New York: Oxford University Press, 1990), 219–25.

Chapter 6

1. Aristotle, *Politics*, trans. Peter L. Phillips Simpson (Chapel Hill: University of North Carolina Press, 1997), 103–5. Aristotle quite famously observes that individuals who have too much power, wealth, virtue, independence, and so on, have historically been ostracized, particularly in democratic regimes. In the best regime, however, an exception should be made for the one case of an individual with preeminent virtue—he should be perpetual king of the city. The principle, for Aristotle, is that anyone who stands out too much from the rest "exceeds proportions" and would be "like a god among human beings." In such cases, ostracism has "a certain political justice to it."

2. Thomas Hobbes, *Leviathan*, ed. Edwin Curley (Cambridge, MA: Hackett, 1994), 207–8. Hobbes, citing Cicero, recommends the banishment of unlawful citizens as a punishment that upholds the rule of law. Banishment should "tend to that benefit of the commonwealth for which all punishments are ordained (that is to say, to the forming of men's wills to the observation of the law)." For those familiar with Hobbes, it will not be surprising for me to suggest that the free spirit would be under threat of banishment. For Hobbes, any citizen who would not

subject himself to the laws of the sovereign in matters of religion, culture, social convention, and so on, is considered unlawful. The free spirit's independence is therefore cause for exile.

3. Consider the exiles of Rousseau or Voltaire from France, for example. Richard Schacht notes that, remarkably, Nietzsche initially dedicated this first work on the free spirit, *Human, All Too Human*, to Voltaire, whom Nietzsche considered the Enlightenment thinker par excellence. Importantly, however, Nietzsche dropped this dedication eight years later, "perhaps because he no longer wanted Voltaire to be taken as paradigmatic of his evolving conception of the 'free spirit.'" Schacht also suggests that the dedication was a direct rebuke to Richard Wagner, soon after Nietzsche had become estranged from the latter. It is also possible, then, that Nietzsche dropped the dedication "because Wagner by then had died, and such gestures were no longer either needed or fitting." See Schacht's introduction to *Human, All Too Human*, by Friedrich Nietzsche, trans. R. J. Hollingdale (Cambridge: Cambridge University Press, 1986), ix.

4. John Christman and Joel Anderson, introduction to *Autonomy and the Challenges to Liberalism*, ed. John Christman and Joel Anderson (New York: Cambridge University Press, 2005), 8.

5. Christman and Anderson identify as one of the major challenges to autonomy "the allegedly hyper-individualism of both autonomy-based liberalism and standard accounts of the autonomous self." Ibid., 2.

6. Some readers will likely disagree with the inclusion of MacIntyre in the camp of communitarians. MacIntrye himself rejected this label. I will address this issue later on.

7. Jack Crittenden, *Beyond Individualism: Reconstituting the Liberal Self* (New York: Oxford University Press, 1992), 19.

8. Patrick J. Deneen, *Why Liberalism Failed* (New Haven, CT: Yale University Press, 2018), 30.

9. Barack Obama, "Dreams from My Father: A Story of Race and Inheritance" (speech, Cambridge Public Library, September 20, 1995). This originally aired as an episode of *The Author Series*, on Cambridge Municipal Television.

10. John Rawls, *A Theory of Justice*, rev. ed. (Cambridge, MA: Harvard University Press, 1999), 98.

11. Charles Taylor, "Atomism," in *Philosophy and the Human Sciences*, vol. 2 of *Philosophical Papers* (Cambridge: Cambridge University Press, 1985), 187. It is highly probable, given Taylor's writings on Rawls elsewhere, that the "successor doctrines" that Taylor has in mind begin with Rawls.

12. Deneen, *Why Liberalism Failed*, 37.

13. John Dewey, "The Ethics of Democracy," in *The Early Works of John Dewey, 1882–1898*, ed. Jo Ann Boydston, vol. 1, *1882–1888* (Carbondale: Southern Illinois University Press, 1969), 241. Emphasis added.

14. Ibid., 240.

15. Woolsey quoted in Charles Merriam, *American Political Ideas: Studies in the Development of American Political Thought, 1865–1917* (New York: Macmillan, 1923), 378.

16. Ibid.

17. Woolsey, like Burgess and Lieber, was influenced by Hegel, so we would do well to remember Hegel's view of the state: "As high as mind stands above nature, so high does the state stand above physical life. Man must therefore venerate the state as a secular deity, and observe that if it is difficult to understand nature, it is infinitely harder to understand the state." Georg F. W. Hegel, *Philosophy of Right*, trans. T. M. Knox (London: Oxford University Press, 1967), 235.

18. Michael J. Sandel, *Democracy's Discontent: America in Search of a Public Philosophy* (Cambridge, MA: Belknap Press of Harvard University Press, 1996), 205.

19. I'm referring to those people who choose to live completely cut off from society, learning to be self-sufficient and residing in mountain huts, desert caves, or some other self-constructed shelter. Clearly this is a very small percentage of the population, but they warrant mention nonetheless.

20. Communitiarians do distinguish communities from one another. Briefly put, there are communities of place (from towns to nations), communities of memories (where shared memories and traditions are the bond, regardless of location), and psychological communities (small, tightly connected communities of trust centered around a common goal). Explicating the differences between these types of communities is outside the purview of this project, but for a more complete summary, see Daniel Bell, "Communitarianism," in *Stanford Encyclopedia of Philosophy*, Fall 2013 ed., ed. Edward N. Zalta, http://plato.stanford.edu/archives/fall2013/entries/communitarianism/.

21. Ibid.

22. Ibid.

23. Sandel, *Democracy's Discontent*, 207.

24. I do not mean to suggest one might disregard the "moral force" of relationships with family and friends. The focus here is on our loyalties and obligations to social traditions and history, and ties to political community.

25. Sandel, *Democracy's Discontent*, 351. Italics mine.

26. Alasdair MacIntyre, *After Virtue: A study in Moral Theory*, 2nd ed. (Notre Dame, IN: Notre Dame Press, 1984), xiv.

27. J. B. Schneewind, "Virtue, Narrative, and Community: MacIntyre and Morality," *Journal of Philosophy* 79, no. 11 (1982): 654.

28. Ibid., 655.

29. MacIntyre, *After Virtue*, 203.

30. Ibid., 218.

31. Ibid., 216.

32. Ibid., 220.

33. Alasdair MacIntyre, *Dependent Rational Animals: Why Human Beings Need the Virtues* (Chicago: Open Court, 1999)
34. Ibid., p. 161
35. Ibid.
36. MacIntyre, *After Virtue*, xv.
37. Ibid., xiv–xv.
38. Ibid., 220.
39. I am indebted to Aloysius P. Martinich for this idea.
40. Friedrich Nietzsche, *The Gay Science*, trans. Walter Kaufmann (New York: Random House, 1974), sec. 270.
41. David Owen, *Nietzsche, Politics and Modernity: A Critique of Liberal Reason* (Thousand Oaks, CA: Sage, 1995), 101.
42. Ibid., 101.
43. Charles Taylor, *Sources of the Self: The Making of the Modern Identity* (Cambridge, MA: Harvard University Press, 1989), 52.
44. Ibid., 18.
45. Ibid., 27.
46. Crittenden, *Beyond Individualism*, 16.
47. Ibid., 18.
48. Taylor, *Sources of the Self*, 27.
49. Ibid., 31.
50. It warrants mentioning that Taylor does not reject individual autonomy, but he does argue that any claims of autonomy must be understood in light of the need to belong to society. In his essay "Atomism," he writes, "I am arguing that the free individual of the West is only what he is by virtue of the whole society and civilization which brought him to be and which nourishes him. . . . And I want to claim finally that all this creates a significant obligation to belong for whoever would affirm the value of this freedom; this includes all those who want to assert rights either to this freedom or for its sake." Taylor, "Atomism," 206.
51. Amy Mullin, "Nietzsche's Free Spirit," *Journal of the History of Philosophy* 38, no. 3 (2000): 387.
52. Nietzsche, *Human, All Too Human*, sec. 226.
53. Mullin, "Nietzsche's Free Spirit," 394.
54. Friedrich Nietzsche, *The Case of Wagner*, in *The Birth of Tragedy, and The Case of Wagner*, trans. Walter Kaufmann (New York: Vintage, 1967), preface, p. 155.
55. Friedrich Nietzsche, *Ecce Homo*, in *The Genealogy of Morals, [and] Ecce Homo*, trans. Walter Kaufmann (New York: Vintage, 1967), pp. 224–25.
56. Ibid. Refer to Nietzsche, *Human, All Too Human*, sec. 34, to find Nietzsche's description of the free spirit as an "at bottom cheerful soul."
57. Daniel Blue, *The Making of Friedrich Nietzsche: The Quest for Identity, 1844–1869* (New York: Cambridge University Press, 2016), 190.

58. Neal Dolan, *Emerson's Liberalism* (Madison: University of Wisconsin Press, 2009), 4.
59. Ibid., 5.
60. Ibid., 8.
61. Ibid., 23.
62. George Kateb, *Emerson and Self-reliance* (Thousand Oaks, CA: Sage, 1994), 178–79.
63. Justin Buckley Dyer and Micah J. Watson, *C. S. Lewis on Politics and the Natural Law* (New York: Cambridge University Press, 2016), 88.
64. Ibid., 97.
65. Johann Peter Eckermann, *Eckermann's Conversations with Goethe*, trans. R. O. Moon (London: Morgan, Laird, 1850), 47.

Conclusion

1. John Stuart Mill, *On Liberty*, ed. Gertrude Himmelfarb (New York: Penguin, 1981), 68.
2. Ibid.
3. Mill, *On Liberty*, 63.
4. Ibid. It should be noted that Tocqueville drew very similar conclusions about the dangers of public opinion. Tocqueville's famous concepts of "soft despotism" and the tyranny of the majority certainly support Mill's arguments, as well as the one being made here.
5. John Gray, *Liberalisms: Essays in Political Philosophy* (London: Routledge, 1989), 264.
6. Søren Kierkegaard, *Either/Or: A Fragment of Life*, trans. Alastair Hannay (London: Penguin, 1992), 43. At the time of Kierkegaard's writing, Denmark was still a monarchy, and freedom of speech was not a protected right.
7. It should also be noted that free spirits are unlikely to gather into communities of their own, that is, we would not expect to see a community of free spirits like we would a community of contemplative monks. Being a free spirit is not only about separation from strong societal influence; it is also about spiritual independence.
8. There may be a rise of skepticism and the scientific perspective in other parts of the world as well, but only in Europe and America might we consider it the dominant worldview. Currently, we are seeing a rise of religion in many parts of the developing world, such as China and Brazil. It remains to be seen whether the rise of religion will be compatible with the continuing rise of science. John Micklethwait and Adrian Wooldridge, *God Is Back: How the Global Revival of Faith Is Changing the World* (New York: Penguin, 2009).

9. Quoted in Richard Dagger, "Autonomy, Domination, and the Republican Challenge to Liberalism," in *Autonomy and the Challenges to Liberalism: New Essays*, ed. John Christman and Joel Anderson (New York: Cambridge University Press, 2005), 199.

10. Friedrich Nietzsche, *Human, All Too Human*, trans. R. J. Hollingdale (Cambridge: Cambridge University Press, 1986), sec. 34.

11. Ibid., sec. 626.

12. Ibid., sec. 625.

13. Ibid., sec. 626. Nietzsche quotes Goethe.

Bibliography

Abbey, Ruth. *Nietzsche's Middle Period*. New York: Oxford University Press, 2000.
Acampora, Christa Davis. "Being Unattached: Freedom and Nietzsche's Free Spirits." In Bamford, *Nietzsche's Free Spirit Philosophy*, 189–206.
Achen, Christopher H., and Larry M. Bartels. *Democracy for Realists: Why Elections Do Not Produce Responsive Government*. Princeton, NJ: Princeton University Press, 2016.
Ansell Pearson, Keith, ed. *A Companion to Nietzsche*. Oxford: Blackwell, 2006.
———. "Beyond Selfishness: Epicurean Ethics in Nietzsche and Guyau." In Bamford, *Nietzsche's Free Spirit Philosophy*, 49–68.
Ansell Pearson, Keith, and Duncan Large, eds. *The Nietzsche Reader*. Oxford: Blackwell, 2006.
Appel, Fredrick. *Nietzsche contra Democracy*. Ithaca, NY: Cornell University Press, 1999.
Aristotle. *Politics*. Translated by Peter L. Phillips Simpson. Chapel Hill: University of North Carolina Press, 1997.
Bamford, Rebecca. "Health and Self-cultivation in *Dawn*." In *Nietzsche's Free Spirit Philosophy*, 85–110.
———, ed. *Nietzsche's Free Spirit Philosophy*. New York: Rowman and Littlefield, 2015.
Bearn, Gordon C. F. *Waking to Wonder: Wittgenstein's Existential Investigations*. Albany: State University of New York Press, 1997.
Bell, Daniel. "Communitarianism." In *Stanford Encyclopedia of Philosophy*, edited by Edward N. Zalta. Fall 2013 ed. http://plato.stanford.edu/archives/fall2013/entries/communitarianism/.
Bennett, John G. "A Note on Locke's Theory of Tacit Consent." *Philosophical Review* 88, no. 2 (1979): 224–34.
Berkowitz, Peter. *Nietzsche: The Ethics of an Immoralist*. Cambridge, MA: Harvard University Press, 1995.
Berry, Jessica N. *Nietzsche and the Ancient Skeptical Tradition*. New York: Oxford University Press, 2011.

Blue, Daniel. *The Making of Friedrich Nietzsche: The Quest for Identity, 1844–1869.* New York: Cambridge University Press, 2016.
Botwinick, Aryeh. *Skepticism and Political Participation.* Philadelphia: Temple University Press, 1990.
Brennan, Jason. *Against Democracy.* Princeton, NJ: Princeton University Press, 2016.
Brennan, Tad. *Ethics and Epistemology in Sextus Empiricus.* New York: Garland, 1999.
Burgess, John W. *Political Science and Comparative Constitutional Law.* Boston: Ginn, 1891.
Catholic Church. "The Sacraments of Christian Initiation." In *Compendium of the Catechism of the Catholic Church.* Vatican: Libreria Editrice Vaticana, 2005.
Ceasar, James W. *Nature and History in American Political Development.* Cambridge, MA: Harvard University Press, 2006.
Christman, John. "Autonomy in Moral and Political Philosophy." In *Stanford Encyclopedia of Philosophy*, edited by Edward N. Zalta. Spring 2011 ed. http://plato.stanford.edu/archives/spr2011/entries/autonomy-moral/.
Christman, John, and Joel Anderson, eds. *Autonomy and the Challenges to Liberalism: New Essays.* New York: Cambridge University Press, 2005.
Church, Jeffrey. *Infinite Autonomy: The Divided Individual in the Political Thought of G. W. F. Hegel and Friedrich Nietzsche.* Philadelphia: Pennsylvania State University Press, 2011.
Clark, Maudemarie. *Nietzsche on Ethics and Politics.* Oxford: Oxford University Press, 2015.
Conway, Daniel W. *Nietzsche and the Political.* London: Routledge, 1996.
———. *Nietzsche's Dangerous Game: Philosophy in the Twilight of the Idols.* Cambridge: Cambridge University Press, 2002.
Crittenden, Jack. *Beyond Individualism: Reconstituting the Liberal Self.* New York: Oxford University Press, 1992.
Dagger, Richard. "Autonomy, Domination, and the Republican Challenge to Liberalism." In Christman and Anderson, *Autonomy*, 177–203.
Daigle, Christine. "The Ethical Ideal of the Free Spirit in *Human, All Too Human*." In Bamford, *Nietzsche's Free Spirit Philosophy*, 33–48.
Danto, Arthur C. *Nietzsche as Philosopher.* New York: Columbia University Press, 1965.
Deneen, Patrick J. *Why Liberalism Failed.* New Haven, CT: Yale University Press, 2018.
Detwiler, Bruce. *Nietzsche and the Politics of Aristocratic Radicalism.* Chicago: University of Chicago Press, 1990.
Dewey, John. "The Ethics of Democracy." In *The Early Works of John Dewey, 1882–1898*, edited by Jo Ann Boydston. Vol. 1, *1882–1888*, 227–49. Carbondale: Southern Illinois University Press, 1969.
Dienstag, Joshua Foa. "Nietzsche's Dionysian Pessimism." *American Political Science Review* 95, no. 4 (2001): 923–37.

Dolan, Neal. *Emerson's Liberalism*. Madison: University of Wisconsin Press, 2009.
Drochon, Hugo Halferty. *Nietzsche's Great Politics*. Princeton, NJ: Princeton University Press, 2016.
———. "The Time Is Coming When We Will Relearn Politics." *Journal of Nietzsche Studies*, no. 39 (2010): 66–85.
Dyer, Justin Buckley, and Micah J. Watson. *C. S. Lewis on Politics and the Natural Law*. New York: Cambridge University Press, 2016.
Eckermann, Johann Peter. *Eckermann's Conversations with Goethe*. Translated by R. O. Moon. London: Morgan, Laird, 1850.
Emerson, Ralph Waldo. *The Essential Writings of Ralph Waldo Emerson*. Edited by Brooks Atkinson. New York: Modern Library, 2000.
———. *Representative Men*. Boston: Phillips, Sampson, 1850.
Fairley, Barker. *A Study of Goethe*. London: Oxford University Press, 1950.
Foot, Phillipa. "Nietzsche: The Revaluation of Values." In Solomon, *Nietzsche*, 156–68.
Fortier, Jeremy. "Nietzsche's Political Engagements: On the Relationship between Philosophy and Politics in *The Wanderer and His Shadow*." *Review of Politics* 78, no. 2 (2016): 201–25.
Franco, Paul. *Nietzsche's Enlightenment: The Free-Spirit Trilogy of the Middle Period*. Chicago: University of Chicago Press, 2011.
Freedman, Ralph. *Hermann Hesse: Pilgrim of Crisis*. New York: Pantheon, 1978.
Frost, Bryan Paul. "Religion, Nature, and Disobedience in the Thought of Ralph Waldo Emerson and Henry David Thoreau." In Frost and Sikkenga, *History of American Political Thought*, 367–87.
Frost, Bryan-Paul, and Jeffrey Sikkenga, eds. *History of American Political Thought*. Lanham, MD: Lexington Press, 2003.
Galbreath, Robert. "Herman Hesse and the Politics of Detachment." *Political Theory* 2, no. 1 (1974): 62–76.
Gaus, Gerald F. "The Diversity of Comprehensive Liberalisms." In *The Handbook of Political Theory*, edited by Gerald F. Gaus and Chandran Kukathas, 100–114. London: Sage, 2004.
Gaus, Gerald, Shane D. Courtland, and David Schmidtz. "Liberalism." In *Stanford Encyclopedia of Philosophy*, edited by Edward N. Zalta. Spring 2018 ed. https://plato.stanford.edu/archives/spr2018/entries/liberalism/.
Gemes, Ken. "Nietzsche on Free Will, Autonomy, and the Sovereign Individual." In Gemes and May, *Nietzsche on Freedom and Autonomy*, 33–50.
Gemes, Ken, and Simon May, eds. *Nietzsche on Freedom and Autonomy*. New York: Oxford University Press, 2009.
Gillespie, Michael Allen. "'Slouching toward Bethlehem to Be Born': On the Nature and Meaning of Nietzsche's Superman." *Journal of Nietzsche Studies*, no. 30 (2005): 49–69.
Glenn, Paul F. "The Politics of Truth: Power in Nietzsche's Epistemology." *Political Research Quarterly* 57, no. 4 (2004): 575–83.

Golomb, Jacob. "Can One Really Become a 'Free Spirit Par Excellence' or an Übermensch?" *Journal of Nietzsche Studies*, no. 32 (2006): 22–40.

Gray, John. *Liberalisms: Essays in Political Philosophy*. London: Routledge, 1989.

———. *Post-liberalism: Studies in Political Thought*. New York: Routledge, 2014.

Gunnell, John G. *The Descent of Political Theory: The Genealogy of an American Vocation*. Chicago: University of Chicago Press, 1993.

Hegel, Georg W. F. *Philosophy of Right*. Translated by T. M. Knox. London: Oxford University Press, 1967.

Heidegger, Martin. *Nietzsche*. Vol. 2, *The Eternal Recurrence of the Same*. Translated by David Farrell Krell. San Francisco: Harper and Row, 1984.

Herold, Aaron L. "Spinoza's Liberal Republicanism and the Challenge of Revealed Religion." *Political Research Quarterly* 67, no. 2 (2014): 239–52.

Hesse, Hermann. *The Glass Bead Game (Magister Ludi)*. New York: Henry Holt, 1943.

———. *Narcissus and Goldmund*. Translated by Ursule Molinaro. New York: Farrar, Strauss and Giroux, 1968.

———. *Steppenwolf*. Translated by Basil Creighton. New York: Holt, Rinehart and Winston, 1963.

Hicks, Stephen R. C. *Explaining Postmodernism: Skepticism and Socialism from Rousseau to Foucault*. Expanded ed. Roscoe, IL: Ockham's Razor, 2011.

Higgins, Kathleen Marie. *Nietzsche's "Zarathustra."* Philadelphia: Temple University Press, 1987.

Hobbes, Thomas. *Leviathan*. Edited by Edwin Curley. Cambridge, MA: Hackett, 1994.

Hollingdale, R. J. "The Hero as Outsider." In Magnus and Higgins, *The Cambridge Companion to Nietzsche*, 71–89.

Janaway, Christopher. "Autonomy, Affect, and the Self in Nietzsche's Project of Genealogy." In Gemes and May, *Nietzsche on Freedom and Autonomy*, 51–68.

Jensen, Anthony K. "Anti-politicality and Agon in Nietzsche's Philology." In Siemens and Roodt, *Nietzsche, Power, and Politics*, 319–46.

Kant, Immanuel. *Practical Philosophy*. Translated and edited by Mary J. Gregor. Cambridge: Cambridge University Press, 1996.

Kateb, George. *Emerson and Self-reliance*. Thousand Oaks, CA: Sage, 1994.

———. "Self-reliance, Politics, and Society." In Levine and Malachuk, *A Political Companion to Ralph Waldo Emerson*, 69–90.

Keirsey, David. *Please Understand Me II: Temperament, Character, Intelligence*. Toronto: Prometheus Nemesis, 1998.

Kierkegaard, Søren. *Either/Or: A Fragment of Life*. Translated by Alastair Hannay. London: Penguin, 1992.

Kirkland, Paul E. "Nietzsche's Honest Masks: From Truth to Nobility 'Beyond Good and Evil.'" *Review of Politics* 66, no. 4 (2004): 575–604.

———. *Nietzsche's Noble Aims: Affirming Life, Contesting Modernity*. Lanham, MD: Lexington Books, 2009.

Kymlicka, Will. *Contemporary Political Philosophy: An Introduction*. New York: Oxford University Press, 1990.

Lampert, Laurence. "'Beyond Good and Evil': Nietzsche's 'Free Spirit' Mask." *International Studies in Philosophy* 16, no. 2 (1984): 41–52.

———. *Nietzsche's Task: An Interpretation of "Beyond Good and Evil."* New Haven, CT: Yale University Press, 2001.

Larmore, Charles. *The Morals of Modernity*. New York: Cambridge University Press, 1996.

Laursen, John Christian. *The Politics of Skepticism in the Ancients, Montaigne, Hume, and Kant*. Leiden: E. J. Brill, 1992.

Leiter, Brian. "Nietzsche and Aestheticism." *Journal of the History of Philosophy* 30, no. 2 (1992): 275–90.

———. "The Truth Is Terrible." *Journal of Nietzsche Studies* 49, no. 2 (2018): 151–73.

Levine, Alan M., and Daniel S. Malachuk, eds. *A Political Companion to Ralph Waldo Emerson*. Lexington: University Press of Kentucky, 2011.

Lewis, C. S. *The Discarded Image: An Introduction to Medieval and Renaissance Literature*. Cambridge: Cambridge University Press, 1964.

———. "Equality." In *Present Concerns*, 17–20. San Diego: Harcourt Brace Jovanovich, 1986.

———. *That Hideous Strength: A Modern Fairy-Tale for Grown-Ups*. New York: Macmillan, 1979.

Locke, John. *Two Treatises of Government*. Edited by Peter Laslett. Cambridge: Cambridge University Press, 1988.

Lomax, J. Harvey. *The Paradox of Philosophical Education: Nietzsche's New Nobility and the Eternal Recurrence in "Beyond Good and Evil."* Lanham, MD: Lexington Books, 2003.

Löwith, Karl. *Nietzsche's Philosophy of the Eternal Recurrence of the Same*. Translated by J. Harvey Lomax. Berkeley: University of California Press, 1997.

Luce, Edward. *The Retreat of Western Liberalism*. Boston: Atlantic Monthly Press, 2017.

MacIntyre, Alasdair. *After Virtue: A Study in Moral Theory*. 2nd ed. Notre Dame, IN: University of Notre Dame Press, 1984.

———. *Dependent Rational Animals: Why Human Beings Need the Virtues*. Chicago: Open Court, 1999.

Magnus, Bernd, and Kathleen M. Higgins, eds. *The Cambridge Companion to Nietzsche*. Cambridge: Cambridge University Press, 1996.

Marini, John. "Progressivism, Modern Political Science, and the Transformation of American Constitutionalism." In *The Progressive Revolution in Politics and Political Science: Transforming the American Regime*, edited by John Marini and Ken Masugi, 221–51. Lanham, MD: Rowman and Littlefield, 2005.

Martinich, A. P. "Four Senses of 'Meaning' in the History of Ideas: Quentin Skinner's Theory of Historical Interpretation." *Journal of the Philosophy of History* 3, no. 3 (2009): 225–45.

May, Simon. "Nihilism and the Free Self." In Gemes and May, *Nietzsche on Freedom and Autonomy*, 89–106.
Merriam, Charles E. *American Political Ideas: Studies in the Development of American Political Thought, 1865–1917*. New York: Macmillan, 1923.
———. *A History of American Political Theories*. New York: Macmillan, 1903.
Micklethwait, John, and Adrian Wooldridge. *God Is Back: How the Global Revival of Faith Is Changing the World*. New York: Penguin, 2009.
Middleton, Christopher, ed. and trans. *Selected Letters of Friedrich Nietzsche*. Chicago: Hackett, 1969.
Mikics, David. *The Romance of Individualism in Emerson and Nietzsche*. Athens: Ohio University Press, 2003.
Mill, John Stuart. *On Liberty*. Edited by Gertrude Himmelfarb. New York: Penguin, 1981.
Mottola, Anthony, trans. *The Spiritual Exercises of St. Ignatius*. Garden City, NY: Image Books, 1964.
Mullin, Amy. "Nietzsche's Free Spirit." *Journal of the History of Philosophy* 38, no. 3 (2000): 383–405.
Nabokov, Vladimir. *Lolita*. 2nd ed. New York: Vintage, 1997.
Nehamas, Alexander. *Nietzsche: Life as Literature*. Cambridge, MA: Harvard University Press, 1985.
Nietzsche, Friedrich. *Beyond Good and Evil: Prelude to a Philosophy of the Future*. Translated by Walter Kaufmann. New York: Vintage, 1989.
———. *The Birth of Tragedy, and The Case of Wagner*. Translated by Walter Kaufmann. New York: Vintage, 1967.
———. *Daybreak*. Translated by R. J. Hollingdale. Cambridge: Cambridge University Press, 1982.
———. "Fate and History: Thoughts." Translated by George Stack. In Ansell Pearson and Large, *The Nietzsche Reader*, 12–15.
———. *The Genealogy of Morals, [and] Ecce Homo*. Translated by Walter Kaufmann. New York: Vintage, 1967.
———. *The Gay Science*. Translated by Walter Kaufmann. New York: Random House, 1974.
———. *Gesammelte Werke*. München: Musarion Verlag, 1923.
———. *Human, All Too Human*. Translated by R. J. Hollingdale. Cambridge: Cambridge University Press, 1986.
———. *Sämtliche Werke: Kritische Studienausgabe*. Edited by Giorgio Colli and Mazzino Montinari. Berlin: Walter de Gruyter, 1986.
———. *Thus Spoke Zarathustra*. Translated by Walter Kaufmann. New York: Viking Penguin, 1966.
———. *Twilight of the Idols, and The Anti-Christ*. Translated by R. J. Hollingdale. New York: Penguin, 1968.

———. *The Will to Power.* Translated by Walter Kaufmann. New York: Random House, 1967.
Nisbet, H. B. "Religion and Philosophy." In Sharpe, *Cambridge Companion to Goethe*, 219–31.
Owen, David. *Nietzsche, Politics and Modernity: A Critique of Liberal Reason.* Thousand Oaks, CA: Sage, 1995.
Owen, J. Judd. *Religion and the Demise of Liberal Rationalism: The Foundational Crisis of the Separation of Church and State.* Chicago: University of Chicago Press, 2001.
Rawls, John. *Justice as Fairness: A Restatement.* Cambridge, MA: Belknap Press of Harvard University Press, 2003.
———. *A Theory of Justice.* Rev. ed. Cambridge, MA: Harvard University Press, 1999.
Reginster, Bernard. "What Is a Free Spirit? Nietzsche on Fanaticism." *Archiv für Geschichte der Philosophie* 85, no. 1 (2003): 51–85.
Roberts, Peter. "Life, Death and Transformation: Education and Incompleteness in Hermann Hesse's *The Glass Bead Game.*" *Canadian Journal of Education* 31, no. 3 (2008): 667–96.
Rousseau, Jean-Jacques. *The Reveries of the Solitary Walker.* Translated by Charles E. Butterworth. Indianapolis: Hackett, 1992.
Saine, Thomas P. "The World Goethe Lived In: Germany and Europe, 1750–1830." In Sharpe, *Cambridge Companion to Goethe*, 6–22.
Salomé, Lou. *Nietzsche.* Translated by Siegfried Mandel. Redding Ridge, CT: Black Swan, 1988.
Sandel, Michael J. *Democracy's Discontent: America in Search of a Public Philosophy.* Cambridge, MA: Belknap Press of Harvard University Press, 1996.
Schacht, Richard. "Nietzsche's 'Free Spirit.'" In Bamford, *Nietzsche's Free Spirit Philosophy*, 169–88.
Schaeffer, Francis. *Back to Freedom and Dignity.* In vol. 1 of *The Complete Works of Francis A. Schaeffer*, 357–84. Westchester, IL: Crossway, 1982.
Schneewind, J. B. "Virtue, Narrative, and Community: MacIntyre and Morality." *Journal of Philosophy* 79, no. 11 (1982): 653–63.
Sextus Empiricus. *Outlines of Scepticism.* Translated by Julia Annas and Jonathan Barnes. Cambridge: Cambridge University Press, 2000.
Sharpe, Lesley, ed. *The Cambridge Companion to Goethe.* Cambridge: Cambridge University Press, 2002.
———. "Goethe and the Weimar Theatre." In *Cambridge Companion to Goethe*, 116–28.
Siemens, Herman W. "Agonal Communities of Taste: Law and Community in Nietzsche's Philosophy of Transvaluation." *Journal of Nietzsche Studies*, no. 24 (2002): 83–112.

Siemens, Herman W., and Vasti Roodt, eds. *Nietzsche, Power, and Politics: Rethinking Nietzsche's Legacy for Political Thought*. New York: Walter de Gruyter, 2008.

Solomon, Robert, ed. *Nietzsche: A Collection of Critical Essays*. Garden City, NY: Doubleday, 1973.

Solzhenitsyn, Alexander. "A World Split Apart—Commencement Address Delivered At Harvard University, June 8, 1978." *OrthodoxyToday*. http://www.orthodoxytoday.org/articles/SolzhenitsynHarvard.php.

Spinoza, Baruch. *Theological-Political Treatise*. Translated by Samuel Shirley. Indianapolis: Hackett, 1998.

Stack, George. "Emerson and Nietzsche: Fate and Existence." *Nineteenth Century Prose* 19, no. 1 (1991): 1–15.

———. *Nietzsche and Emerson: An Elective Affinity*. Athens: Ohio University Press, 1992.

Strong, Tracy B. *Friedrich Nietzsche and the Politics of Transfiguration*. Expanded ed. Berkeley: University of California Press, 1988.

Sullivan, William M. *Reconstructing Public Philosophy*. Berkeley: University of California Press, 1982.

Taylor, Charles. *The Malaise of Modernity*. Toronto: House of Anansi Press, 1991.

———. *Philosophy and the Human Sciences*. Vol. 2 of *Philosophical Papers*. Cambridge: Cambridge University Press, 1985.

———. *A Secular Age*. Cambridge, MA: Belknap Press of Harvard University Press, 2007.

———. *Sources of the Self: The Making of the Modern Identity*. Cambridge, MA: Harvard University Press, 1989.

Thiele, Leslie Paul. *Friedrich Nietzsche and the Politics of the Soul: A Study of Heroic Individualism*. Princeton, NJ: Princeton University Press, 1990.

Thoreau, Henry David. *Walden and Other Writings*. Edited by Brooks Atkinson. New York: Modern Library, 1950.

Tocqueville, Alexis de. *Democracy in America*. Edited and translated by Harvey C. Mansfield and Delba Winthrop. Chicago: University of Chicago Press, 2000.

Waldron, Jeremy. "Moral Autonomy and Personal Autonomy." In Christman and Anderson, *Autonomy*, 307–29.

Wikipedia. "Liberalism." Last modified January 20, 2019. https://en.wikipedia.org/wiki/Liberalism.

Wilson, W. Daniel. "Goethe and the Political World." In Sharpe, *Cambridge Companion to Goethe*, 207–18.

Young, Julian. *Friedrich Nietzsche: A Philosophical Biography*. Cambridge: Cambridge University Press, 2010.

Zakaras, Alex. *Individuality and Mass Democracy: Mill, Emerson, and the Burdens of Citizenship*. New York: Oxford University Press, 2009.

Zuboff, Arnold. "Nietzsche and Eternal Recurrence." In Solomon, *Nietzsche*, 343–57.

Index

abolitionist movement
  Emerson and, 85–88
  Fugitive Slave Law of 1850 and, 85–86
  Thoreau and, 85
academic philosophy, 30–31
Acampora, Christa Davis, 45
Achen, Christopher, 47
aesthetic bliss, 108
aesthetic distance, 107, 109–110, 112–113
aesthetic perspective
  art in, 107–108
  for Emerson, 81–82, 111
  eternal recurrence doctrine and, 108–110, 112–113
  of free spirits, 102–113
  hedonism and, 106
  individuality and, 111–112
  liberal society and, 102–113
  life as aesthetic phenomenon, 105–106
  narrative unity and, 157
  spiritual fullness and, 102–113
  "terrible truths" and, 107–108
  time and, 112
affective attachment, 179n22
  liberalism and, 16–17
  spiritual fullness and, 16–17

affective component, of community, 160
After Virtue (MacIntyre), 153, 155–156
Anderson, Joel, 130–131
animating principle, spirit and, 8
The Anti-Christ (Nietzsche), 27–28, 53, 55, 186n42
antidogmatism, 78
Aristotle, 119, 151, 200n1
  on individual autonomy, 14
  on spiritual fullness, 12–13
  on virtue, 12–13
art, in aesthetic perspective, 107–108
ataraxia (tranquility), 33, 35–38
  cheerfulness and, 37
  spiritual fullness and, 38
Atkinson, Brooks, 84, 192n94
atomistic liberal theories, 148–149
atomization of society, 148–149
attachment. *See* affective attachment; existence
"audacious manliness," 30
autonomous consent, 139–140
autonomy, for individuals
  Aristotle on, 14
  basic, 131
  challenges to, 13–14
  in classical liberal theory, 3

autonomy, for individuals *(continued)*
  creative activity and, 128
  cultivation of drives and, 128–130
  definition of, 131
  desirability of, 15
  ethical, 131
  free spirits and, 127–128, 137
  gardening metaphor for, 127–129
  Hegel on, 14
  ideal, 131
  in liberal governments, 117–126
  liberalism and, 13, 113, 130–131
  local, 131
  as member of the state, 14, 48–49
  moral, 131–133, 135–138
  personal, 131–133
  Plato on, 14
  political, 131
  in political theory, 118–119
  practicable sense of, 126–138
  Rawls on, 124
  Rousseau on, 14
  self-development and, 129–130, 138
  self-mastery and, 138
  social, 131–132
  social contract theory and, 15, 123–124
  sovereign individuals, 133–136, 157–158
  spiritual, 45
  spiritual emptiness as result of, 15–16
  spiritual fullness, 159–163
  Taylor on, 203n50
  types of, 131

"bad" free spirits, 167–168
Bamford, Rebecca, 128
banishment, of individuals, 145
Bartels, Larry, 47
Bearn, Gordon, 180n20

being, Nietzsche on, 25–26
Bennett, John, 141
Berry, Jessica, 29, 32–33, 181n40, 182n47
Beyle, Marie-Henri, 91
Beyond Good and Evil (Nietzsche), 34, 53–54, 109, 129
The Birth of Tragedy (Nietzsche), 104–105, 107
Blue, Daniel, 162–163
Brennan, Jason, 47–48
Brown, John, 86
Buchholtz, F. F., 63
Burgess, John, 14, 122

Came, Daniel, 105
Carl August (Duke), 60–62
Catholicism, tacit consent and, 142, 200n62
character, 37–38
  temperament as distinct from, 37
"Character" (Emerson), 78–79
cheerfulness
  ataraxia and, 37
  free spirits and, 35–39
  skepticism and, 35–39
Christianity
  evangelical thought, 71–72
  for Lewis, C. S., 71, 74–75
  Nietzsche's rejection of, 28, 162–163
Christman, John, 130–131
"Circles" (Emerson), 79
citizens
  freedom for, 3
  liberal, 3
  as self-owners, 3
"Civil Disobedience" (Thoreau), 84
civil society, community and, 150–151
civil state, 121
classical liberal theory, 3
communal values, 163–165

Index

communitarianism
  on atomization of society, causes of, 148–149
  free spirits and, 17
  on liberal democracy, 146–147
  MacIntyre and, 153–154
  on meaningful attachment, 147–152
community
  affective component of, 160
  civil society and, 150–151
  communal values, 163–165
  definition of, 150
  free spirits and, 42–43
  liberal values and, 163–166
  meaning through, 152–159
  membership in, 151
  narratives in, 152–159
  political cooperation as distinct from, 152
  politics and, 41
  shared elements of, 151–152
  spiritual freedom and, as obstacle to, 160–161
  types of, 151–152, 202n20
conformity
  liberal political order influenced by, 101
  in liberal society, 97, 99
consciousness, 8
consent
  autonomous, 139–140
  explicit, 141–142
  tacit, 141–142, 200n62
Conversations (Goethe), 61
cooperation
  classical liberal theory and, 3
  political, community as distinct from, 152
creativity, individual autonomy and, 128
Croly, Herbert, 14, 119
cultivation of drives. *See* drives

Daigle, Christine, 19, 179n3
Deneen, Patrick, 2, 146, 148–149, 177n3
Dependent Rational Animals (MacIntyre), 154–155
detachment. *See* politics of detachment
Dewey, John, 118–119, 149–150
  on state as social organism, 14–15
Dienstag, Joshua Foa, 25, 170n19
Dionysian pessimism, 25
The Discarded Image (Lewis, C. S.), 74–75
disengaged self, 158–159
disposition, temperament and, 22
dogmata, 31–32
dogmatic philosophy, 30–31
dogmatism, 33–34
  antidogmatism, 78
Dolan, Neal, 164
drives, cultivation of, 38, 98
  development of self and, 129–130
  freedom and, 129–130
  individual autonomy and, 128–130
Dyer, Justin, 71

Ecce Homo (Nietzsche), 23, 52, 161–162
eccentricity, in liberal society, 92–93
Eckermann, Johann Peter, 61
economic freedom, 3
Emerson, Ralph Waldo, 24, 43, 59, 85–89
  in abolitionist movement, 85–88
  on aesthetic perspective, 81–82, 111
  antidogmatism and, 78
  Brown and, defense of, 86
  "Character," 78–79
  "Circles," 79
  as free spirit, 78
  idealism of, 191n66
  on individualism, 78

Emerson, Ralph Waldo (*continued*)
    on injustice of slavery, 85
    Kant as influence on, 78
    on natural laws, 78
    politics of detachment and, 78, 81
    Pyrrhonism and, 79–80, 191n74
    "Self-reliance," 81
    on self-reliance, 80, 87
    skepticism of, 79
    spiritual fullness and, 78
    transcendentalism and, 77–82,
        84–85
    "The Transcendentalist," 80
    on wonder, 82
"energetic natures." *See* free spirits
enlightened rationalism, 54
Epicureans, 31
epistemic truth, 26
epistemological skepticism, 30,
    185n34
epoché (suspension of judgment), 33,
    35–36
    spiritual fullness and, 38
equality, classical liberal theory and, 3
"Equality" (Lewis, C. S.), 75
eternal recurrence doctrine, 108–110,
    112–113
ethical autonomy, 131
ethical imperatives, 26
The Ethics of Democracy (Dewey),
    14–15, 118–119
evangelical thought, 71–72
exile, of individuals, 145, 201n3
existence, attachment to
    Rousseau on, 11
    Schopenhauer on, 24
    spiritual fullness as affirmation of,
        103–104
    Taylor on, 11
experimental free spirits, 161, 163
explicit consent, 141–142

Fairley, Barker, 62–63
fanaticism, 99–101
    free spirits as alternative to, 6,
        99–100
Fichte, Johann, 122
Forest, Rainer, 131
Fortier, Jeremy, 52
Franco, Paul, 56, 127–128, 194n49
free spirits. *See also* Emerson, Ralph
    Waldo; Goethe, Johann Wolfgang
    von; Hesse, Hermann; Nietzsche,
    Friedrich; spiritual fullness;
    Thoreau, Henry David
    aesthetic perspective of, 102–113
    as autonomous individuals,
        127–128, 137
    "bad," 167–168
    characteristics of, 88
    cheerfulness and, 35–39
    Christian doctrine for, 28
    communitarianism and, 17
    community and, 42–43
    conformity for, 97
    cultural goals of, 51
    definitions of, 5–6
    Emerson as, 78
    experimental, 161, 163
    fanaticism and, as alternative to, 6,
        99–100
    as free riders, 168
    ideology and, loosening of, 6
    independence of mind for, 6, 171
    intellectual freedom of, 4
    invention of, 54
    knowledge for, 44–45
    liberal political order and, 88–89,
        139
    in liberal society, 99–102
    liberalism and, 13–17
    negative liberty and, 6
    political philosophy and, 5, 50–57

politics and, 42–44, 46–51
politics of detachment and, 6, 57
in popular culture, 5–6
as positive role models, 169
progressivism and, 17
protection from public opinion, 169–170
protection of, 116–117
as relative concept, 20
skepticism and, 5–6, 27–39
spectrum of, criteria for, 19–20
spiritual freedom of, 6, 99–100
spiritual fullness of, 6, 17, 23, 102–113, 161–162
spiritual seeking by, 21
temperament for, 24, 27, 37–38
Ten Commandments for Free Spirits, 44–46
"terrible truths" for, 23–24, 28–29
tolerance of, 175
transcendentalism and, 82–83
free will, 128–130, 135. *See also* autonomy
Freedman, Ralph, 66
freedom. *See also* intellectual freedom; spiritual freedom
cultivation of drives and, 129–130
Kant's principles of, 133
for liberal citizens, 3
negative, 92
political, 3
positive, 92
Frost, Brian-Paul, 77–78, 87
Fugitive Slave Law of 1850, 85–86

Galbreath, Robert, 57, 65–68, 70–71
The Gay Science (Nietzsche), 107, 181n26, 194n49
Gemes, Ken, 129
genius, Nietzsche on, 51
German political thought, 122

Gillespie, Michael, 55, 109–110
The Glass Bead Game (Hesse), 68–70, 178n19
Glenn, Paul, 51–52, 185n34
Goethe, Johann Wolfgang von, 43
Carl August and, 60–62
Conversations, 61
as free spirit, 59, 64
in *Human, All Too Human*, 59–60
on monotheists, 64
on pantheists, 64
political detachment of, 62–63
political participation of, 60–62
on polytheists, 64
privacy for, insistence on, 63
as skeptic of philosophy, 64
solitude for, 63–64
The Sorrows of Young Werther, 62, 188n15
support of liberal values, 165–166
in Weimar Republic, 61–62
Goldsmith, Oliver, 1
Golomb, Jacob, 187n1
Gray, John, 170
Gresham, Douglas, 72

harm principle, 76, 165, 168
hedonism, 106
Hegel, Georg Wilhelm Friedrich, 122
on history as rational process, 126
on individual autonomy, 14
herd mentality, 97–98
Hesse, Hermann, 43
on Arab aggression in Israel, 67
banning of literature, in Nazi Germany, 65, 88
dual citizenship for, 65
as free spirit, 65
The Glass Bead Game, 68–70, 178n19
Narcissus and Goldmund, 67

Hesse, Hermann *(continued)*
   pacifism of, 66
   on politics, negative effects of, 66
   politics of detachment for, 64–66, 71, 189n43
   public silence on Nazi Party, 66–67
   on spiritual freedom, 67–68
   Steppenwolf, 67–68
Himmelfarb, Gertrude, 92
Hobbes, Thomas, 120–121. *See also* social contract theory
   civil state for, 121
   Leviathan, 115, 121, 200n2
   on rights of nature, 197n11
   social compact for, 121
Human, All Too Human (Nietzsche), 21, 44, 52–53, 102, 127–128, 187n1, 201n3
   Goethe in, 59–60
   political perfectionism in, 49
   temperament in, 37
humans, as illogical beings, 21
Humboldt, Wilhelm von, 63
hyper-individualism, 146

ideal autonomy, 131
identity, loss of, spiritual fullness and, 7
ideology, free spirits and, 6, 99
Ignatius of Loyola (Saint), 9–11, 178n15
inclusiveness, of spirituality, 8
independence of mind
   for free spirits, 6, 171
   in liberal society, 92–93, 96–97
individual autonomy. *See* autonomy
individual rights, in inverted social contract, 139–140
individualism. *See also* autonomy
   aesthetic perspective and, 111–112
   Emerson on, 78
   herd mentality and, 97–98
   hyper-individualism, 146

   Mill, J. S., on, 97–98, 138
   radical, 42
   skepticism and, 42
   spiritual emptiness and, 146
   for Thoreau, 78
institutional politics, 72, 74, 81
intellectual culture, in liberal society, 93
intellectual freedom
   of free spirits, 4
   spiritual freedom and, 4, 173
internal culture, in liberal society, 93
inverted social contract, 138–143
   autonomous consent in, 139–140
   explicit consent in, 141–142
   formation of, 139–140
   individual rights in, 139–140
   natural rights and, 139
   for non-free spirits, 140–141
   scope of, 138–139
   tacit consent in, 141–142

Janaway, Christopher, 134–135
Jefferson, Thomas, 115
Jensen, Anthony K., 52
Jesus, as historical figure, 28
justice theory, 197n22

Kant, Immanuel, 191n66
   Emerson influenced by, 78
   ethical imperatives, 26
   on freedom, 133
Kateb, George, 87, 165
Keirsey, David, 37
Kennedy, Anthony (Justice), 1
Kierkegaard, Søren, 171
Kirkland, Paul, 53–54
knowledge
   for free spirits, 44–45
   theory of, 31

Lampert, Laurence, 53–54

Larmore, Charles, 12
Laursen, John, 36
Leiter, Brian, 23–24, 180n23
Leviathan (Hobbes), 115, 121, 200n2
Lewis, Clive Staples (C. S.), 43
  Christianity of, 71, 74–75
  The Discarded Image, 74–75
  "Equality," 75
  on evangelical thought, 71–72
  on liberal political order, advocacy of, 75–76
  on liberalism, 165
  political detachment of, 74–76
  on politics, personal disdain for, 72–75
  skepticism and, 71, 75
  social contract theory and, endorsement of, 76, 165
  spiritual freedom for, 72, 76
  That Hideous Strength, 73–74
Lewis, Warnie, 72
liberal governments. *See also* liberal political order
  individual autonomy in, 117–126
  institution of natural laws in, 121–122
  legitimacy of, 126
  origins of, 117–126
  social contract theory in, 121–122
liberal nation-states. *See* nation-states
liberal political order. *See also* liberalism; nation-states
  conformity as negative influence on, 101
  critical attacks on, 1–2
  free spirits and, 88–89, 139
  Lewis, C. S., advocacy of, 75–76
  literature on, 1
liberal society
  aesthetic perspective and, 102–113
  conception of, 91–92
  conformity in, 97, 99
  eccentricity in, 92–93
  free spirits in, 99–102
  independent belief and thought in, 92–93, 96–97
  intellectual culture in, 93
  internal culture in, 93
  Mill, J. S., on, 92–102, 140
  negative freedoms in, 92
  outsiders in, embrace of, 98–99
  positive freedoms in, 92
  spiritual fullness and, 102–113
  Tocqueville on, 94–96
  tolerance in, 95–96, 99
  tyranny in, 93–95
liberal theory. *See* classical liberal theory
liberal values, 163–166
  Goethe and, 165–166
liberalism
  affective attachment and, 16–17
  atomization of society through, 148–149
  classical liberal theory and, 3
  communitarianism and, 146–147
  community and, 163–166
  critics of, 1–2, 14–15
  definition of, 138
  foundational principles of, 147
  free spirits and, 13–17
  individual autonomy and, 13, 113, 130–131
  inverted social contract and, 138–143
  Lewis, C. S., on, 165
  MacIntyre's opposition to, 156
  materialism of, 177n3
  moral aims of, 3
  moral autonomy and, 133
  nation-states and, 115
  Nietzschean critiques of, 20
  personal autonomy and, 133
  as political philosophy, rejection of, 16

liberalism *(continued)*
  social contract theory and, 120–121
  Solzhenitsyn as critic of, 2
  spiritual defense of, 2
  spiritual emptiness as result of, 2, 146–147
  spiritual impoverishment as result of, 2
  state of nature and, 120–121
  Taylor on, 14
  unencumbered self and, 125
  voluntarist self-image and, 125–126
liberty. *See also* freedom
  Locke on, 120–121
  negative, 6
  political philosophy and, 3
  politics and, 3
  self-preservation through, 120–121
liberty theory, 92–94
Lieber, Francis, 122
life, as aesthetic phenomenon, 105–106
"Life without Principle" (Thoreau), 83
local autonomy, 131
Locke, John, 76, 165. *See also* social contract theory
  on liberty, 120–121
Lolita (Nabokov), 108
Lomax, J. Harvey, 55–56
love, new forms of, 184n14

MacIntyre, Alasdair, 14, 146
  After Virtue, 153, 155–156
  as communitarian, 153–154
  Dependent Rational Animals, 154–155
  opposition to liberalism, 156
May, Simon, 129–130
meaning, definition of, 177n7
Merriam, Charles, 14, 119, 122
metaphysics
  Nietzsche's repudiation of, 104–105
  skepticism and, 27–28

Mill, James, 93
Mill, John Stuart, 91
  harm principle, 76, 165, 168
  on individualism, 97–98, 138
  on liberal society, 92–102, 140
  On Liberty, 92, 93–94
  on liberty, theory of, 92–94
  on politics, 47
  on spiritual freedom, 93
  on tyranny, 92–95
modernity, spiritual fullness and, 7
monotheists, 64
moral autonomy, 131–133, 135–138
  promise-making and, 136–137
moral truth, 26–27, 179n12
morality, liberalism and, aims of, 3
Müller, Friedrich von, 64
Mullin, Amy, 20, 51, 161

Nabokov, Vladimir, 108
Nachlass (Nietzsche), 32–33
Narcissus and Goldmund (Hesse), 67
narrative unity, 156–160
  aesthetic perspective and, 157
  spiritual fullness and, 7
narratives
  in community, 152–159
  virtue ethics theory and, 153–154
nation-states
  civil state, 121
  ethical life in, 118
  hierarchies in, 118
  liberalism and, 115
  as living organism, 119
  as social organism, 119–120
  Spinoza on, 116
  Treaty of Westphalia and, 115
natural laws
  Emerson on, 78
  through liberal governments, institution of, 121–122
  transcendentalism and, 82

natural rights, 122, 197n11
  inverted social contract and, 139
Nazi Germany
  Hesse's literature banned in, 65, 88
  Hesse's public silence on, 66-67
negative freedoms, 92
negative liberty, 6
Nehamas, Alexander, 103-104, 195n67
new philosopher, 51-52
  Übermensch and, 54-55
Nietzsche (Nehamas), 103-104
Nietzsche, Friedrich
  aestheticism of, 103-104
  The Anti-Christ, 27-28, 53, 55, 186n42
  ataraxia and, 33, 35-38
  on being, 25-26
  Beyond Good and Evil, 34, 53-54, 109, 129
  The Birth of Tragedy, 104-105, 107
  on Christianity, critiques of, 28, 162-163
  cultivation of drives, 38, 98
  on Dionysian pessimism, 25
  Ecce Homo, 23, 52, 161-162
  elitism of, 51
  epoché and, 33, 35-36, 38
  eternal recurrence doctrine, 108-110, 112-113
  as free spirit, 54-55
  on free spirits, 7, 19-24, 43-50, 116-117
  on free will, 128-130, 135
  The Gay Science, 107, 181n26, 194n49
  on genius, 51
  herd mentality, 97-98
  Human, All Too Human, 21, 37, 44, 49, 52-53, 59-60, 102, 127-128, 187n1, 201n3
  on Jesus, as historical figure, 28
  on liberalism, critiques of, 20
  on love, new forms of, 184n14
  Lutheran influences on, 105
  metaphysics and, repudiation of, 104-105
  on moral truth, 26-27, 179n12, 181n26
  Nachlass, 32-33
  new philosophers and, 51-52, 54-55
  nihilism and, 105, 154
  On the Genealogy of Morals, 134, 157
  perspectivism and, 33-34
  on philology as interpretive art, 33
  philosophical nominalism of, 26
  political philosophy of, 50-57
  on politics, free spirits and, 46-50
  Pyrrhonism and, 32-34, 182n47
  on radical individualism, 42
  Schopenhauer as influence on, 23-24
  skepticism of, 27-30, 32, 46, 181n36
  on solitude, 54
  sovereign individuals and, 133-136, 157-158
  on substance, 25-26
  on temperament, 22, 24, 37-38
  Thus Spoke Zarathustra, 54-56
  Twilight of the Idols, 34, 56, 59-60, 187n1
  Übermensch and, 54-55, 186n38
  on understanding of immediate environment, 25
  Will to Power, 195n67
nihilism, 105, 154
Nisbet, H. B., 64
nominalism. *See* philosophical nominalism
non-free spirits, 140-141

Obama, Barack, 145-146
Oliver, Mary, 78

On Liberty (Mill, J. S.), 92, 93–94
On the Genealogy of Morals (Nietzsche), 134, 157
Outlines of Skepticism (Sextus), 30–31
Owen, David, 157

pacifism, of Hesse, 66
pantheists, 64
Pearson, Keith Ansell, 71
personal autonomy, 131–133, 135–138
personality, spirit and, 8
perspectivism, 33–35
  skepticism and, 34–35
pessimism. *See* Dionysian pessimism
philology, as interpretive art, 33
philosophical nominalism, of Nietzsche, 26
philosophy, political. *See also* academic philosophy; dogmatic philosophy; skeptical philosophy
  free spirit and, 5, 50–57
  liberalism as, rejection of, 16
  liberty and, 3
  of Nietzsche, 50–57
  politics as distinct from, 50
physical experiences, spirituality and, 8
Plato, 149
  on individual autonomy, 14
Platonists, 31
political autonomy, 131
political freedom, 3
Political Liberalism (Rawls), 124
political philosophy. *See* philosophy
political theory, spiritual fullness in, 4
politics
  community and, 41
  direct engagement in, for Lewis, C. S., 75
  free spirits and, 42–44, 46–50
  Goethe and, active engagement in, 60–62
  Hesse on negative effects of, 66
  indirect engagement in, for Lewis, C. S., 75
  institutional, 72, 74, 81
  for Lewis, C. S., personal disdain for, 72–75
  liberty and, 3
  Mill, J. S., on, 47
  political philosophy as distinct from, 50
  practical, 50
  skepticism towards, 48
  spiritual freedom and, 48–49
  Thoreau on, negative effects of, 83–84
Politics (Aristotle), 151, 200n1
politics of detachment
  Emerson and, 78, 81
  free spirits and, 6, 57
  for Goethe, 62–63
  for Hesse, 64–66, 71, 189n43
  for Lewis, C. S., 74–76
polytheists, 64
populist movements, 1
positive freedoms, 92
progressive theory, 122
progressivism
  free spirits and, 17
  social contract theory and, 125
promise-making, 136–137
public opinion
  free spirits protected from, 169–170
  skepticism and, 170
  tyranny of the majority, 169, 204n4
Pyrrhonism
  academic philosophy and, 30–31
  ataraxia and, 33, 35–36
  dogmatic philosophy and, 30–31
  Emerson and, 79–80, 191n74
  epoché and, 33, 35–36
  Nietzsche and, 32–34, 182n47

perspectivism and, 33–34
skeptical philosophy and, 30–31
skepticism and, 29–31, 35, 177n6

radical individualism, 42
rationalism. *See* enlightened rationalism
Rawls, John, 122–124, 147
   on individual autonomy, 124
   justice theory, 197n22
   on liberal citizens, 3
   veil of ignorance, 123
reciprocity, 124
Reconstructing Public Philosophy (Sullivan), 119
Reginster, Bernard, 100–101
Reinbeck, Georg von, 63
The Reveries of the Solitary Walker (Rousseau), 10–11
rights. *See* natural rights; individual rights
Roberts, Peter, 70
Rousseau, Jean-Jacques
   attachment to existence for, 11
   exile of, 201n3
   on individual autonomy, 14
   "noble savage" and, 13
   on spiritual fullness, 10–11, 13
Royce, Josiah, 152
Russell, Bertrand, 19

safe spaces, 193n30
Saine, Thomas, 61–62
Sandel, Michael, 14, 125, 146
Sarton, May, 145
Schacht, Richard, 53, 201n3
Schaffer, Francis, 74
Schopenhauer, Arthur, 23–24, 41
   condemnation of existence, 24
science, skepticism as result of, 174, 204n8
scientific perspective, 107

self
   development of, 129–130, 138
   disengaged, 158–159
   strong evaluator, 158–159
self-mastery, 138
self-preservation, through liberty, 120–121
"Self-reliance" (Emerson), 81
self-reliance theory, 80, 87
Sextus, 30–32, 181n38
   dogmata, 31–32
shared values, 163–164
Sharpe, Lesley, 61
Siemens, Herman W., 50
skeptical philosophy, 30–31
skepticism
   of "audacious manliness," 30
   cheerfulness and, 35–39
   demands for certainty and, 28
   of Emerson, 79
   epistemological, 30, 185n34
   free spirits and, 5–6, 27–39, 170–171
   goals of, 31
   of Goethe, over philosophy, 64
   individualism and, 42
   of Lewis, C. S., 71, 75
   metaphysics and, 27–28
   of Nietzsche, 27–30, 32, 46, 181n36
   perspectivism and, 34–35
   Platonists and, 31
   politics and, 48
   post-Cartesian, 30
   practice of, 29
   public opinion and, 170
   Pyrrhonism and, 29–31, 35, 177n6
   through science, 174, 204n8
   Sextus and, 30–31
   spiritual freedom and, 36
   theory of knowledge and, 31
Skinner, B. F., 74
slavery, injustice of, 85. *See also* abolitionist movement

Smith, Adam, 99
social autonomy, 131–132
social compact, 121
social contract theory
  individual autonomy and, 15, 123–124
  inverted social contract, 138–143
  Lewis, C. S., endorsement of, 76, 165
  in liberal governments, 121–122
  liberalism and, 120–121
  natural rights and, 122
  political power in, 199n46
  rejection of, by progressives, 125
social cooperation, 124
soft despotism, 204n4
solitude
  for Goethe, 63–64
  for Nietzsche, 54
Solzhenitsyn, Alexander, as critic of liberalism, 2
The Sorrows of Young Werther (Goethe), 62, 188n15
the soul, 8
sovereign individuals, 133–136, 157–158
Spinoza, Baruch, 115–116, 196n5
  on liberal nation-states, 116
spirit, spirituality and
  as animating principle, 8
  consciousness and, 8
  etymology of, 8
  inclusiveness of, 8
  personality and, 8
  as physical experiences, 9
  scope of, 8–9
  the soul, 8
  subjective experience and, 8
spiritual autonomy, 45
spiritual emptiness
  from individual autonomy, 15–16, 147–152

  individualism and, 146
  from liberalism, 2, 146–147
  spiritual fullness as distinct from, 11
Spiritual Exercises (St. Ignatius of Loyola), 9–10
spiritual freedom, 171–176. *See also* free spirits
  community as obstacle to, 160–161
  definitions of, 2–4
  degrees of, 39
  of free spirits, 6, 99–100
  Hesse on, 67–68
  intellectual freedom and, 4, 173
  for Lewis, C. S., 72, 76
  Mill, J. S., on, 93
  model of, 20
  political participation and, 48–49
  protection of, 116–117
  skepticism and, 36
  spiritual fulfillment from, 4
  spiritual fullness and, 173
  transcendentalism and, 84–85
spiritual fulfillment, from spiritual freedom, 4
spiritual fullness, 4–13
  aesthetic perspective and, 102–113
  affective attachment and, 16–17
  affirmation of existence and, 103–104
  Aristotle on, 12–13
  ataraxia and, 38
  classical Greek approach to, 12–13
  definition of, 9–11
  desirability of, 17
  Emerson and, 78
  epoché and, 38
  for free spirits, 6, 17, 23, 102–113, 161–162
  individual autonomy and, 159–163
  liberal society and, 102–113
  loss of identity and, 7

modernity and, 7
narrative unity and, 7
in political theory, 4
Rousseau on, 10–11, 13
scope of, 8–9, 11–12
sources of, 4
spiritual emptiness as distinct from, 11
spiritual freedom and, 173
St. Ignatius of Loyola on, 9–11
success and, as criterion for, 7
Taylor on, 9
virtues and, 12
the state. See also nation-states
individual autonomy as member of, 14, 48–49
as social organism, 14–15, 119–120
spiritual role of, 149–150
Steppenwolf (Hesse), 67–68
strong evaluator, 158–159
subjective experiences, spirituality and, 8
substance, Nietzsche on, 25–26
Sullivan, William, 119
superman/superwoman. See Übermensch
suspension of judgment. See *epoché*

tacit consent, 141–142, 200n62
Catholicism and, 142
Taylor, Charles, 146, 158–159
on existence, 11
on individual autonomy, 203n50
on liberalism, 14
on spiritual fullness, 9
temperament
character as distinct from, 37
disposition and, 22
as fixed, 37
for free spirits, 24, 27, 37–38
internal, 37
Nietzsche on, 22, 24, 37–38

Ten Commandments for Free Spirits, 44–46
"terrible truths"
aesthetic perspective and, 107–108
epistemic truth, 26
for free spirits, 23–24, 28–29
moral truth, 26–27
That Hideous Strength (Lewis, C. S.), 73–74
Theognis, 52
A Theory of Justice (Rawls), 124
Thiele, Leslie Paul, 110, 183n7–8
Thoreau, Henry David, 43, 59, 77–78, 82–85
in abolitionist movement, 85
antidogmatism and, 78
"Civil Disobedience," 84
individualism for, 78
"Life without Principle," 83
on political participation, negative effects of, 83–84
transcendentalism for, 83
Walden, 110–111
Thus Spoke Zarathustra (Nietzsche), 54–56
time, aesthetic perspective and, 112
Tocqueville, Alexis de, 101
on liberal society, 94–96
soft despotism, 204n4
tyranny of the majority, 169, 204n4
tolerance
of free spirits, 175
in liberal society, 95–96, 99
tranquility. See *ataraxia*
transcendentalism
Emerson and, 77–82, 84–85
free spirits and, 82–83
natural laws and, 82
spiritual freedom and, 84–85
Thoreau and, 83
"The Transcendentalist" (Emerson), 80

trigger warnings, 193n30
Twilight of the Idols (Nietzsche), 34, 56, 59–60, 187n1
tyranny, in liberal societies, 92–95
　resistance to, 95

Übermensch (superman/superwoman), 54–55, 186n38
unencumbered self, 125

values
　communal, 163–165
　liberal, 163–166
　shared, 163–164
Viroli, Maurizio, 175
virtue ethics, theory of, 153–154
virtues
　Aristotle on, 12–13
　Classical Greek approach to, 12
　spiritual fullness and, 12
voluntarist self-image, 125–126

Wagner, Richard, 201n3
Walden (Thoreau), 110–111
Waldron, Jeremy, 132, 134, 137
Watson, Micah, 71
Webster, Daniel, 87
Weimar Republic, Goethe in, 61–62
Why Liberalism Failed (Deneen), 2
Will to Power (Nietzsche), 195n67
Wilson, Daniel, 60, 62
wonder, 82
Woolsey, Theodore, 150, 202n17

Zakaras, Alex, 80, 92, 111
Ziolkowski, Theodore, 70